Social Care, Service Users and User Involvement

RESEARCH HIGHLIGHTS 55

Research Highlights in Social Work Series

This topical series examines areas of particular interest to those in social and community work and related fields. Each book draws together different aspects of the subject, highlighting relevant research and drawing out implications for policy and practice. The project is under the editorial direction of Professor Andrew Kendrick, Head of the School of Applied Social Sciences at the University of Strathclyde, Scotland.

other recent books in the series

Social Work Education and Training
Edited by Joyce Lishman
ISBN 978 1 84905 076 0
eISBN 978 0 85700 262 4
RESEARCH HIGHLIGHTS IN SOCIAL WORK 54

Substance Misuse
The Implications of Research, Policy and Practice
Edited by Joy Barlow
ISBN 978 1 84310 696 8
eISBN 978 0 85700 219 8
RESEARCH HIGHLIGHTS IN SOCIAL WORK 53

Youth Offending and Youth Justice
Edited by Monica Barry and Fergus McNeill
ISBN 978 1 84310 689 0
eISBN 978 0 85700 195 5
RESEARCH HIGHLIGHTS IN SOCIAL WORK 52

Leadership in Social Care
Edited by Zoë van Zwanenberg
ISBN 978 1 84310 969 3
eISBN 978 0 85700 204 4
RESEARCH HIGHLIGHTS IN SOCIAL WORK 51

Public Services Inspection in the UK
Edited by Howard Davis and Steve Martin
ISBN 978 1 84310 527 5
eISBN 978 1 84642 830 2
RESEARCH HIGHLIGHTS IN SOCIAL WORK 50

Co-Production and Personalisation in Social Care
Changing Relationships in the Provision of Social Care
Edited by Susan Hunter and Pete Ritchie
ISBN 978 1 84310 558 9
eISBN 978 1 84642 721 3
RESEARCH HIGHLIGHTS IN SOCIAL WORK 49

Developments in Social Work with Offenders
Edited by Gill McIvor and Peter Raynor
ISBN 978 1 84310 538 1
eISBN 978 1 84642 682 7
RESEARCH HIGHLIGHTS IN SOCIAL WORK 48

Social Care, Service Users and User Involvement

Edited by
Peter Beresford and Sarah Carr

Foreword by Simon Denegri

RESEARCH HIGHLIGHTS 55

Jessica Kingsley *Publishers*
London and Philadelphia

The SCIE has kindly given permission for the quotes in Chapter 2.
Figure 10.1 on p.182 from Barnes, Mercer and Morgan (2001) has been reprinted with permission from Disability Press.
Table 10.1 on p.185 from Barnes, Mercer and Morgan, (2000) has been reprinted with permission from Disability Press.
Table 10.2 on p.186 from Morgan, Barnes and Mercer, (2001) has been reprinted with permission from Disability Press.
Crown Copyright material is reproduced with the permission of the Controller of HMSO and the Queen's Printer for Scotland.
Figure 13.2 on p.232 has been reproduced with kind permission from Shaw, C., Brady, L.M., and Davey, C. of the National Children's Bureau.

First published in 2012
by Jessica Kingsley Publishers
116 Pentonville Road
London N1 9JB, UK
and
400 Market Street, Suite 400
Philadelphia, PA 19106, USA

www.jkp.com

Copyright © Jessica Kingsley Publishers 2012
Foreword copyright © Simon Denegri 2012

Library of Congress Cataloging in Publication Data
Social care, service users and user involvement / edited by Peter Beresford and Sarah Carr ; foreword by Simon Denegri.
    p. cm. -- (Research highlights ; 55)
Includes bibliographical references and index.
ISBN 978-1-84905-075-3 (alk. paper)
1. Social service--Great Britain. I. Beresford, Peter. II. Carr, Sarah, 1971-
HV245.S6143 2012
361.941--dc23
                            2012029186

British Library Cataloguing in Publication Data
A CIP catalogue record for this book is available from the British Library

ISBN 978 1 84905 075 3
eISBN 978 0 85700 264 8

Printed and bound in Great Britain

Peter:
Dedicated to the memory of my friend, Chris Harrison, fellow member of the Coordinating Group of Survivors Speak Out, psychiatric system survivor and blind person and pioneer of both the disabled people's and the survivor movement. He understood and was an expression of the best of both of them.

Sarah:
Dedicated to the life, work and memory of Nasa Begum 1963–2011. Sister, struggler, survivor. Inspiration and friend.

Peter and Sarah both wish a warm welcome to the book's 'production babies' and congratulations to Angela Sweeny, Louca-Mai Brady, Kath Browne and Helen Bowers.

Contents

Foreword

Simon Denegri

Where does public participation and user involvement in social care stand today?

On the one hand, the breaking waves of national and local consultations and initiatives with their crowns of participatory language, give the impression that public participation and user involvement is now part of mainstream thinking and activity. On the other, the ebb and flow of this tide can seem to do little more than leave the participation and involvement agenda obscured if not stranded in ever deeper and murkier pools of stagnated policy and policy-making.

We hear both views expressed equally forcefully. Indeed, in the current climate of reform, restructure and unsettling austerity, we can forgive ourselves for oscillating between these opinions in our own minds, sometimes on the same day.

Yet, given the opportunity to pause and sit a moment, and if I look back over my own ladder of involvement – beginning at the Alzheimer's Society in the nineties as people with dementia found their voice and challenged the prevailing consensus about their needs as defined by others, to the world I inhabit now as Chair of INVOLVE and NIHR National Director for Public Participation and Engagement in Research – I would argue strongly that the shoreline of social care has changed because of public participation and user involvement.

But with progress comes new challenges to add to existing ones. Alongside the all too familiar institutional and cultural barriers, the need for practical tools fit for our time, as well as our own search for definition, identity and confidence, we must add that thing called 'impact'. Or rather proof of impact; driven as much by our own desire for improvement and learning as it is by the need for providers, commissioners and policy-makers to justify their actions. It requires reflection rather than reaction. It must be built on evidence rather than simple opinion such as mine expressed above.

Who better to provide us with the means and the opportunity to reflect in this way, to present such evidence as well as contextualise it, than Peter Beresford and Sarah Carr? Two of the country's leading and most respected voices and practitioners in user involvement as well as much-admired colleagues.

In the latest 'Research Highlights' series, looking at 'Social Care, Service Users and User Involvement,' Peter and Sarah have thoughtfully collated and deftly introduce this collection of research-based contributions by experts in their field. The common theme that binds them together is their examination of the impact of user involvement as well as the difference that can be made by service users in its research and evaluation.

It is a timely and important book. These are unique and absorbing perspectives. They will provoke new thought and further debate. For the practically minded, each presents fresh and actionable insights and new learning in an area which is challenging and exacting. All of the contributions could stand alone on their own merits.

But, tempted though the reader might be to simply 'dip in' to this book as you might another collection, I hope you will consume it in its entirety as I did. For, regardless of the specific role or reason that led you here, you will emerge with a better understanding of user involvement in the whole, in its current surrounds. And with that better understanding we have a greater chance of seeing an environment unfold in which service users are able to transform the social care landscape in ways which better meet their needs.

Simon Denegri
Chair, INVOLVE, and NIHR National Director for
Public Participation and Engagement in Research

Introduction

Peter Beresford and Sarah Carr

The aim of this book is to explore both service user views and user involvement to share up-to-date research-based knowledge. All the contributions in this book are research-based, drawing on the latest knowledge, provided by experts in their fields. The book addresses both theoretical and practical issues in relation to service user perspectives and involvement. In choosing contributions, as editors we have sought to ensure that the book addresses issues which have emerged as central and of long-term importance. The book is also positioned to take account of the implications of key developments in its field, such as personalisation and the Equality Act 2010, as well as more established issues and concerns.

There is growing interest in the 'impact' of and 'outcomes' from user involvement, as well as in its practice, theory and ideology. The book addresses and distinguishes between user views and involvement in processes and in outcomes and their measurement. The book includes findings regarding user involvement in relation to:

- services, their delivery and provision
- practice and practitioners
- research and evaluation.

These provide a basis for the book's final form. To encourage readers and increase access the book is organised according to key current themes. It includes service user voices as well as explorations of their involvement and the difference it can make.

The context of the book

There is barely a word in the title of this book, *Social Care, Service Users and User Involvement*, which is not heavily contested. While these terms have come to be widely used in professional and policy discussions and developments, they are also frequently criticised for being poorly defined and jargonistic. Surveys have repeatedly highlighted that there is very low 'public recognition' of 'social care' – or put simply, it is not a term that most people understand or are even familiar with. 'What' or 'who' is a 'service user', is a common response to the use of this terminology. 'User involvement' is perhaps the most opaque of the terms, advanced by some as a route to personal liberation, while seen by others as a tokenistic dead-end. Yet all these terms have come to occupy an increasingly central place in the policy lexicon along with new associated terminology such as 'co-production'. They also impact in both subtle and direct ways on people's lives, having an increasing role and importance in them, especially in the context of personalisation reforms in health and social care. This is particularly true given the evidence that major demographic changes mean that more and more people are likely to need to turn to social care policy and provision for support now and in the future.

These issues about terminology in this field not only provide the context for this book. They also create the rationale and need for it. This makes it all the more important to subject such terms to careful scrutiny and that is one of our aims in this edited book, where we will attempt to set out and explore competing interpretations and understandings, rather than just adding our own.

A key purpose of the Research Highlights series is to explore issues through research. In this way it seeks to develop the knowledge or evidence base of its subject. This is very much the aim here in this book, where the focus is 'user involvement'. However, user involvement also raises a range of additional issues of its own in taking forward this task. This is because such user involvement is not only the focus of the book. It also has major implications for the research on which it draws. User involvement has had an impact on research as well as becoming a subject of study. Thus the spotlight is turned on to both the nature of the subject matter and the nature of the research exploring it. We are therefore not only concerned with the insights and impact to be gained on user involvement through research and development, but also with the part that user involvement can and increasingly does play in research itself. There is also an additional relationship to take into consideration: the role and effect that user involvement in research may have on the knowledge or evidence that is gathered about involvement or indeed any other subject.

In putting this book together, we have sought to interpret the boundaries of social care, social and community work broadly and flexibly to offer readers as much help as possible in analysing and making sense of these issues. We have looked at user involvement in different settings: in quality assessment, commissioning and service provision, practice development, research and evaluation, standard setting and more, although our focus has necessarily not been exhaustive. Many different groups of service users are included and also contribute, ranging from children and young people to older people, people with life limiting conditions and addiction problems, learning difficulties, physical and sensory impairments and mental health problems. There are local, national and international examples and experiences of user involvement. We have sought to explore issues of equality and diversity. These not only relate to the equality issues of ethnicity, sexuality, gender, disability and age, but also to a range of other exclusions and barriers which people are liable to experience as service users, for example, through their housing circumstances, contact with the criminal justice system, through communicating differently and so on. The studies we have included draw on and explore different kinds of research: qualitative, quantitative and mixed methods research, as well as illustrating different approaches to involvement in research and elsewhere, from user-controlled research, through partnership, to user consultation. They raise complex issues of identity, experience and knowledge. Contributors also look at some of the personal and professional issues raised by being a 'service user researcher' as well as the dynamics of service users undertaking research in partnership with professional researchers.

The structure of the book

We have organised the book according to some of the key areas and issues that it explores. Thus we have structured the 12 contributions that make up the main body of this book according to five themes. Readers may feel it could have been organised differently. We would agree with this, because each chapter highlights many different issues. Our concern in organising the book has been to try and bring out some of the broader issues that individual contributions raise, as well as helping the reader develop their understanding through the course of a wide range of different approaches, examples and methodologies of user involvement and user involvement research.

Thus, for example, while we have identified three chapters to include under the heading of 'Inclusion and addressing diversity', there are others which also centrally address this issue. This includes, for example, Karen Newbigging and colleagues' account of the involvement of service users from black and minority ethnic communities in a systematic research review and Phil Cotterell's contribution on involving people at the end of life in research. Equally we are not saying that the book exhaustively covers all issues relating to user involvement in this field. There might have been additional chapters about user involvement in education and training, professional practice and processes for complaint. Having said that, we have sought to address key issues and to embrace as wide a range of focuses and issues for user involvement as possible in this book, while at the same time, we hope, ensuring that discussions are sufficiently detailed, grounded and substantial to be helpful for readers.

We begin with two general chapters by the editors. The first aims to provide an introductory overview to the theory and philosophy of user involvement. The second focuses on the impact user involvement may have and some of the evidence on factors which may help or hinder change as a result of participation. This is then followed by a series of contributions which we have organised according to five key themes. These are:

- exploring user involvement
- user involvement in quality and standard setting
- involving people in research and evaluation
- user-led service provision
- inclusion and addressing diversity.

Exploring user involvement
Jennie Fleming

In her chapter, Jennie Fleming looks at what different dimensions of user involvement can mean in the lives of service users, highlighting the impact that the presence or absence of involvement in one aspect of a person's life can have on other aspects of it. To do this she draws upon the 'Standards We Expect' project, a four-year participatory research and development project supported by the Joseph Rowntree Foundation whose focus was 'person-centred support', or 'personalisation' as it has more often come to be called in social care. The aim of the project was to support the development of such person-centred support through exploring its meaning, identifying barriers in its way and how these might be overcome. She considers the relation between individual and collective involvement and what service user participarion could look like, given the frequent limitations of prevailing practice. She provides a standard for participation that was developed by the Standards We Expect project.

Martin Hoban

Martin Hoban, in this chapter, focuses on community work approaches to involvement for social care. He defines such approaches, providing a background to community work and critiquing three influential modern approaches to it: community development, community action and community planning. He considers the directive as well as liberatory potential of such community work. He makes the case, drawing on his own practice, research and experience, that if community work is to offer service users and their organisations a helpful approach to involvement, it is necessary to reclaim its practice by developing a more participatory approach to it.

Involving people in quality and standard setting
Arne Kristiansen

The focus of this chapter by Arne Kristiansen is on how user-led organisations in the drug addiction field can develop forms of quality assurance from a service user perspective, more appropriate for appraising their organisations. The chapter offers an international perspective as it reports on experience in Sweden. There is an increasing emphasis on quality assurance generally; however, prevailing approaches to the setting and measurement of quality standards tend to be based on managerialist and professional understandings and perspectives. Rainbow is an umbrella organisation of service user organisations in the Swedish drug addiction field. The 'Rainbow Quality System' (RQS) is a user-led approach to standard setting, which includes user involvement and which builds on a partnership between academic and service user organisations. The chapter examines the development of RQS, the form it takes, how it works in practice and results and experiences with it.

Helen Bowers and Anita Wilkins

Helen Bowers' and Anita Wilkins' chapter focuses on the involvement of older people in setting standards and defining 'outcomes'. While older people constitute the largest group of social care service users, they are often overlooked in research and in discussions about user involvement, which is why it is particularly helpful to be able to include this chapter in the book. The chapter reports the experiences and lessons from working with older people and other key stakeholders in three initiatives over a period of five years concerned with improving older people's life chances through the development and delivery of improved public services. The chapter also explores issues of co-production because of its interest in partnership working, particularly with older people who have support needs. It pays specific attention to discussions about user-defined outcomes which involve older people and which have impacted on policy and practice.

Involving people in research and evaluation
Karen Newbigging, Alastair Roy, Mick McKeown and Zemikael Habte-Mariam

The authors, Karen Newbigging, Alastair Roy, Mick McKeown and Zemikael Habte-Mariam, highlight that relatively little has been written about the involvement of black and minority ethnic mental health service users in the research process or the involvement of service users in the technical intricacies. Their chapter helps fill this gap by addressing the participation of this key marginalised group. It is particularly concerned with African and Caribbean men with mental health problems. The methodology, particularly the participation methodology of a Social Care Institute for Excellence knowledge review, looks at mental health advocacy services for this group. It shows that not only can you involve people often assumed not to be 'involveable', but it also involves them in a systematic review, that is to say secondary research. It also shows the importance and feasibility of a university research department working in equal partnership with an ethnic minority organisation, while acknowledging some of the tensions.

Angela Sweeney

Angela Sweeney's focus in her chapter is the 'double identity' of the 'survivor researcher' and what if any difference it may make to research.

She considers how it can affect the topic, process and results of research. She explores this through the subject of mental health service users' experiences of 'continuity of care', a key issue for both services and service users, although so far one that has been inadequately defined and which has been understood and explored mainly from a professional perspective. Angela seeks to define it from a service user perspective, to enable a new understanding of its meanings and experience for them. She generates a measure of 'continuity of care' employing a 'survivor controlled' research process, which uses both qualitative and quantitative research methods and reports her results and reflections in her chapter.

Phil Cotterell and Mandy Paine

This chapter is concerned with involving a group that faces particular barriers and exclusions, people with life limiting illnesses and conditions. It is jointly written by a researcher, Phil Cotterell, and Mandy Paine, an activist with a life limiting condition. While there has been an increasing emphasis in health and social care on user involvement, one group where this has been slow to develop and where there have been particular concerns that it might not be possible or appropriate is people with life limiting or palliative care conditions. The chapter explores and takes account of the complex practical and emotional issues that are raised where people are involved in research and other activities at end of life. While the emotional insights which it offers may have a particular relevance in addressing the issues raised by and for this group of service users, they are of relevance and importance for involvement more generally.

User-led service provision

Colin Barnes

In the UK and internationally, since the 1980s, there has been a shift away from the provision of services by the state to a welfare pluralist approach which places a greater emphasis on diverse sources of service supply. This chapter explores a parallel and related development, beginning with the emergence of the international disabled people's movement and the social model of disability and philosophy of independent living. It examines the contribution of disabled people's organisations to the design and delivery of services to enable service users to achieve the goals of independent living. It offers a discussion of the political and social context in which such user-led services (such as centres for independent living) evolved in the 1980s, in particular the critique of the welfare state and the promotion of user involvement in public services. It discusses the findings from a major mixed method user controlled national research project exploring user-led services and considers the implications of recent developments in the promotion of user-led services in the policy context of direct payments and personal budgets.

Patsy Staddon

In her chapter, Patsy Staddon, coming from a dual position of lived experience and academic study, challenges conventional understandings and treatment of 'alcoholism'. She draws on an emancipatory research perspective and the social model of disability, to question traditional medicalised understandings of alcohol dependency in relation to women, looking at the services based on them and problems associated with them. She examines the user-led support service that developed from her research and women's understandings of dominant models of alcohol dependence as well as their own interpretations, experience and viewpoints. Her chapter begins a process of reconceptualising alcohol problems from a social model perspective.

Inclusion and addressing diversity
Kath Browne, Leela Bakshi and Jason Lim

The lesbian, gay, bisexual and transgender (LGBT) local community-led research project, 'Count Me In Too', which Kath Browne, Leela Bakshi and Jason Lim report, explores how partnership working right from the beginning of research could empower marginalised LGBT people and still impact on dominant agendas. The project was shaped by activists and academics. It highlights the importance of partnership working with marginalised communities, academics and commissioners, in ensuring that research makes a difference to service provision and accessibility, while highlighting that the impact can still vary because of the multiple forms of marginalisation that can operate in LGBT communities. It provides an important reminder of the importance of acknowledging the context of both research and user involvement and showcases an example of applied research designed to directly inform service provision and commissioning practice.

Louca-Mai Brady, Catherine Shaw, Rachel Blades and Ciara Davey

In their chapter, Louca-Mai Brady, Catherine Shaw, Rachel Blades and Ciara Davey discuss the involvement of children and young people in research within the broader context of their rights and models of child participation. They offer a model for involvement developed by the National Children's Bureau (NCB) Research Centre and look at its practical application through three core projects. These were concerned with involving young people in public health research, evaluating the 'Youth4U – Young Inspectors' programme with a team of young evaluators and involving young people in a study exploring why children who had been in care were disproportionately likely to be remanded or sentenced to custody. The authors look at the implications of these projects for children and young people's involvement in research and social care policy and practice.

Maggie Brennan, Vic Forrest and Jennifer Taylor

This chapter is jointly written by two people with learning difficulties, Maggie Brennan and Jennifer Taylor, and their supporter, Vic Forrest. All are researchers and they write from their particular viewpoints and experience about involving people with learning difficulties in research and self-advocacy. They write from their first-hand experience in their own voices, discussing self-advocacy more generally. They examine the social model of disability and discuss what they see involving people with learning difficulties as meaning and why it is important. They set out some of the barriers created by unhelpful involvement and ways of overcoming them, examining the role and importance of a skilled supporter, how such support can go wrong and ways of avoiding this.

Conclusion

Public participation and user involvement have now been part of the political, policy and professional scene for more than a generation in western societies. They have become embodied in political and policy rhetoric, with requirements for them built into legislation, guidance and good practice manuals. They are to be found in every kind of policy, from social care to education, public health, to housing. However, at a time when severe cuts are being made in public finances and public and social policy are undergoing major regressive restructuring, much confidence is being lost in the value and effectiveness of such public participation and user involvement. Consultations, listening exercises and the rest to involve public, patients and service users, continue, but people increasingly see them having little influence on the policy process and service provision, which largely seem to be unaffected by them. It is hoped that the detailed examples in this book and the practical, philosophical and theoretical issues they raise and illustrate will show that user involvement has an important part to play, even if policy drivers for such involvement changes.

User involvement and public participation have come a long way from the early requirements for 'comment and complaints procedures' first established in the 1990 NHS and Community Care Act or in the pioneering provisions of public participation in planning legislation of the late 1960s. While there is still frequently a failure to acknowledge or to learn from all this experience, much of it can now be found distilled in the diverse contributions included in this book. Between them they provide practical, philosophical and theoretical insights, as well as offering guidance and case study examples of research methods and methodology. There is thus both a wide range of evidence and knowledge to be drawn upon from research as well as research-based findings to learn from and draw upon.

CHAPTER 1

The Theory and Philosophy Behind User Involvement

Peter Beresford

Introduction

A fundamental problem affecting user involvement and participation is that the terms tend to be poorly defined and carelessly used. They seem to suffer the same problem as other related 'feel-good' terms such as 'community', 'neighbourhood', 'self-help', 'voluntarism' and 'mutuality'. Because the assumption often is that they delineate something positive and helpful; because they relate to contested political and policy discourses and because they engage many different, sometimes competing interests and perspectives, there is more likely to be disagreement than consensus about their meaning. Thus terms such as 'participation' and 'user involvement' are routinely used to include as diverse a range of activities as volunteering, campaigning, pressure group politics, consultation, satisfaction surveys and lobbying.

While ideas of participation and user involvement connect with the disciplines and discourses of politics and political philosophy; of democracy and power; of citizenship rights and responsibilities, they often tend to be abstracted from these and treated in isolation as a technical rather than ideological matter. However participation and user involvement are far from value-free and neutral issues amenable to technical solutions. Instead they need to be understood in their historical, political, ideological, and cultural contexts. It is important that any concern with involvement is clearly connected with existing knowledge and experience. Otherwise its ambiguities and contradictions are likely to remain unrecognized and unresolved. Ultimately discussions of participation which are not grounded in an understanding of its practice and politics, are likely to be unhelpful and deficient. It is this thinking which underpins this book and its contributions. The aim has been to engage with practice, connect it with theory and values, particularly drawing on knowledge from research to do so.

Contextualizing user involvement

In their broadest sense participation and user involvement are part of wider discussions about democracy that go back to ancient Greece. More specifically they can be seen to be linked with attempts to move from representative democracy, embodied in the UK in the parliamentary system and local government, to participatory democracy, which seek to enable people's direct involvement in political, policy, administrative and other processes which can affect them in society. From the late 1990s, there have been a range of such developments, including citizen juries, referenda, official petitions and of course consultative and other participatory structures and arrangements provided at European, UK, national, regional and local levels.

A longstanding issue, which is still not adequately resolved, is how such participatory provisions relate to the representative structures for formal democracy. We have seen this under the coalition government where an official petition for a referendum on UK membership of the European Community has not been taken forward in policy because it conflicts with the government's position on the subject. From the late 1960s, provision for public participation was introduced in land use planning and development legislation. While these were established parallel to the structures of formal local and national representative democracy, the two were not integrated. The process of planning and participation was not related to the wider political process. Research suggested that the public participation which followed from these arrangements was limited and biased (Sheffield University, 1974–1978). As a result, Norman Dennis (1972), writing about public participation in planning, advised people instead to go through the conventional structures of representative democracy, via their councillor or MP, to get their views heard and achieve change, on the basis that these were more likely to be effective than add-on participatory arrangements. This problem and tension has continued with the widespread introduction of arrangements for user involvement, which are mainly consultative and advisory in purpose, rather than ensuring people an effective influence. This has resulted in frequent complaints from service users and their organizations that much formal user involvement achieves little and does not ensure them an adequate voice. Discussions about participation and user involvement often ignore or underplay structural issues, yet as Kath Browne and her colleagues highlight in their chapter, the context of and structural constraints affecting user involvement are crucial.

The modern history of participation really begins with those provisions for public participation in planning. Overlapping and subsequent developments have included community development, followed from the 1980s by user involvement. Participation has been a key element of community work and community development since the 1970s, however their capacity to achieve participation has been limited. Such participation, as we will see in Martin Hoban's chapter in this book, has often been seen as 'a means to an end rather than central'; it has frequently only engaged 'the usual suspects' and control has tended to remain with the professionals, rather than the public.

The 1980s saw the emergence of a new focus for participation and new terminology – user involvement. This reflected a desire to move away from service or provider-led public provision to more user-centred and user-led services and support. The desire was for different, better, more responsive services. User involvement became the unifying idea underpinning this development (Croft and Beresford, 1996, pp.184–5). By increasing user involvement it would be possible to move beyond traditional top-down paternalistic approaches associated with the welfare state, to more user-centred provision. While user involvement became the buzz term of this development, what it meant and the values and ideology underpinning it, were largely left unclear and unagreed.

Models of participation

Stephanie McKinley and Sarah Yiannoullou's recent observation about user involvement in mental health could be applied much more generally now to public policy. They say:

> It is a '*must do*' for the mental health system and an '*opportunity to do*' for those using mental health services... Over the past 10 years, service user involvement has finally become enshrined in

policy. The government has made it a requirement... (McKinley
and Yiannoullou, 2012, p.115)

They followed a longstanding and popular approach to exploring user
involvement by framing it in terms of *models* of participation. They
referred to a particularly influential and early established model, the
'ladder of participation' developed by Sherry Arnstein in the context of
planning and development (Arnstein, 1969). This identifies a number
of positions on a continuum, from control and citizen power, through
consultation and tokenism to manipulation and non-participation. But
as McKinley and Yiannoullou observe, although still widely cited, this
has come to be recognized as having major limitations because of its
linear and uni-dimensional nature (Tritter and McCallum, 2006, p.165).
Participation is not necessarily as simple as that. Arnstein's ladder and its
derivatives generally do not take account of the fact that participation is
a complex and interactive process (which citizens can manipulate too),
that is essentially political in nature and takes place in a broader political
context.

The origins of interest in user involvement

User involvement is usually associated with participation in the public
rather than personal or private sphere, although its operation in social
care, where the two can converge, as policies intervene in the intimacies
of people's lives, raises particular issues. At least four developments have
been identified from the 1970s which have led to increased interest in
such participation (Taylor, 1996, p.181). These are the emergence of the
disabled people's and other service users' movements; the re-emergence
of interest in ideas of 'human need', with a particular concern with
social participation; the rekindling of interest in the idea of citizenship,
particularly linked with concerns about 'social exclusion'; and finally,
postmodernism, where the highlighting of diversity has also encouraged
concerns with the equal rights, inclusion and participation of different
groups and identities. We can also add to this:

- emerging public disquiet in the late twentieth century about the
  inadequacy and poor quality of welfare and other public services

- struggles for equal opportunities which highlighted the frequent
  failure of public services to ensure equal access, opportunities
  and provision

- progressive professionals and other service workers who wanted to work in more positive ways

- the emergence of new kinds of support services from women's, black and LGBT organizations and movements, showing how things could be different

- the emergence of new philosophies highlighting ideas of participation and inclusion, like 'normalization' and 'independent living'.

(Croft and Beresford, 1996, p.185)

However, the two contemporaneous developments which have perhaps had the most powerful and direct influence on the development of user involvement have been the ideological shift to the political right over the last 30 years in UK governments and beyond and the emergence of the new social or liberatory movements, like the women's, civil rights and LGBT movements. These have also been associated with the emergence of health and welfare service user movements, notably that of disabled people. Mike Oliver, the disability activist and academic identified four characteristics associated with such new social movements:

- They tend to be located at the periphery of the traditional political system and sometimes are deliberately marginalized.

- They offer a critical evaluation of society as part of a 'conflict between a declining but still vigorous form of domination and newly emergent forms of opposition' (Boggs, 1986, p.4).

- They are concerned with the quality of people's life as well as narrowly materialist needs.

- They tend to focus on issues that cross national boundaries and thus they become internationalist.

(Oliver, 1990, pp.118–123)

Thus the most frequent analytical discussion over the nature of participation has been concerned with the ideological distinction between the consumerist or managerialist/consumerist approach, which has its origins in the market-led politics of the new right, and the democratic or emancipatory approach advanced by the disabled people's and service users' movements and their supporters, which is grounded in a commitment to collective self-advocacy.

The dominant discussion about user involvement has been the managerialist/consumerist one, which in western countries such as the

UK has gained uninterrupted political support from the time of Mrs Thatcher, through New Labour to the current coalition government. Much of the modern discussion about participation has been framed in terms of having choice within a market economy or mixed economy of welfare. The consumer or service user is thus enabled to decide what (public) service they receive, just as they might expect to have a choice in relation to the commercial provision of other goods and services. This has been reflected in the methodology of this approach to user involvement, which has mainly been structured in terms of arrangements for consultation and market research. Consumerism starts with the idea of buying the goods and services we want, commodifying our needs, instead of making collective provision for them, to secure rights and entitlements. There is an irony here in the belief that market solutions applied to state and collective action offer helpful ways to improve them, when the state sector and the welfare state developed significantly to counter the inequalities and inadequacies of market-led economies.

Such a consumerist approach is fundamentally different from the understanding of the service user movements, who see participation very much in terms of challenging people's disempowerment and redistributing power and control. Service users are also much more interested in people's lives than services. They start with an interest in improving those lives rather than just trying to improve services that may impact on them (Campbell and Oliver, 1996).

However, while these two approaches to involvement are in essence very different from each other there are cross-overs between them and each has had effects on the other. For example, Marian Barnes and colleagues have argued that some mental health service user groups have adopted a consumerist approach to involvement (Barnes *et al.*, 1999). Similarly, the development of managerialist/consumerist approaches to involvement in public policy from the 1990s, provided levers and opportunities for service users and their movements to advance their ambitions for the democratization of services and their own empowerment. At the same time, the very real differences between these two approaches should not be underestimated. There is a big gulf between the liberatory goals of the service user movements, particularly the disabled people's movement and its development of the social model of disability with its associations with leftist politics, and right wing consumerism.

This gulf has often been blurred by their shared reliance on the common language of participation and involvement. But the same words have come to be used to mean very different things. This is undoubtedly a cause of confusion and misapprehensions among and between service users and those seeking to involve them, where there can be genuine misunderstandings about what is on offer and what the purpose of involvement actually is. The aim for state and service system is often merely to gain people's views to inform their own policy and decision-making processes. For service users, on the other hand, as repeatedly emerges from surveys and consultations exploring this issue, most people get involved in order to 'make a difference' and to be able to influence and change existing arrangements (Branfield *et al.*, 2006).

Social care and service users

However, as we noted in the book's introduction, it is not only the term 'user involvement' whose definition needs to be considered more carefully. The same applies to the other two key terms we are concerned with here, 'social care' and 'service users'. Social care has been helpfully defined as:

> The provision of services to adults who require assistance with aspects of daily living as a result of disability, illness or ageing. Social care is an all-embracing term for the personal social services. (Barton, 2000, p.318)

But this is by no means an agreed definition. Some commentators also include work with children and families while others challenge assumptions that social care can and should be seen only as a distinct and separate policy area. Instead they highlight the role that a range of other policies can play in providing social support and having a social care function, including housing, education and training, income maintenance and of course health. This is a point that has been particularly highlighted in relation to ideas like 'place-shaping' and 'total place' where the idea is to unify activities to promote people's wellbeing (Beresford *et al.*, 2011, pp.16–18; HM Treasury, 2010).

The term 'service user' is even more contentious. While it was developed to replace terminology which some people found oppressive, for example, words like 'patient', 'client' and 'customer', it has also come in for criticism for the association of the word 'user' with illegal drug use and for presenting people in passive terms and emphasizing their relation with services at the expense of other key aspects of their identity. There is, however, no agreed language in this field. What suits one person may offend another (Beresford, 2005). As Clare Allan, writer and mental health service user/survivor has written:

> All words are labels, categories in the great linguistic filing cabinet. And as such they are both including and excluding. Language is general, it has to be, but we write and read it as individuals and therein lies the problem. But language is also what links individuals. And however precarious the bridge, we have to keep striving to cross it. (Allan, 2011, p.2)

Shaping Our Lives, the national user-controlled organization and network has tried to develop a definition of service user which acknowledges the term's complexity and political nature and which may cause minimal offence. It says:

> The term 'service user' can be used to restrict your identity as if all you are is a passive recipient of health and welfare services. That is to say that a service user can be seen to be someone who has things 'done to them' or who quietly accepts and receives a service. This makes it seem that the most important thing about you is that you use or have used services. It ignores all the other things you do and which make up who you are as a person. This is *not* what Shaping Our Lives National User Network means when we talk of 'service users'. Shaping Our Lives National User Network sees 'service users' as an active and positive term, which means more than one thing. It is important that 'service user' should always be based on self-identification. But here are some of the things we think it means.
>
> It means that we are in an unequal and oppressive relationship with the state and society.
>
> It is about entitlement to receive welfare services. This includes the past when we might have received them and the present. Some people still need to receive services but are no longer entitled to for many different reasons.
>
> It may mean having to use services for a long time which separate us from other people and which make people think we are inferior and that there is something wrong with us.
>
> Being a service user means that we can identify and recognise that we share a lot of experiences with a wide range of other people who use services. This might include, for example, young people with experience of being looked after in care, people with learning difficulties, mental health service users, older people, physically and/or sensory impaired people, people using palliative care services and people with drug and alcohol problems.

This last point about recognising our shared experiences of using services, whoever we are, makes us powerful and gives us a strong voice to improve the services we are given and to give us more control and say over what kind of services we want. (Shaping Our Lives, 2012)

This is how we have sought to use the term in this chapter and book.

Participation and power

Participation is an issue inseparable from power, although this is not always made explicit and is certainly not always acknowledged in consumerist debates about user involvement. However, it is why discussions of empowerment and participation, especially among service users, closely overlap. Discussions and developments about participation generally, and user involvement specifically, also tend to be associated with people experiencing disempowerment. People want to get involved to exert an influence and to make change – personally and for others like themselves. That is why 'having a say' and 'getting involved' are often treated as synonymous, although they are not necessarily so in the actual practice of involvement. The political philosopher Steven Lukes reminds us that power is exercised when one party gets another to act as it wants it to, regardless of what it might want to do. These parties may be individuals, groups or institutions. But he also highlights 'the complex and subtle ways in which the inactivity of leaders and sheer weight of institutions – political, industrial and educational' can keep people out of the process and 'from even trying to get into it' (Lukes, 1974, pp.24, 38).

This problem can operate at all levels and in many different situations. Arrangements for involvement can challenge it, but we also need to remember that many people may be discouraged from, or not even have a sense of the possibility of, challenging their exclusion and disempowerment, to get involved. John Gaventa, the political sociologist, used Lukes' model of power to explain why poor Appalachian farmers appeared to accept domination and oppression by large corporations (Gaventa, 1980). People may not know what's possible, how to get involved, may not like to ask for too much, or be reluctant to complain. Understanding this can help us to make sense of why participatory initiatives are often very partial in who they engage, and are frequently limited to the most confident and assertive of people, and reflect dominant patterns of exclusion and inequality, for example, in relation to age, class, culture, belief, gender, sexuality and disability.

Two components seem to be essential if people are to have an equal and realistic chance of getting involved effectively. These are *access* and *support*. Access means having ways into political, organizational and decision-making structures which take account of people's physical, communication, cultural and other needs. Such provisions need to be ongoing, flexible and entail zero cost in all senses. Provisions for support arise from the issues highlighted by Lukes and Gaventa and address the need for:

- personal development – to increase people's expectations, assertiveness, self-confidence and self-esteem

- skill development – to build the skills people want and need to get involved and to develop their own preferred approaches to involvement

- practical support – to be able to take part, including access to information, child and respite care, transport, meeting places, advocacy etc.

- support for people to get together and work collectively in groups – including administrative support and funding, capacity building, payment for workers, training and development costs.
                                         (Croft and Beresford, 1996, p.193)

Involvement, diversity, inclusion and solidarity

Throughout the contributions in this book, we will see how providing such access and support is what makes it possible for the wide range of people who get involved to participate.

This concern with inclusion and diversity also has important links with the emergence of new social movements in the 1970s and 1980s. These came in for criticism from some quarters, as leading to an unhelpful move away from class analysis and action and the opportunities they were seen to offer for united action. There have also been concerns that their focus on different identities would result in conflict and fragmentation rather than unity and concerted action (Meiksens-Wood, 1986). Thus while, as has been said here, some commentators have seen postmodernism as one of the forces generating pressure for participation and collective action for change (through its highlighting of diversity, encouraging the equal rights, inclusion and the involvement of different groups and identities), others have seen this as creating divisions and weakening solidarity (Best, 2002; Heywood, 2007).

However, the experience of Shaping Our Lives, the independent national service user organization and network, in which I am involved, points to a very different conclusion. Shaping Our Lives has long worked hard to address issues of inclusion and diversity in both how it works and in its objectives. It works across (and is made up of) a wide range of service users and sees access as an equality issue, identifying three key areas for access:

- physical/environmental access
- cultural access
- communication access.

In addition Shaping Our Lives has carried out research projects exploring issues of diversity and inclusion. The evidence-based conclusion it has come to from such research, is that addressing diversity and working in more inclusive ways actually helps to *strengthen* solidarity, as well as making possible more inclusive and effective involvement (Beresford and Branfield, 2012).

The ambiguity of user involvement

As has been reported here, the issue of power is central to participation. This is also key to an understanding of the potential *ambiguity* of user involvement. Participatory initiatives and arrangements can result in the redistribution of power, changed, more equal relationships and the creation of opportunities for influence. Equally they often also serve in practice as a means of *keeping power from* people and giving a false impression of its transfer. This is frequently articulated in service users' complaints about user involvement being used to 'rubber stamp', 'tick boxes', 'tokenize' and 'incorporate' them. Participatory schemes can be used for these two conflicting purposes according to whether their initiators aim to hold on to power, or to share it.

Concerns about the regressive role of user involvement have raised suspicions about it and led to it being devalued, distrusted and in some cases rejected. But this leaves many people's desire to be more involved and have a greater say in society unsupported and vulnerable. A more helpful first step to dealing with the potential ambiguity of user involvement, is to analyse it carefully, as we have sought to here. This can help us understand why it is often treated as little more than a rhetorical flourish, rather than as a serious policy like any other. It can also help us respond to and take forward 'user involvement' in more effective and positive ways.

This is particularly important at a difficult time like the present, when major changes are being imposed on public policy from the top and centre by a government committed to both significant ideological change and large-scale public expenditure cuts. At this point it may therefore be helpful to draw some further distinctions. Getting involved and user involvement can mean two different but overlapping things. They may mean:

- people getting involved in *other people's* (for example, state, services, organizations) structures and arrangements for involvement

- people initiating *their* own activities and arrangements to seek to influence the latter (state, services, organizations).

Both of these may happen on an:

- individual basis

- collective basis.

The repeated message from service user movements is that it is likely to be much more effective to get involved on a collective basis. Also perhaps the weakest and most vulnerable position to be in, is to be trying to influence an organization as an individual. The lesson from the disabled people's and service users' movements tends to be that if we first develop our own collectivity, our own ideas, proposals and demands, we are then much more likely to be able to exert an influence with them, either directly through our own proactive initiatives, or on services, policymakers, local and central state, through responding to their participatory schemes (Beresford, 1999; Campbell and Oliver, 1996).

The shifting emphasis of user involvement

While the talk of user involvement continues unabated under the current coalition government, with, for example, its NHS slogan (appropriated and individualized from the disabled people's movement), 'Nothing about me without me', such calls now carry less and less conviction with public, patients and service users, seeing frontline services cut arbitrarily, despite innumerable consultations and 'listening events', their growing protests and resulting hardship. Government consumerist calls for 'user involvement' are being met with increasing wariness. The unprecedented public spending cuts from 2011, being made in the name of the 'public deficit' have brought user involvement's contradictions into stark relief.

Faced with the loss of welfare benefits, housing and services, service users are finding their voice in opposition, action and protests. Because they may have physical and sensory impairments, because they are frail through age, or isolated through mental distress, traditional forms of involvement and campaigning may not be open to them, or familiar or comfortable. Over the years they have developed new accessible forms of involvement, which now increasingly draw on the new technologies and forms of social networking that have become available. Service users and their organizations are creating new meanings to collectivity and community, direct action and protest. They work alone and together, with people with shared experience, as well as with allied causes. Service users are joining mainstream anti-cuts campaigns, linking up with them and forming their own. They are taking to the streets, to the blogosphere and are a growing presence on social networking sites (Beresford, 2011). While some service users are still excluded from the new digital and internet age, others are at the cutting edge. Such service users are blogging, vlogging, podcasting, tweeting and forming their own Facebook groups. The 'Spartacus' report, researched, written and published by disabled people and other service users, challenging government welfare reform, epitomizes this development (Campbell *et al.*, 2012). 'The social media storm [it] stirred up...has motivated many disabled people to campaign for the first time' (Dhani and Winyard, 2012, p.33).

A shift in emphasis is taking place. This represents a real innovation in user involvement. Instead of just getting involved in official provisions for user involvement, service users are more and more developing their own initiatives and campaigns and connecting with traditional structures of representative democracy and new inclusive forms of lobbying and networking to achieve their objectives.

Priorities for the future

The contributions in this book reflect these emerging understandings and approaches to user involvement. They are not narrowly concerned with responding to calls to get involved from the state and/or services. Yet at the same time some of their discussions do offer help and support to people and groups seeking to do this. There are examples which explore and develop skills and models which link with conventional arrangements for involvement, like quality assurance and standard setting. But these are also relevant where people are seeking to make their own independent efforts to have an influence and have their voices heard. Thus contributions are concerned with both proactive and reactive approaches to involvement, and activities and issues where the two may converge. They connect with both consultation and campaigning and recognize the potential for links between the two.

What they perhaps highlight most is the importance for people and groups seeking to increase their involvement and to take forward user involvement, to advance their own skills, understanding and knowledge about it. This emphasizes the key role that learning and training have to play here. The educationalist Alan Hurst has written:

> Education has the key role to play in the growth of participation – and this involves participation in the process of learning, learning how to participate and learning about participation. (Hurst, 1998, p.303)

This is one of the key ways in which service user knowledge or knowledges may be developed and shared. Training for 'user trainers' and the development of 'user trainers' (notably in the field of social work) are a key expression of this. Another key way forward, as is also emphasized in this book, is through the development of user involvement in research, collaborative and user-led research. There are a number of such examples reported and discussed here. Such research not only extends the evidence-base of user involvement, but also offers another systematic route to the advancement of service user knowledge(s).

This is likely to have an increasingly important part to play both in understanding and advancing user involvement. In the early days of user involvement, the moral argument that it was important to involve people, or technicist assumption that such involvement would necessarily improve products and services, tended to hold sway. Over the last five to ten years, much greater emphasis has been placed on demonstrating the 'impact' of involvement, that is to say, evidencing what effects it actually has. (This is the subject of the next chapter by Sarah Carr.) This discussion about impact has become increasingly important, but it is still at a relatively early stage, so far as its intellectual development is concerned. What it means, the domains in which it needs to be tested and whose judgements should apply, continue to be subjects for discussion. What we can probably expect is that interpretations of impact are likely to vary according to whose viewpoint is offered. This is another important reason for ensuring that the experiential knowledge of the diverse range of service users is included in this, whether accessed systematically through research, or through other forms of knowledge sharing and development.

Marian Barnes and Phil Cotterell in the conclusion to their book about user involvement offer a helpful reminder that 'all social phenomena are subject to competing interpretations of meanings and significance and reality itself can be considered to be socially constructed' (Barnes and Cotterell, 2012, p.225). This can also be seen as part of the inheritance of postmodern discussions which have a more general bearing on user involvement. It is a further reminder of the complexity of perspectives on user involvement and the different, multi-faceted and overlapping identities associated with user involvement and its development. This is strongly demonstrated in our book where we encounter people collaborating from different standpoints, as well as embodying multiple perspectives in their own complex individual identities.

At the same time, we know that imbalances of power mean that some perspectives and identities are more powerful than others. Experience as a long-term social care service user usually signifies disempowerment. If we are to get the benefit of all these different standpoints, experiences and knowledges, if they are to be able to collaborate on more equal terms in future to advance our understanding of the theory and practice of user involvement, then more needs yet to be done to challenge the barriers that still face service users and their experiential knowledge to ensure user involvement that is truly and equally inclusive of all service users. This ranges from those devalued as 'the usual suspects', to those increasingly acknowledged as being 'seldom heard voices'. Our hope is that this book may serve as one more resource to help make this happen.

References

Allan, C. (2011) 'On Mental Health, It's Wise To Choose Your Words Carefully.' *Society Guardian*, 6 September, p.2.

Arnstein, S. (1969) 'A ladder of citizen participation.' *Journal of the American Institute of Planners 35*, 4, 216–224.

Barnes, M. and Cotterell, P. (eds) (2012) *Critical Perspectives On User Involvement*. Bristol: Policy Press.

Barnes, M., Harrison, S., Mort, M. and Shardlow, P. (1999) *Unequal Partners: User Groups and Community Care*. Bristol: Policy Press.

Barton, R. (2000) 'Social Care.' In M. Davies (ed.) *The Blackwell Encyclopaedia of Social Work*. Oxford: Blackwell.

Beresford, P. (1999) 'Making Participation Possible: Movements of Disabled People and Psychiatric System Survivors.' In T. Jordan and A. Lent (eds) *Storming the Millennium: The New Politics of Change*. London: Lawrence and Wishart.

Beresford, P. (2005) '"Service user": regressive or liberatory terminology?' Current Issues, *Disability and Society 20*, 4, 469–477.

Beresford, P. (2011) 'Society's Hidden Have Found Their Protesting Voice.' Second Thoughts, *Society Guardian*, 5 January, p.4.

Beresford, P. and Branfield, F. (2012) 'Building Solidarity, Ensuring Diversity: Lessons from Service Users and Disabled People's Movements.' In M. Barnes and P. Cotterell (eds) (2012) *Critical Perspectives On User Involvement*. Bristol: Policy Press.

Beresford, P., Fleming, J., Glynn, M., Bewley, C., Croft, S., Branfield, F. and Postle, K. (2011) *Supporting People: Towards a Person-centred Approach*. Bristol: Policy Press.

Best, S. (2002) *Introduction to Politics*. London: Sage.

Boggs, C. (1986) *Social Movements and Political Power*. Philadelphia: Temple University Press.

Branfield, F., Beresford, P. with Andrews, E.J., Chambers, P., Staddon, P., Wise, G. and Williams-Findlay, B. (2006) *Making User Involvement Work: Supporting Service User Networking and Knowledge*. York: Joseph Rowntree Foundation, York Publishing Services.

Campbell, J. and Oliver, M. (1996) *Disability Politics: Understanding our Past, Changing our Future*. London: Routledge.

Campbell, S.J., Anon, M.E., Marsh, S., Franklin, K., Gaffney, D., Anon, Dixon, M., James, L., Barnett-Cormack, S., Fon-James, R., Willis, D. and Anon (2012) *Responsible Reform: A Report on the Proposed Changes to Disability Living Allowance. Diary of a Benefit Scrounger. Spartacus*. Available at www.ekklesia.co.uk/files/response_to_proposed_dla_reforms.pdf, accessed on 20 June 2012.

Croft, S. and Beresford, P. (1996) 'The Politics of Participation.' In D. Taylor (ed.) *Critical Social Policy: A Reader*. London: Sage.

Dennis, N. (1972) *Public Participation and Planning Blight*. London: Faber.

Dhani, J. and Winyard, S. (2012) 'Disabled Unity.' Letter, *The Guardian*, 20 January.

Gaventa, J. (1980) *Power and Powerlessness: Quiescence and Rebellion in an Appalachian Valley*. Oxford: Clarendon.

Heywood, A. (2007) *Political Ideologies: An Introduction*. Basingstoke: Palgrave Macmillan (Fourth edition).

HM Treasury (2010) *Total Place: A Whole Area Approach to Public Services*. London: HM Treasury and Department of Communities and Local Government.

Hurst, A. (1998) 'Review of D. Taylor (ed.) (1996) *Critical Social Policy: A Reader*.' *Disability and Society 13*, 2, 301–304.

Lukes, S. (1974) *Power: A Radical View*. Basingstoke: Macmillan.

McKinley, S. and Yiannoullou, S. (2012) 'Changing Mind: Unleashing the Potential of Mental Health Service Users – A Critical Perspective on Current Models of Service User Involvement and their Impact on Wellbeing and "Recovery".' In M. Barnes and P. Cotterell (eds) (2012) *Critical Perspectives On User Involvement*. Bristol: Policy Press.

Meiksens-Wood, E. (1986) *The Retreat From Class: A New True Socialism*. London: Verso.

Oliver, M. (1990) *The Politics of Disablement*. Basingstoke: Macmillan.

Shaping Our Lives (2012) Definitions available at www.shapingourlives.org.uk/definitions.html, accessed on 20 June 2012.

Sheffield University (1974–1978) *The Linked Research Project into Public Participation: Interim Research Papers, 1–13*. Sheffield: Department of Extra-Mural Studies, Sheffield University.

Taylor, D. (ed.) (1996) *Critical Social Policy: A Reader*. London: Sage.

Tritter, J.Q. and McCallum, A. (2006) 'The snakes and ladders of user involvement: moving beyond Arnstein.' *Health Policy 76*, 2, 156–168.

CHAPTER 2

Participation, Resistance and Change

Examining Influences on the Impact of Service User Participation

Sarah Carr

Introduction

It is important to note that the desire to change things and make a difference is perhaps the chief motivating factor for those involved in all the projects and initiatives described by the various contributors to this book. This chapter aims to set a context by looking at some of the broader issues for achieving meaningful change through service user participation and examines some of the key UK literature on organisational resistance, power dynamics and conflict in the process. It also outlines the emergence of the 'co-production' approach in relation to service user participation and change and concludes by asking questions about the future while reflecting on past evidence.

McKinley and Yiannoullou note in their assessment of the impact of current models of mental health service user participation on wellbeing and recovery that:

> Being 'involved' should have a positive impact on how the service is used, perceived and experienced by the stakeholders in receipt of them and should enhance their wellbeing. They are obviously the people best placed to know what they need and what works.

> The impact of involvement is influenced by the purpose, presence
> and process and measuring the...impact of any type of service user
> involvement is critical to its success. (McKinley and Yiannoullou,
> 2012, p.117)

Here the authors refer to a useful set of evidence-based principles which
form a framework for service user participation. These are purpose,
presence, process and impact (Faulkner, 2010). The discussion that
follows examines how the middle two elements influence the final
element – that is to say how presence and process can determine impact
and therefore achieve change.

'Has service user participation made a difference to social care services?': selected findings from a research synthesis

*The Social Care Institute for Excellence Position Paper 3: Has Service User
Participation Made a Difference to Social Care Services?* (Carr, 2004) is a
'review of reviews' designed to provide one of the first comprehensive
sources of evidence on the overall impact of service user participation
on social care service development, design and provision in England and
Wales. It is a synthesis of four directly commissioned literature reviews
(older people, children and young people, disabled people and people
with learning disabilities, with attention to diversity across all groups)
and two NHS Service Delivery Organisation (NHS SDO) programme
literature reviews on mental health and user participation in change
management (Rose *et al.*, 2002).

    The production of the report itself included service user participation
wherever possible which required developing a methodology for service
user participation in the commissioning process as well as with the
teams conducting each research review – relatively new approaches in
research commissioning and review. The extent of control that service
users had in the production of each report differed, with only one of
the four studies being fully user-controlled and authored. Inclusive
commissioning, tendering and peer review processes were developed as
part of this work and later set standards for research commissioning
(particularly with INVOLVE, an NHS National Institute for Health
Research organisation supporting public and patient involvement in
health and social care research (see INVOLVE, 2003) as well as inclusive
systematic or literature review methodology (Carr and Coren, 2007;

Coren and Fisher, 2006), more fully demonstrated by Newbigging and colleagues in Chapter 7 of this book. In this particular instance the report was given additional credibility by the explicit acknowledgement of the service user status of the author.

The research synthesis revealed what will become a consistent theme in this chapter – that certain participation strategies do not necessarily accommodate service user voices or knowledge or result in user-led change. The research review showed that although organisational participation processes were monitored, the impact and outcome of participation were seldom evaluated and fed back to participants. There were strong indications of a lack of organisational responsiveness to issues identified by service users and a lack of clear commitment to change and its evaluation as a result of service user participation. Many of the contributors to this book demonstrate that this situation is now slowly changing, particularly with projects such as those described by Browne and colleagues in Chapter 12, Bowers and Wilkins in Chapter 6 and Kristiansen in Chapter 5 of this book. However, these authors also describe the distinct challenges of realising meaningful change through participation, which has a long-term, positive impact on people's lives through improving services and support.

Most relevant for the discussion in this chapter are the report findings on organisational commitment and responsiveness, power relations, diversity and marginalisation and conflict and expectations. As suggested above, there was a distinct lack of organisational responsiveness to service user participation, suggesting that a fundamental political commitment should be driving participation initiatives. Power issues were at the heart of the majority of identified difficulties with achieving change and:

> exclusionary structures, institutional practices and professional attitudes can still affect the extent to which service users can influence change. It appears that power sharing can be difficult within mainstream structures, formal consultation mechanisms and traditional ideologies. (Carr, 2004, p.vii)

As regards attention to the diversity of service users in terms of race, sexual orientation, culture and even disability, mainstream services and participation initiatives were found wanting. This finding related to both diversity within service user groups and the relative lack of knowledge about participation for marginalised people:

> Service users who are marginalised from mainstream services can also be found to be under- or unrepresented in the participation intended to develop those services. (Carr, 2004, p.21)

Finally, conflict emerged as an important but often avoided part of participation. Although this was sometimes due to unclear expectations of the process and its outcomes from both sides, it was often rooted in deeper tensions. The findings on conflict and change were subsequently explored further in a journal paper, which is discussed next.

Conflict and change: a further analysis of report findings

The *Critical Social Policy* paper 'Participation, power, conflict and change: theorising dynamics of service user participation in the social care system of England and Wales' (Carr, 2007) represents a further analysis of some key findings on the power dynamics inherent in service user participation from the Social Care Institute for Excellence (SCIE) report outlined above. It is a deeper analysis of the dynamics between social care organisations and service users who are participating in change. Research suggests that conflict has a role in service user participation strategies but the response of organisations has sometimes been to avoid conflict and resist change. The paper examines how organisational ideology, language, structure and mechanism can exclude service users who are perceived as 'too political' or 'too emotional', or where lived experience as expertise is not recognised. However, it is argued that if service users' own understanding of participation is accounted for, it should be recognised as a political act rather than compliance with a process.

The political theories of Chantal Mouffe (Mouffe, 2002) are used to examine the wider influence of the dominant liberal democratic culture on organisational behaviour in relation to user-led change. Her argument that liberal democracy demands 'rational consensus' and 'regulates dissidence', is one which can be applied to social care organisations engaged in service user participation. Mouffe's assertion is that 'antagonism' or conflict is inevitable when there is a plurality of ideas and experience, some of which are expressed in more personal or emotional ways. For the line of argument in this paper, this means service users challenging the rational professional consensus and doing so in ways which do not always fit with the dominant organisational language or process. The suggested solution, in the light of Mouffe's ideas, is not to resist or exclude people, but to change the process and terms of discourse, so that different voices are heard and there is an opportunity to form what she calls 'collective forms of identification' (Mouffe, 2002). The conclusion of the paper is that service users and frontline practitioners should be supported to find a continuity of common understanding, based on their experience at the frontline of adult social care delivery. It is argued that change informed by common understandings and experience between service users and frontline practitioners can occur as a result of open dialogue rather than artificial 'rational' consensus, which can exclude or marginalise certain voices or experiences. The argument and conclusion of this paper somewhat anticipates later ideas about 'co-production' in adult social care, to be discussed later in this chapter.

Barnes and colleagues also share the observations made in the paper about the operation of power and discourse in service user participation. They come to similar conclusions after examining responses to the emotional expression and experience of mental health service users in professionally or bureaucratically determined participation forums (Barnes, 2002; Barnes, 2008; Barnes, *et al.*, 2006). Barnes explicitly discusses what was implied by Hodge's conclusions about certain topics and modes of expression being 'off limits' (Hodge, 2005) in terms of often unacknowledged 'rules of engagement' as defined by the services or professionals which can exclude or delegitimise the types of 'contested knowledges' brought by service users. Such rules, according to Barnes, should not exclude 'the bearers of such knowledges' and if they 'are to be included within processes previously determined by rules governing dialogue on the basis of scientific evidence, bureaucratic procedures and/or party political debate, then this may require rethinking those rules in order to accommodate them' (Barnes, 2002, p.323). Barnes perceives that rules of the game do not only work to exclude 'contested knowledges', but also militate against emotional expression. Again, using evidence from case studies, Barnes argues that:

> public officials find any emotion – whether it be anger, pain or despair, difficult to handle in the context of deliberation directed at issues of policy or service delivery. The onus on managing emotions thus rests with the service users or citizens taking part, officials can invoke institutional rules and norms to define what is acceptable in contexts they control. (Barnes, 2008, p.472)

Rethinking the rules: some theories and observations from a brief UK literature review

This section presents a brief UK literature review, mainly starting from the twenty-first century, of some of the main theoretical pieces on the power dynamics and discourses in service user participation in adult mental health and social care to further illustrate the discussion on change and resistance in service user participation.

A tendency towards organisational and professional resistance to implementing change generated by service user participation was strongly evidenced by the SCIE research synthesis report which included an important literature review on user and carer involvement in a mental health context (Rose *et al.*, 2002). In their literature review Rose *et al.* conclude that for promoting democracy, representation and cultural change, 'resistant organisational or professional cultures and embedded power differentials are seen as primary obstacles to user involvement in formal representative structures' (p.9). The report authors identify the problem of incompatible understandings of 'the service user' as discussed above – that is the tension between the models of 'consumer' and 'citizen' – as being influential here, defining the problem as follows:

> A central framework for analysing the stakeholder relation in mental health services turns on the distinction between users and carers as consumers and citizens. The aims of user movements, however, are not always consonant with or limited to consumerist interests... Service users may have a dual identity as consumers of services, and as citizens to whom such services are accountable... The user movement calls for a more robust range of citizenship rights than those found in the customer relation. (p.12)

The report also identifies two issues which are relevant for the discussion of the theoretical analyses which follow: understandings of democratic process and ambivalence about service user involvement and the 'hidden' obstacles posed by structural and power differentials in the participation forum. The literature generating theories deriving from case studies analysis and other research into user participation in adult social care and mental health, identified for this section, has three main themes:

- understandings of representative democracy
- user voice, experience, expression and identity
- power differentials, discourse and rules.

These themes and the associated theories and findings are now examined.

As Beresford demonstrates in his chapter on the theory and philosophy behind user involvement for this book, there is a central political tension between the policy construction of the service user as a consumer and the service user movement's recognition of the broader citizenship of people who use social and mental health services. This tension also relates to wider issues of political agency and more general understandings and expectations of different democratic processes, of which service user participation is one. In their literature review, Rose *et al.* reveal a problem that service users often encounter in the participation process, one which was also surfaced in the SCIE report:

> It appears to be a particular problem that users and carers are asked to be more 'representative' than any other group of stakeholders in the change management process. Articulate users may be criticised as unrepresentative because 'ordinary' users are often not seen as articulate. Other stakeholder groups, in contrast, will not be subject to such challenges – articulate and assertive professionals and managers, for instance, are not likely to be questioned as 'unrepresentative'. (Rose *et al.*, 2002, p.14)

For those whom citizenship can be complex, conditional or contingent (Flint, 2009; Morris, 2004; Morris, 2005; Rummery, 2006) and who ally themselves with political and 'new social movements' such as the disability or mental health survivor movement, participation can be a difficult process in spaces determined by services and professionals. As Hodge has argued, 'the inadequacies of service-led attempts to give service users a voice in the policy-making process are contrasted with the activities of user-controlled organisations, both in developing their own alternatives to mainstream provision and in campaigning for change within mainstream services on their own terms' (Hodge, 2005, p.165). The notion of service user 'representativeness', as Rose *et al.*, evidence, is often used to resist participation and change (see also Bochel *et al.*, 2007). Barnes *et al.*'s definition of 'representative' and 'deliberative' models of democracy and democratic engagement aims to draw an important distinction between the understanding of how representative democracy should function in general governance and how a form of deliberative democracy should characterise the activity of specialist participatory decision-making forums (Barnes *et al.*, 2007). Service user participation in the decision-making process about services very rarely fits with the elected representative model, and yet the expectation is often that service user participants be representative when they may perceive participation as an opportunity to exercise their right to be critical citizens: 'Such initiatives require [professionals] to share their power with others who they may think ill-informed, lacking legitimacy and scarcely representative of the communities they claim to speak for' (Rao quoted in Barnes *et al.*, 2007, pp.41–42). While recognising its limitations, deliberative democracy, Barnes *et al.* surmise, can offer a participative form of governance and decision making which is more useful for understanding service user participation:

> advocates argue it can generate a stronger democracy with citizens empowered in relation to both politicians and public officials. The practice of deliberative democracy is intended to open knowledge previously restricted to specific scientific or other communities to lay scrutiny, as well as open up political arenas to more direct processes of citizen involvement... Underlying such initiatives is the belief that technical or expert knowledge alone is inadequate to the resolution of policy problems, since the issues such problems raise are also political and ethical. (pp.35–36)

However, the chief limitation of deliberative democracy for understanding service user participation, Barnes argues, is the fact that the conditions of social parity, equality of access, capacity and opportunity and the type of power sharing required for it to function properly do not exist in reality. Instead she argues that 'we need a practice of deliberation which explicitly recognises and encompasses inequalities of power and diversity of experience and expression, rather than assuming that such inequality and diversity will be accommodated within processes governed by universalist notions of fairness and competence' (Barnes, 2002, p.324).

Drawing on the SCIE report to demonstrate the lack of evaluation of the impact of service user participation in adult social care, Webb argues that the 'concept has been consistently under-theorised in both research and policy remits' (Webb, 2008, p.271). He also discusses the political dimension of participation in terms of 'representational and participatory democracy'. However, he asserts that such understandings of service user participation are too simplified and he is critical of the way 'social care research has engaged in too general discussions of participation such that they cannot be operationalised' (p.269). Instead, Webb offers a social network analytic model for evaluating the extent and impact of service user participation in service development and change, arguing that 'traditional approaches to participation based on outcome evaluation have failed to capture the impact and qualitative nature of relationships of participation' (p.284). However, Bochel *et al.*'s observation that organisations evaluating the impact of service user participation have tended to focus on 'output' (process) rather than 'outcome' (impact and change) suggests that outcomes of service user participation are not always evaluated (Bochel *et al.*, 2007), also echoing the findings of Rose *et al.* Lewis' analysis of how power relations function in participation processes draws on human rights perspectives, and she argues that 'recognition is not just socio-political but also personal, with a strong moral dimension to the issue' (Lewis, 2009, p.259). Her analysis focuses on the effects of the non-recognition of mental health user and survivor perspectives and knowledge which is 'undermining of [their] personhood and humanity [and] can work to have a deleterious effect on interpersonal and therefore self-respect' (p.267). She argues that 'psychiatrising', or the pathologising of service user and survivor contributions, is a form of this 'misrecognition' which perpetuates and even deepens the injustice that participation initiatives in mental health seek to address, and points to the need to challenge 'institutionalised patterns of cultural values which impeded participation' (p.270).

Analysis of case studies in the participation of mental health service users shows how user voices and experiences can be marginalised or downplayed. This is not always by a conscious strategy of exclusion, but rather as the consequence of the interplay of power and identity in participatory processes and decision-making forums that are professional spaces into which service users are 'invited'. From the perspective of the 'critical professional', Batsleer and Humphries have located this difficulty in the construction of welfare discourse more generally: 'the discourses of welfare mark social division, inclusion and exclusion: mark 'us' and 'them' in changing and shifting ways' (Batsleer and Humphries, 2000, p.2). Hodge's examination of the workings of a mental health service user forum centres on the analysis of power dynamics and discourse (Hodge 2005). She shows how 'power is exercised discursively in various, apparently trivial, ways, ensuring that the forum's discourse remains within established normative boundaries and serving, ultimately, to reinforce existing institutionally defined power relations' (p.164). Her research leads her to decide that certain negative experiences of treatment (such as electroconvulsive therapy or ECT), suggestions for service change, alternative understandings of mental distress and practitioner personal agreement 'if not off-limits, are incapable of being incorporated into the forum's discourse in any meaningful sense. They clearly fall outside the discursive boundaries that have been set' (p.170). She concludes that by examining linguistic interaction 'it is possible to demonstrate precisely how power is used to exclude certain voices, to give legitimacy to the status quo and…to reinforce existing structural power inequalities between service users and officials' (p.165).

The construction of co-production: an overview

The difficulties of the exercise of power and influence by service users in spaces created and controlled by professionals and their services have also been reflected in the construction of policy terminology used to describe a certain sort of service user participation. 'Co-production' is a policy term that first appeared as an official government strategy for service user participation in the 2007 *Putting People First* concordat for adult social care reform in England:

> the first public service reform programme which is co-produced, co-developed, co-evaluated and recognises that real change will only be achieved through the participation of users and carers at every stage. (HM Government, 2007, p.1)

Since then, the term 'co-production' has become embedded in current policy language for adult social care and health reform in England, with the Think Local Act Personal (TLAP) partnership using it in relation to the evaluation and development of personalised social care and community services and support (TLAP, 2011).

Elsewhere, in practice, co-production is being used to define an approach to participation which aims to create a situation where frontline staff and service users can come together to share expertise and develop solutions to mutually identified problems (Needham, 2007; Farr, 2012). Its influence for social care and mental health practice is evident in Chapter 6 of this book, where Bowers and Wilkins discuss defining co-production with older people and acknowledge difficulties with the concept's 'excessive elasticity'. In their chapter they refer to work by Needham and Carr which aims to define a model of co-production in adult social care which could promote change or transformation:

> It repositions the service user as one of the experts and asks what assets they can contribute to collaborative relationships which will transform provision. It takes 'a whole life focus', incorporating broader quality of life issues, rather than just clinical or service

issues. The people who use services can be involved in shaping the ethos of care and in empowering frontline staff as well as themselves. However, some people are already able to be active citizens and take advantage of the opportunities that co-productive approaches will offer, whereas others are very disadvantaged, both socially and personally. This situation needs to be carefully considered when developing transformative approaches for different people and different social care contexts. (Needham and Carr, 2009, p.9)

Despite the term becoming embedded in policy language as a way of describing an approach to service user participation in the reform, development and delivery of adult social care, co-production is a concept originally associated with the generation of social capital (Cahn, 2001; Cummins and Miller, 2007; Whitaker, 1980). Cummins and Miller's brief definition is useful as a starting point for understanding co-production: 'basically, services have to learn how to *work with* rather than *do unto* service users' (Cummins and Miller, 2007, p.7). In addition and as is clear from Needham and Carr's definition, 'service users should be regarded as an asset encouraged to work alongside professionals as partners in the delivery of services' (Boyle and Harris, 2009, p.15). Co-production was explored by Barnes and colleagues as a way to manage community care services and user participation in 1999 (Barnes *et al.*, 1999) and resurfaced after the theoretical approach was conceived as part of personalisation (Beresford, 2009; Carr, 2010; Glasby and Littlechild, 2009). The work of Leadbeater is most evident in the construction of the policy concept of co-production as a way of describing 'deep' personalisation in the Demos think-tank report *Personalisation Through Participation* (Leadbeater, 2004) which outlined his potential 'new script' for public services. Leadbeater emphasises the direct participation of the people who use services: 'By putting users at the heart of services, by enabling them to become participants in the design and delivery, services will be more effective by mobilising millions of people as co-producers of the public goods they value' (Leadbeater, 2004, p.19). Leadbeater's co-production appears to be a concept posited as a coherent policy solution, then adopted as a part of the New Labour reform package of adult social care services, of which personalisation was the central driving force (Carr, 2010; HM Government, 2007).

Hunter and Ritchie explore the implications of co-production and personalisation for changing relationships in social care and provision of welfare services, giving examples of existing practice (Hunter and

Ritchie, 2007). They describe co-production as 'a particular approach to partnership between people who rely on services and the people and agencies providing those services' (p.9), which moves from organisational partnership in strategy and governance to the service users and practitioners at the frontline. Notably, Hunter and Ritchie argue that a key problem in social care services is located in the nature of human relationships, which a co-production approach could address: 'Many people are under-served by the human service system. Some of this results from the orientation and focus of services, with people's important needs not being addressed at all, or with services actually compounding people's problems' (p.13). They refer to the place of co-production as 're-engineering' approaches to the design and delivery of social care and support following the 'philosophical reorientation' by the disability and independent living movements and by policy developments in consumerism. They argue that the collaborative relationship between the practitioner and service user and the bringing together of their expertise has the potential to solve particular (and often local, 'site specific') problems in social care service design and delivery.

In response to the emerging developments in government policy, a series of practice explorations, political position papers and further conceptual work focusing on co-production have appeared (Bovaird, 2007; Boyle, Clark and Burns, 2006; Cummins and Miller, 2007; Needham, 2007; New Economics Foundation, 2008; Stephens and Ryan-Collins, 2008). Some argue at a political 'macro level' for a new understanding of market economy, social capital and the value of people's 'assets' (knowledge, experience, ideas) (New Economics Foundation, 2008; Stephens and Ryan-Collins, 2008) while others evaluate practical implementation issues and highlight good practice points (i.e. Boyle et al., 2006). Most authors conclude, along with Hunter and Ritchie, that a re-evaluation, new understanding and re-configuring of frontline relationships and relative expertise and assets are vital. However, co-production as a way to reform wider public services has been the focus of a 'public sector innovation lab' work programme and a series of reports from the National Endowment for Society and the Arts (NESTA) in partnership with the New Economics Foundation (NEF) (see Boyle et al., 2010; Boyle and Harris, 2009; Boyle, Slay and Stephens, 2010). While this work aims to define co-production for public service reform and identify and evaluate practice, the project activity is essentially at the level of 'policy makers...those who have the political, organisational or professional power to determine the overall philosophy or strategic direction of the policy process' (Bochel *et al.*, 2007, p.202). It does not appear to include those identified in theory and research as key players in co-production, service users, carers and frontline practitioners, in highest level strategic discussions about policy development and implementation. This in itself exemplifies some of the challenges for service user participation in policy making and organisational change identified by those analysing the operation of service user participation and how user knowledge and expertise is valued and conceptualised (Beresford, 2003). Indeed, as Farr has argued, co-production as a 'new' way of conceptualising and undertaking service user participation, may yet be beset by the same difficulties as previous strategies unless there is the genuine political commitment to power sharing identified in the SCIE report:

> co-production and co-design projects engage with service users' experiences, emotions and skills and promote collective dialogue to catalyse reflection and action, involving both staff and users in improvement processes. However, organisational politics, cultures, policies and procedures may restrict impact and influence. (Farr, 2012, p.88)

Conclusion

To return to the framework for service user participation introduced at the beginning, 'purpose, presence, process and impact' (Faulkner, 2010), the chapter sought to set out and examine some of the evidence and discussion about how presence and process can influence impact. The overview of some of the key UK evidence showed that presence is an area of particular tension in user participation and is often characterised by degrees of conflict and subject to different types of (often unrecognised and sometimes unintentional) control which can limit the extent to which user-driven change can be achieved. This situation means that 'current practices limit the effectiveness of user involvement and mean that the pace of change is slow' (Shaping Our Lives *et al.*, 2007, p.3). However, the evidence presented here can act as a starting point for recognising and addressing some of the more difficult power and value dynamics in service user participation. Moreover, the remaining chapters in this book all show how some of these issues are being tackled in practice and constitute a significant contribution to the next wave of evidence on how service user participation could result in change that makes a real difference to people's lives.

References

Barnes, M. (2002) 'Bringing difference into deliberation? Disabled people, survivors and local governance.' *Policy and Politics 30*, 3, 319–331.

Barnes, M. (2008) 'Passionate participation: emotional experiences and expressions in deliberative forums.' *Critical Social Policy 29*, 3, 374–397.

Barnes, M., Davis, A. and Rogers, H. (2006) 'Women's voices, women's choices: experiences and creativity in consulting women users of mental health services.' *Journal of Mental Health 15*, 3, 329–341.

Barnes, M., Harrison, S., Mort, M., Shardlow, P. and Wistow, G. (1999) 'The New Management of Community Care: User Groups, Citizenship and Co-production.' In G. Stoker (ed.) *The New Management of Local Governance.* Basingstoke: Palgrave.

Barnes, M., Newman, J. and Sullivan, H. (2007) *Power, Participation and Political Renewal: Case Studies in Public Participation.* Bristol: Policy Press.

Batsleer, J. and Humphries, B. (2000) *Welfare, Exclusion and Political Agency.* London: Routledge.

Beresford, P. (2003) *It's Our Lives: A Short Theory Of Knowledge, Distance And Experience.* London: OSP for Citizen Press.

Beresford, P. (2009) 'Social care, personalisation and service users: addressing the ambiguities.' *Research, Policy and Planning 27*, 2, 73–84.

Bochel, C., Bochel, H., Somerville, P. and Worley, C. (2007) 'Marginalised or enabled voices? "User participation" in policy and practice.' *Social Policy and Society 7*, 2, 201–210.

Bovaird, T. (2007) *Beyond Engagement and Participation: User and Community Co-Production of Services.* London: Carnegie Trust.

Boyle, D., Clark, S. and Burns, S. (2006) *Hidden Work: Co-Production by People Outside Paid Employment.* York: Joseph Rowntree Foundation.

Boyle, D., Coote, A., Sherwood, C. and Slay, J. (2010) *Right Here, Right Now: Taking Co-Production into the Mainstream.* London: NESTA.

Boyle, D. and Harris, M. (2009) *The Challenge of Co-Production: How Equal Partnerships Between Professionals and the Public are Crucial to Improving Public Services.* London: NESTA.

Boyle, D., Slay, J. and Stephens, L. (2010) *Public Services Inside Out: Putting Co-Production into Practice.* London: NESTA.

Cahn, E. (2001) *No More Throwaway People: The Co-Production Imperative.* Washington, DC: Essential Books.

Carr, S. (2004) *Social Care Institute for Excellence Position Paper 3: Has Service User Participation Made a Difference to Social Care Services?* London: SCIE/Policy Press.

Carr, S. (2007) 'Participation, power, conflict and change: theorising dynamics of service user participation in the social care system of England and Wales.' *Critical Social Policy 27*, 2, 266–276.

Carr, S. (2010) *Personalisation: A Rough Guide.* London: SCIE (Second revised edition).

Carr, S. and Coren, E. (eds) (2007) *Collection of Examples of Service User and Carer Participation in Systematic Reviews.* London: SCIE.

Coren, E. and Fisher, M. (2006) *The Conduct of Systematic Reviews for SCIE Knowledge Reviews.* London: SCIE.

Cummins, J. and Miller, C. (2007) *Co-production, Social Capital and Service Effectiveness.* London: OPM.

Farr, M. (2012) 'Collaboration in Public Services: Can Service Users and Staff Participate Together?' In M. Barnes and P. Cotterell (eds) *Critical Perspectives on User Involvement.* Bristol: Policy Press.

Faulkner, A. (2010) *Service User and Carer Involvement in the National Mental Health Development Unit: Scoping Report.* London: NSUN.

Flint, J. (2009) 'Subversive Subjects and Conditional, Earned and Denied Citizenship.' In M. Barnes and D. Prior (eds) *Subversive Citizens: Power, Agency and Resistance in Public Services.* Bristol: Policy Press.

Glasby, J. and Littlechild, R. (2009) *Direct Payments and Personal Budgets: Putting Personalisation into Practice.* Bristol: Policy Press (Second edition).

HM Government (2007) *Putting People First: A Shared Vision and Commitment to the Transformation of Adult Social Care.* London: HM Government.

Hodge, S. (2005) 'Participation, discourse and power: a case study in service user involvement.' *Critical Social Policy 25*, 2,164–179.

Hunter, S. and Ritchie, P. (2007) *Co-Production and Personalisation in Social Care: Changing Relationships in the Provision of Social Care.* London: Jessica Kingsley Publishers.

INVOLVE (2003) *Report of the Commissioning Workshop 2nd July 2003.* Eastleigh, Hants: INVOLVE.

Leadbeater, C. (2004) *Personalisation Through Participation: A New Script for Public Services.* London: Demos.

Lewis, L. (2009) 'Politics of recognition: what can a human rights perspective contribute to understanding users' experiences of involvement in mental health services?' *Social Policy and Society 8*, 2, 257–274.

McKinley, S. and Yiannoullou, S. (2012) 'Changing Minds: Unleashing the Potential of Mental Health Service Users – A Critical Perspective on Current Models of Service User Involvement and their Impact on Wellbeing and "Recovery".' In M. Barnes and P. Cotterell (eds) *Critical Perspectives on User Involvement.* Bristol: Policy Press.

Morris, J. (2004) 'Independent living and community care: a disempowering framework.' *Disability and Society 19*, 5, 427–442.

Morris, J. (2005) *Citizenship and Disabled People: A Scoping Paper Prepared for the Disability Rights Commission.* London: DRC.

Mouffe, C. (2002) *Politics and Passions: The Stakes of Democracy.* London: Centre for the Study of Democracy.

Needham, C. (2007) 'Realising the potential of co-production: negotiating improvements in public services.' *Social Policy and Society 7*, 2, 221–231.

Needham, C. and Carr, S. (2009) *Social Care Institute for Excellence Research Briefing 31: Co-Production: An Emerging Evidence Base for Adult Social Care Transformation.* London: SCIE.

New Economics Foundation (2008) *Co-production: A Manifesto for Growing the Core Economy.* London: NEF.

Rose, D., Fleischmann, P., Tonkiss, F., Campbell, P. and Wykes, T. (2002) *User and Carer Involvement in Change Management in a Mental Health Context: Review of The Literature – Report to the National Co-ordinating Centre for NHS Service Delivery and Organisation R and D (NCCSDO.)* London: NCCSDO.

Rummery, K. (2006) 'Disabled citizens and social exclusion: the role of direct payments.' *Policy and Politics 34*, 4, 633–650.

Shaping Our Lives, National Centre for Independent Living and University of Leeds Centre for Disability Studies (2007) *SCIE Knowledge Review 17: Developing Social Care – Service Users Driving Culture Change.* London: SCIE.

Stephens, L. and Ryan-Collins, J. (2008) *Compass Think Piece 44: The Wealth of New Time – How Timebanking Can Help People Build Better Public Services.* London: Compass.

Think Local Act Personal (2011) *Think Local, Act Personal: Next Steps for Transforming Adult Social Care.* London: TLAP Partnership.

Webb, S. (2008) 'Modelling service user participation in social care.' *Journal of Social Work 8*, 3, 269–290.

Whitaker, G. (1980) 'Co-production: citizen participation in service delivery.' *Public Administration Review 40*, 3, 240–246.

CHAPTER 3

Service User Involvement – What It Is and What It Could Be

Lessons from the Standards We Expect Project

Jennie Fleming

Introduction

The focus of this chapter is service user involvement in decisions that affect them. In the context of this chapter this means people's individual involvement in decisions about their day-to-day support and the chapter also considers how groups of people can be actively involved in the design, delivery and evaluation of services to ensure they better meet needs individually and collectively.

The chapter draws on a four-year national project funded by the Joseph Rowntree Foundation – the 'Standards We Expect' (for more information about the Standards We Expect and the full findings see Beresford *et al.*, 2011). The project was a change and development project, which worked closely with eight local adult care services and their users to explore person-centred support, the barriers to its development and ways in which they may be overcome. Key elements were to share learning about empowering approaches to person-centred support with a wider network and to explore opportunities for bringing about change in services.

The project was undertaken by a consortium, led by Shaping Our Lives, the national service user organisation and network, and included two university centres and a voluntary organisation. In total nine individuals were involved in undertaking the work. The team included people with experience as service users, academics, voluntary project workers, current and past practitioners and people with expertise in equality and diversity issues.

The project specifically focused on the views and experiences of service users and face-to-face workers – two groups who are often marginalised in research – as well as service managers. We were committed to involving as wide a range of people as possible. The approach underpinning this project was a rights-based one informed by the social model of disability; it was a participatory project. Standards We Expect was based on the belief that if real change is to take place, then it will have to be owned by all the key stakeholders involved.

Starting with service users' and practitioners' own definitions, the aims and objectives of Standards We Expect were to:

- identify the barriers that operate against person-centred approaches, preventing people who use services from taking control of their own lives

- identify the techniques and methods which enable and promote person-centred approaches and empower service users and workers

- share knowledge and expertise to facilitate the development of services that people want

- identify structural issues and problems and suggest possible solutions.

(Branfield *et al.*, 2004)

As well as the eight projects we worked closely with there was a looser network of a further 12 projects. These 20 participating sites included a wide variety of partnerships and services – statutory (health and local authority), independent and voluntary sectors. They provided a range of services for adults including, for example, residential and day provision, advocacy, advice and social work support, support with employment, housing and information technology. There were no user-controlled organisations included in the project sites.

How we describe those of us who use services has changed over time with different words and phrases being more acceptable than others (McLaughlin, 2008). In the Standards We Expect we used the term 'service user' and understood its meaning to be people who receive or are eligible to receive health, social care and welfare services. This could be on a voluntary or compulsory basis. Many in the projects had long-term experience of using such services. Whilst practitioners, managers and carers were included in the research, this chapter focuses on issues raised by service users and all quotations in this chapter come from service users.

What is in a word – service user involvement or participation?

Much has been written in policy and legislation about service users having choice and control and people having as much control as they want over decisions that affect them. The right to make our own decisions is enshrined in UK law through the Mental Capacity Act 2005, the Human Rights Act 1998 and also internationally in the United Convention on the Rights of Persons with Disabilities which the British government ratified in 2009.

The Care Services Improvement Partnership (CSIP) urged services to involve service users in making improvements: 'It is vital to listen to and involve service users and carers who are the "experts by experience". They can very often identify small changes or service improvements, which make a big impact' (CSIP, 2008, p.38).

Despite these directives for increased involvement and participation of service users the terms can cover many forms and can be undertaken in many different ways. There is no single agreed definition of participation. Robson *et al.* (2008, p.13) write 'There are many words related to participation – engagement, consultation, involvement, inclusion, access and representation, for example'. They go on to say that this results in no universal understanding of what these words mean which can confuse understanding of what participation is. Some people who took part in the project felt this confusion.

> Gobbledegook, I'm sorry I'm very anti all this rubbish language they are coming out with, why are they doing it, is it to confuse us? To make us seem confused, all right we are elderly but we still have a bit of grey matter.

Adams (2008, p.31) brings some clarity as he distinguishes between 'involvement' of service users and 'participation'. He writes that

> involvement refers to the entire continuum of taking part, from one-off consultation through equal partnership to taking control. Participation refers to that part of the continuum of involvement where people play a more active part, have greater choice, exercise more power and contribute significantly to decision-making and management.

Elements of involvement can be seen as disempowering and tokenistic, and so participation may be seen as a more powerful approach. Few of the people in the Standards We Expect project had experience of participation as defined here.

SCIE identifies that service user involvement operates at different levels, 'from individual control over day-to-day decisions about what to wear, what to eat and how to spend one's time to collective decisions about how services are run and commissioned' (SCIE, 2008, p.3). For both they identify – and this was strongly confirmed in our research – that involvement should not just be 'about being present and taking part but also about having an influence over decisions and actions' (SCIE, 2008, p.3). Both individual and collective involvement should improve the quality of the services and have a positive impact on the lived lives of the people who use them.

Standards We Expect have taken service user involvement to mean any activity that ensures the views of the people who use the services have the chance to be heard in order to make real, sustainable changes to the support they receive and the services that provide it. The following sections of this chapter will look at each of these two areas in turn.

Individual control over day-to-day decisions

Notwithstanding the legal, policy and moral drivers for service user involvement in Standards We Expect people told us much about how they felt limited in decision making in their daily lives. Many factors were seen by people who use services to affect their ability to make the decisions they wanted about their own lives.

Good relationships with the workers were seen as crucial. Staff attitudes could be very supportive to people making decisions for themselves. The quality of staff was very variable – from the exceptional to the very poor. Staff were seen as a key to empowering service user involvement.

> Oh yes, very good, I can talk to her. She is very understanding and listens to your point of view.

However this was not always the case; staff were also seen as a barrier to people making their own decisions:

> It can be hard to get support for what you want to do, not what they want you to do.

> Sometimes you talk to the worker and they start talking before you even stop talking.

Mostly, not being listened to had significant consequences:

> I don't think reviews are very helpful, it's just people talking about you. They sort of decide and make decisions for you and at the end of the day you feel out-voted and your voice doesn't get heard.

> You sort of say to them 'oh, I want a shower and wet room', and they write it all down and then come and put a bath in, and you get a bath seat and you go 'yeah, thanks but a bath's totally useless'.

As with staff, family members also could have a positive and negative impact on people's ability to make their own decisions. Many people, particularly, but not exclusively, older people, depended very much on loved ones – spouses, children, friends to provide care for them or to advocate on their behalf with services.

> I have got a family and they will decide what happens to me when the time comes… Oh yes, you have got to talk to them before about it and they are quite in agreement.

We also often heard of carers and family limiting the autonomy of people – particularly young adults, people with learning difficulties and, in contrast with above, older people.

> Because I am new here, my mum at the moment doesn't think I can do some of the things I am doing and she doesn't like the fact that I am trying. It makes it very difficult.

The following quotation shows how difficult family relationships can sometimes be.

Because I am getting more confident and things, I'm getting a say. My decisions are becoming real in my head, and I'm saying to my parents 'you know you're not the ones making my decisions and at the end of the day it's me'. And I'm sticking and because I'm gaining more independence and I have got the independent skills and the confidence, and when things come up I'm the first to say yes I'll do that, that's why I think [accommodation] is for me.

For some people the support of others was needed to help try to sort things out.

What somebody said earlier – your parents are a massive thing but they need, especially when you go into a residential home, they need to know that yeah they can care for you and yeah they can do what they like for you, but they need to know that you want your space and…it's like this morning I was talking about my money when we talked about our human rights and how my mum's put most of my money into an ISA now I can't get access to it because she won't let me have the pass book because she thinks I can't deal with it. But the [place] are trying to help me do that but they can't do parts of that unless she's prepared to give me the money for them to help me do that.

Service users highlighted the consequence that assumptions made by both face-to-face workers and family carers could have as they often thought they knew what was right for them. Such assumptions could preclude the possibility of hearing and including what service users had to say.

They believe they know what we need and they don't accept it when we say they are wrong or tell them what we really need.

These situations do raise questions as to how families are encouraged to support family members to greater independence and person-centred support.

Access to mainstream services such as college, transport and housing was a major limiting factor for people and was a considerable barrier to people being able to make the decisions they wanted.

They don't understand it from our point of view, they don't know what it's like to be a wheelchair user.

Access is not so good. Cos you have to open doors. I have to have people open doors for me; you have to have stuff moved out of the way sometimes cos they are blocking where you want to get to, and that makes it really awkward. I think if they had electric [doors] I'd be fine. They are too heavy (the doors). If they had electric doors that would solve all the problems like getting to class and that. I'd be fine.

One young woman told of being unable to go to college for more than a year because of a difficulty over insurance and her having only an indoor wheelchair.

I'm nearly in my twenties and it's not fair. I should be out there enjoying my life, not indoors. I can't even go outside. It's just driving me around the bend, can you imagine being in four walls 24/7 with nowhere to go? I want to do my course, catch up with my education. To me it is important… It is a big thing for me. The reason I decided to come back here is to be independent.

Inaccessible – or inconsistently accessible – public transport affected people's ability to make decisions about how they lived their lives. This was particularly true in rural areas.

Lack of accessible public transport. [Transport] would take up a huge chunk (of your money) if you're living in a rural area.

This is a huge problem. [Place] has wheelchair-friendly buses but half the time they don't work. Bus drivers are apathetic and unhelpful. Inconsistency means people can wait for a bus and then it doesn't have a ramp.

Things like transport haven't changed and it is still quite hard work to go anywhere.

Limited access to suitable housing affected the decisions people had to make about where they could live and this in turn had a profound effect on how people could lead their lives. This was a a huge problem for people. We heard of authorities with housing policy committed to building new affordable housing – but nothing for disabled people. This made it very difficult for people to even think about moving from residential accommodation to more independent living at all – let alone to think about having any form of choice as to where they might live. In one area, people had to wait for a long time for any accommodation to be offered and if they refused it (for example because there was not space for a residential PA) they were returned to the end of the waiting list.

Resources, most specifically finances, appropriate staff and suitable services also limited people's ability to make the decisions about their everyday lives that they wanted to make.

> Whether it will happen or not is a different thing. I don't know. A lot depends on the money.

> If you want to go somewhere they try to help. I think a lot of it revolves around staff absence, so in a lot of ways we can't do things that we'd like to. There always has to be one person in the building at all times.

> Funding is a problem, there is talk of my respite ending. I will have to pay for it.

People told us they have had to stop doing some things because they can no longer afford them. This has a negative effect on their quality of life. People pointed out that being on a fixed income means that when charges for services increase it means 'your pot gets smaller and smaller so it limits what you can do. It's not just one thing, it's everything'.

Concerns about risk and health and safety severely affect people's ability to make the decisions they wanted. This affected all people in some way.

> It restricts me, it takes over.

> I think health and safety has too much power.

These restrictions were often felt to be overwhelming for those living in residential care. Concerns about risk affected people's ability to make decisions for themselves ranging from whether to have a cup of tea to when and where they could go out to socialise, what banks they could use, work or education they could undertake.

> If we are going out, and we won't be back for dinner but we want it later, we're not allowed to microwave it because of health and safety. To me that means we can't go out unless we want our dinner first or we don't go out which to me is a bit sad.

> We're not allowed to go in our fridge in our own home to get the milk out because our manager says it's all to do with health and safety. I'm sure no one says that to you in your home, so why is it different here?

A further limitation on people's abilities to make day-to-day decisions related to the lack of flexibility of some services and the feeling they were developed to a 'one size fits all' model.

> I was working full time and I was told the only slot they could fit me into in the morning was 10.30 and I have been getting to work at 7.30 in the morning but I just couldn't cope on my own any more. And they said 'Oh well we can slot you in at 10.30 there is no other time available'.

> I have Homecare, but I could occasionally do with more. I have very good weeks and very bad weeks, it would be nice to say I don't need services when I'm good and have them back when I'm bad, but you can't do that, you have to keep it going all the time, otherwise you lose it.

Much was made of language and culture limiting the decisions people could make by carers and practitioners; service users themselves had less to say about it.

> I wish there was some more, I'm not having a go at the staff, but I wish there was a course in looking after black skin. If they had thought about it before I moved in that would have been fine.

Day-to-day decisions cover a wide range of situations, those that might appear to be small daily choices – like what to wear and when to eat – to bigger choices about education or where to live. We heard of people being limited and restricted in the choices they had and so unable to make the decisions and live the lives they wanted to across a wide diversity of circumstances.

Participation in decisions affecting lives beyond day-to-day support – collective participation

The previous section considered how people often have to fight to be able to freely make their own decisions about their daily lives and care. One way to challenge these daily individual challenges is for people who use services to be actively involved in the design, delivery and evaluation of services to ensure they better meet needs individually and collectively. Ensuring services are informed by collective participation would have an impact on the big picture and also make a difference to how individuals experience services.

Service users had an expectation that their views should be listened to and valued. They felt they should be treated in a respectful way. They wanted to hear what action was taken and how their involvement had been used in reaching decisions. However this was far from always the case.

People we spoke to had considerable experience of being involved in participative activities – most particularly consultations. Whilst the negative experiences were the predominant experience – this was not always the case. A small number of people spoke about being involved at every level of the organisation, alongside managers and practitioners, and felt that service users' views and perspectives influenced the whole organisation.

> They are doing their best to improve and they are very open to suggestions from us. We are in contact with them the whole time.

> Any decision that happens within the centre is passed through the management committee. If we don't like the idea it doesn't happen.

> They are doing their best to improve and they are very open to suggestions from us. We are in contact with them all the time.

However, it has to be said that many also expressed frustrations at how their views and opinions were sought and for what purpose.

Service users gave some examples of changes that had occurred without any involvement from them – changes happening to their care and services they used which they had not even been aware might happen – let alone been consulted about. This had led to frustration and anger and, for some, considerable distress.

> They just come in and announce a change and there's not been any consultation on it, and it's just introduced.

Some people felt there was not a real commitment to their involvement.

> They're not actually coming down to our level, it's more information from up there to down here. We should all be working together instead of having one higher one and lower one.

People spoke of their experience of tokenism and of being expected to be involved in inappropriate ways. This included people being put off by the formality of meetings and finding it hard to say what they wanted to say in such circumstances.

> It's quite daunting. Sort of like you feel intimidated.

> I'd like to change the meetings. Sometimes I get bored. [It is] difficult to understand what people are saying.

For others consultations were felt to be tokenistic as the practical arrangements for supporting their involvement were not adequate and some organisations did not fully meet the range of access requirements of service users and so they could not all be included equally. People said that being involved takes time and energy, and for some people being actively involved can result in physical discomfort or pain. Others also pointed out that organisations often did not make allowances for service users' wider needs, such as differences in background and life experiences.

People told us that often the timescales allowed for consultations are unrealistic – being too short to enable meaningful involvement. Service users may need time to arrange support to attend a meeting, for example, or may need to spend time with a supporter going through papers before the meeting takes place. Being hurried does not support their involvement and can leave people feeling undervalued or that their involvement is an afterthought.

Service users commented that the regular questionnaires they were sent to find out their views were usually uninviting to use and difficult to understand.

> [I fill it in] if it's simple because a lot of questionnaires are very long winded and you don't kind of know what they are saying.

> Sometimes I fill it in, depends if the questions are interesting. If they are I'll answer them.

A small number of people expressed concerns about possible repercussions of speaking up. They were concerned that expressing critical views could single them out for negative treatment from workers or managers; this could lead to people not being honest or open or deter them from taking part in consultations.

> Sometimes people are afraid to speak out because they are in fear it will jeopardise their opportunities.

People wanted to be involved to improve support for themselves and others and so were incredibly frustrated at the lack of feedback they received following their involvement.

> Disabled people need feedback – what happens to our ideas?

We go to a lot of meetings and you are discussing things and you never hear anything about it afterwards. You never know where that discussion went or what did head office think to it, what they had to say about it, what is going to be done about it. So very often you feel I have just wasted my time going to it.

If things aren't possible then explanation needs to be given as to why.

Feeling in the lurch, being made clowns of, we've done it but haven't been told what is in the report. We would like to see it. It concerns us.

Many service users expressed extreme dissatisfaction about the lack of change resulting from their involvement. They often felt that nothing changed at all.

It's true, you bring something up and you do get ignored. [...] You go to the meetings and you don't get anything done.

You report things and they give you a date but nothing is ever done right... I'm actually on the residents action committee for [organisation], I take complaints. It goes up to another level. It goes from there, it's like going round in a circle.

Service user involvement – what it could be

Overall the findings of Standards We Expect paint a bleak picture of the state of user involvement both in individual decisions about how people live their lives on a daily basis and also in being collectively involved in decisions about how support is designed, delivered and evaluated. From a lack of involvement to a lack of feedback and a lack of perceived change, many service users have had negative and frustrating experiences of being 'involved' and many could not see that their involvement had led to any positive change.

Nevertheless participants continued to place a strong emphasis on the importance of involvement and of getting it right. They had clear ideas about how involvement could be improved and what good service user involvement would look like. People told us how they thought they could have more control individually over the day-to-day decisions in their lives.

One question which care planners should ask themselves is 'What would I want, if this was my own situation?'

Support was seen as a vehicle – a means of ensuring choice and control for individual service users.

> Being able to decide for yourself what you want to do and not letting anyone decide for you. Other people may have good intentions for what you need but you might know better how to achieve it.

Service users identified the importance of the relationship between an individual service user and their carers, supporters or key-worker to them being able to make their own decisions. Participants emphasised the importance of listening.

> Listening, *really* listening.

Some people felt very strongly that the values of carers and workers were crucial – they must value people and focus on the positives.

> By believing in people's value and giving all people a chance.

Flexibility emerged as a key issue to enabling people to make the decisions they wanted about how they received services and lived their lives. People need services that can respond to individual needs and adapt to personal choices. Flexibility implies the service's ability to adapt as people's needs change or they decide to pursue different goals.

> Remembering everyone is different and has different needs.

Service users made it clear that for them the most important way of overcoming the barriers to them being able to be involved in decisions that affected their lives was through more effective user involvement or participation. Whilst this does relate to individual involvement, they particularly emphasised collective involvement through working in service user groups and organisations.

> You cannot get anywhere just speaking on your own.

Several service users thought that there was strength in numbers and that this offered a way of having more control over decisions. Working together, people were seen as being able to have an impact where an individual could not.

> We can have more say by becoming stronger together.

The Standards We Expect findings led to the drawing together of 12 standards that should inform good practice for person-centred support (Beresford *et al.*, 2011). Standard 12 relates to participation and states:

Standard 12: participation

Service users should be centrally involved in the planning, development, management, commissioning and evaluation of services and support. This should be made possible for all service users, addressing diversity and including people with all forms of impairment, addressing physical, communication and cultural access requirements. This demands support for both individual and collective involvement, including the adequate resourcing of service user controlled organisations. (Beresford *et al.*, 2011, p.31)

We went on to develop a collection of principles for successful involvement that would be applicable across a wide range of situations and levels of involvement. If service providers are to ask service users to participate in their organisations they must ensure that they have in place the support and provision needed for all to be able to do so effectively. To this end as part of Standards We Expect we offered training to service users about their rights to be involved in decisions about their lives, and for workers and managers as well. We also produced publications to support involvement for service users (Bewley *et al.*, 2011) and practitioners (Croft *et al.*, 2011).

This guidance suggests a wide range of actions that can be taken to maximise the involvement of service users. It proposes that before starting, people consider thinking about the purpose of the involvement, what it is seeking to achieve, as well as realistic timescales. It is crucial that people understand what they are being involved in and what this might entail and vitally how much power and control over decisions people actually have. It is a good idea to involve service users at this early stage to ensure the whole process benefits from their knowledge and experience.

Care should be taken about who to involve and ensuring equal access for all who may want to take part – this includes, for example, considering how to communicate with service users and access to both materials and venues. People's safety and ability to speak honestly without fear of repercussion also need to be considered.

Ensuring feedback and also action as a result of involvement is essential. This does have some financial implications – service user involvement done well does cost money and so it is important to identify a budget and make decisions about the costs of payment, expenses and personal assistance.

CSIP pointed out that the involvement of service users should be the 'norm in every aspect of service planning, redesign and improvement' (2008, p.6). However important such involvement is, it is essentially 'participation by invitation' (Fitzpatrick, Hastings and Kintrea, 1999, p.12) or what Barnes calls 'officially sponsored deliberative forums' (2008, p.463), that is, service users being invited to take part in participation where the agenda is set by organisations and service providers. Along with many others Shaping Our Lives points out the limitations of this and says that service user involvement should mean service users setting the agenda themselves.

> There is a big difference between feeding into someone else's ideas and organisations and developing your own. This distinction needs to be recognised. The first approach can be a very individualistic exercise, requiring no more than that people fill in a form or go to a meeting. But the second represents a new departure. It means people getting together and working things out for themselves and developing their own agendas. (Branfield and Beresford, 2006, p.x)

Much service user involvement has increasingly become removed from the aspirations of the disability movement (Oliver, 1990). Where disabled people do set the agenda the issues of most concern to them are often different to those identified by organisations. 'We Are Not Stupid' (Taylor *et al.*, 2007) is a research project by people with learning difficulties finding out 'what was happening in the lives of people with learning difficulties' (p.19); the issues this research identified were bullying, racism, sexual abuse, having relationships, choice and independence and staff – when they are setting the agenda these are the things they want to change. Hodge (2005) writes of how service users can be controlled within forums and writes of mental health service users wanting to discuss Electroconvulsive Therapy (ECT), but this being resisted by staff and so though the topic was raised there was 'no potential for it to become the subject of debate orientated to changing policy' (2005, p.173).

Involvement in decisions is itself a right for disabled people and those who use services in the long term. However more importantly participation is the means by which all other human rights are best achieved. It is the means by which inequality and oppression can be addressed. Service user involvement and participation are not themselves the outcome to be achieved; service user involvement is the means to address challenges and issues people face. In Standards We Expect we heard of a range of human rights not being met. These included, for example, the right to a private and family life, a normal life – 'a life like any other', the right to say what you think and be listened to, the right to freedom of association and the right not to be discriminated against (Human Rights Act 1998). These injustices will not be addressed without the effective involvement of service users in decisions about the provision of support.

If service user involvement is to go forward and make a progressive contribution to the lives of service users then two things need to happen. First, where service user involvement has an organisational focus it must be based on a real commitment to listen to what service users say, act on what they say and power sharing. Second, participation of disabled people and service users need to also move beyond the current predominant organisational focus on issues and concerns identified by providers and address the agendas service users themselves identify. In this way service user involvement can move beyond being tokenistic or seen as an end in itself, and lie at the heart of improving the lives of service users.

Acknowledgements

First I would like to acknowledge all the partners of Standards We Expect – Peter Beresford, Catherine Bewley, Fran Branfield, Suzy Croft, Michael Glynn, Charles Patmore and Karen Postle and all the people who took part in the project. I also want to acknowledge how extremely useful I found the literature review undertaken by Jackie Martin for her PhD transfer report in informing the discussion about service user involvement, participation and empowerment.

References

Adams, R. (2008) *Empowerment, Participation and Social Work.* Hampshire: Palgrave Macmillan (Fourth edition).

Barnes, M. (2008) 'Passionate participation: emotional experiences and expressions in deliberative forums.' *Critical Social Policy 29,* 3, 461–481.

Beresford, P. *et al.* (2011) *Supporting People: Towards a Person Centred Approach.* Bristol: Policy Press.

Bewley, C., Branfield, B., Glynn, M., Beresford, P., Croft, S., Fleming, J., Postle, K. (2011) *Person-Centred Support: A Service Users' Guide.* Available at www.shapingourlives.org.uk/documents/SWEx-Serviceusers.pdf, accessed on 4 April 2012.

Branfield, F. and Beresford, P. (2006) *Making User Involvement Work: Supporting Service User Networking And Knowledge.* York: Joseph Rowntree Foundation.

Branfield, F., Collins, J., Beresford, P. and Fleming, J. (2004) *Proposal Registration Form: The Standards We Expect.* London: Shaping Our Lives.

Croft, S., Bewley, C., Beresford, P., Branfield, B., Fleming, J., Glynn, M. and Postle, K. (2011) *Person-Centred Support: A Guide to Person Centred Working for Practitioners.* Available at www. shapingourlives.org.uk/documents/SWEx_Practitioners.pdf, accessed on 4 April 2012.

CSIP (Care Services Improvement Partnership) (2008) *High Impact Changes for Health and Social Care: An Inspirational Collection of Organisational Initiatives which are Changing Health and Social Care Services and the Lives of People who Use Them.* London: Department of Health.

Fitzpatrick, S., Hastings, A. and Kintrea, K. (1999) 'Young people's participation in urban regeneration.' *Child Right 154,* 11–12.

Hodge, S. (2005) 'Participation, discourse and power: a case study in service user involvement.' *Critical Social Policy 25,* 2, 164–179.

McLaughlin, H. (2008) 'What's in a name: "Client", "Patient", "Customer", "Expert by Experience", "Service User" – what's next?' *British Journal of Social Work 39,* 6, 1–17.

Oliver, M. (1990) *The Politics of Disablement.* London: McMillan Education.

Robson, P., Sampson, A., Dime, N., Hernandez, L. and Litherland, R. (2008) *Seldom Heard: Developing Inclusive Participation in Social Care.* London: Social Care Institute for Excellence.

SCIE (2008) *The Participation of Adult Service Users, Including Older People, in Developing Social Care.* London: SCIE.

Taylor, J., Williams, V., Johnson, R., Hiscutt, I. and Brennan, M. (2007) *We Are Not Stupid.* London: Shaping Our Lives.

CHAPTER 4

Reclaiming Community Work for Involvement in Social Care

Martin Hoban

In this chapter, I will address a number of questions. What have been the main approaches to community work and how successful have they been in involving poor and excluded people? Can community work be a helpful strategy for promoting involvement in social care? In doing so I will try to give some sense of the continuing dialogue within myself about community work. I will draw from my own learning as a community worker and researcher in Rhondda Cynon Taff in South Wales.

My starting point

At the outset, it is important to start by sharing some of my own background and to state what I mean by a community work approach. My first experience of collective action was in the trade union movement in the Republic of Ireland. After I left school, I worked as a telephone technician and became active within the union movement. My personal experience of physical impairment led to my involvement with the formation of the disability rights movement in Ireland in the late 1970s. Both of these involvements led to engagements in wider social movements concerned with anti-poverty and community work. I left my job as a technician and undertook full-time education in community work. This form of education was designed to enable activists to become full-time paid community workers. Around this time, both youth and community work in Britain and Ireland were becoming paid activities. I emigrated to Britain in the 1980s and worked as a community worker in Newcastle upon Tyne and in the South Wales Valleys. I became a community worker because I believe that the practice is fundamentally about involving people in bringing about social change. In this sense, community work is very much about human journeys. People get involved in the issues that affect their lives and work with others to achieve positive changes.

At this point, it is also important to say what I mean by an approach. As practitioners, we choose to intervene in the lives of poor and excluded people using a range of approaches. For me, an approach is crucially a form of intervention that draws on a particular set of ideas or values in terms of both what we are trying to achieve and how we go about doing it. A community work approach is essentially a planned intervention at the level of groups and communities. For my purpose here, I will use the generic term 'community work' rather than 'community development'. In essence, community workers use a range of approaches, one of which is community development.

Background and approaches

There has been a long history of people getting involved and forming groups and associations at community level. People are motivated to act out of feelings of anger, frustration and concern for others. For many, a starting point is to engage with the issues where they live. Together with neighbours and others, they organise collectively to improve local services or to campaign for changes. In this way, they often combine collective forms of self-help (Holman, 2000) with local political action (Cooke and Shaw, 1996; O'Malley, 1977). Political activists have also seen the 'community' as a potential site for generating local opposition to the local state (Curno, 1978). There has also been a long history of external intervention into the lives of poor and excluded people. Philanthropic and state agencies have long been preoccupied with the moral and physical renewal of 'poor people' and 'poor areas'. The Victorian middle class intervened through organisations such as the utilitarian Charity Organisation Society, the Settlement Movement and the churches (Cunningham, 2001).

Community workers (paid and unpaid) who supported such initiatives have drawn on different values and theories (Smith, 1981). There has also been much controversy as to whether community work is a profession or a social movement (Smith, 1980). There have been various attempts to explain community work in terms of different approaches (Popple, 1995; Rothman, 1970). Despite differing political influences, many community workers have sought to find common ground. There has also been a concern to agree a common definition of community work and since 2010 to devise occupational standards (NOS, 2010). Contemporary community workers have a diverse range of job titles such as development workers, project workers, enterprise workers, community co-ordinators, community education workers, community arts workers and so on. They are increasingly employed by the state and the third sector. In recent times, there has also been a significant growth in community work consultancies and university-based courses.

The three main approaches

As noted above, there have been various attempts to explain the increasing complexity of activities undertaken by practitioners and activists within community settings. Although an increasing range of approaches have been devised to explain the practice the main ones can still be explained in terms of community development, community action and community planning. I will start with community development.

Community development

This approach has its roots in a range of other professional practices such as social, youth, pastoral and development work. It has been influenced by pluralist and consensual values that promote a professional intervention, the pursuit of small-scale changes at local level, improved service delivery, self-help, personal and skill development, and rebuilding 'community' (Calouste Gulbenkian Foundation, 1968; Twelvetrees, 2002). If we trace its history, we find it originated within the British Foreign Office. Following World War II, many former British colonies were starting the process of national independence and self-government. The term 'community development' emerged as a policy designed to support this process with the purpose of linking local programmes to a national policy agenda (Jones, 1981). This approach was later introduced to Europe as a means of tackling urban and rural problems particularly at local level. Since the 1950s, the term has been used by a wide variety of interest groups including governments, aid agencies and voluntary organisations. The approach still has a significant influence on contemporary work in both Britain and Ireland and overseas.

If we examine the community development model we find that this approach, as defined by central government policy, has limited potential to extend involvement beyond the locality. Instead, its primary aim is to create a process of 'development' from *within* the locality through the creation of individual leadership, group formation and self-help. One of the main assumptions underlying this approach is that 'community' has broken down, confidence has to be restored and localised support needs to be established (Henderson and Thomas, 1987). Therefore, 'involvement' is perceived in terms of enabling and supporting local people to identify and solve their own problems within a clearly defined 'community' of place or interest. Individuals involved in these initiatives may achieve important gains for the locality and undergo significant personal and psychological changes. However, the gains achieved rarely extend beyond 'the project' or into a critical domain that can pose a sufficient challenge to external forces or policies that impact on the locality (Powell and Geoghegan, 2004).

Community action

I will now turn to the community action approach. This approach has been influenced by the political and cultural traditions of the tenants' movement, the civil rights movement, trade unions, disability and mental health survivor movements, feminist and anti-racist struggles (Campbell and Oliver, 1996; Ledwith, 2005). In the main, radical and alternative theories have been the main influence on this approach. Community workers who adhere to this tradition share many of the values of community development such as starting in the locality and achieving concrete gains at local level. However, they also see themselves as part of a wider political struggle for change that takes place beyond the locality. These workers tend to be more concerned with addressing the structural causes of poverty and inequalities.

If we take a closer look at the community action approaches of the 1970s we find that the key aims of this approach were to secure gains for and to politicise the working class (Smith, 1981). This model involved confronting the local power holders with specific demands. The result would often lead to inevitable conflicts between activists, community workers and representatives of the local state. Small groups of activists would gain a great deal from their involvements in local protests and struggles. For instance, local activists learned political and organisational skills and often an awareness of the power relationships between themselves and the local state. For example, the radical element of the community development projects of the 1970s tended to define poverty in class terms and used an action-research approach to tackle local issues and campaigns (Bennington, 1970). Much of historical and contemporary working class protest has been about opposition to an external threat. One of the features of such protests is that they were often led by charismatic individuals and small groups. Usually, the wider community (people outside this core) are mobilised by these more committed and politicised leaders (Gilligan, 2011). Therefore, it could be argued that this model was significant in involving individual leaders and small groups, in its ability to respond quickly to external threats and in achieving concrete gains for poor areas. However, a significant limitation was in seeking to involve wider groups of people. Over the past 20 years, and as the state has integrated community work into its own policy making, the more radical forms of community work have gradually declined and there has been a corresponding decrease in paid community workers supporting local campaigns. Workers who have used these approaches have either moved on to other things or accommodated themselves within contemporary development and planning approaches.

Community planning

Having considered the development and action approaches, I will now turn to community planning which has been generally associated with initiatives from the state. Henderson and Thomas (1987) describe it as an 'attempt to bring to community work the expertise, technologies, and comprehensiveness of rationalist approaches to planning' (p.327). The 'planning' approach has its origins in classical management theory and emphasises organisation, management and control. Those who promote this approach contend that a range of planning and diagnostic techniques can be developed for assessing collective need within a given geographical area and that these can be met by means of various projects and programmes (Thomas, 1978). The main aims of this approach are usually to create more efficient and accessible service delivery. Such an approach assumes that the needs of local people can be identified and appropriate 'joined up' resources applied to plug the gaps.

There have been a number of previous government interventions associated with this approach. These include regeneration initiatives such as City Challenge in England and the ongoing Communities First programme in Wales. For example, in New Labour's neighbourhood renewal programme, increasing numbers of community workers were employed to rediscover, renew and regenerate 'community'. The rhetoric of 'involvement' was also a key feature of this policy. In this discourse, 'involvement' was defined in terms of opportunities, social entrepreneurialism, and 'community leadership' (SEU, 1998; SEU, 2001). A key objective of this approach was to promote involvement through the market place by providing employment opportunities for *individual* residents. Those who were excluded within poor areas would be 'involved' by creating training and employment opportunities. This thinking was apparently in line with the overall philosophy of the New Labour project that the cultivation of individual opportunities and the elimination of poverty went together (Blair, 1998). As part of this policy, local networks, 'the community', would establish localised services to meet the needs of individuals. This approach was very much in line with the Blairite vision of a 'community' that seeks to 'revive the notion of solidarity, government, and action by the community to advance the individual' (Blair, 2000).

However, at a deeper level, this raises deeper questions in relation to involvement. In the wake of major regeneration initiatives and the riots across major English cities in August 2011 can we honestly say that people in our poorest areas are more involved now than they were in 1997 (Anti-Poverty Network Cymru, 2006; Holman, 2002)? Indeed, it could be argued that to emphasise the involvement of *individual* residents over more collective approaches have only led to opportunities for the very few. If we examine just one very relevant aspect of this policy, we find that a strategy that seeks to educate and train local activists on university courses to be qualified community workers implies no guarantee that their 'community' will benefit. Having qualified, they may quite naturally decide to seek paid employment and use their skills in other areas. Therefore, it is still unclear how a form of involvement that is essentially about the creation of individual opportunities can contribute to the overall objective of neighbourhood renewal and this raises major issues related to equity and non-equity. Certainly, such a policy may not support lofty ideals of community planning. It may in fact even lead to the depletion of essential human resources from the locality and result in the increasing ghettoisation of those with the greatest needs (Hoban and Beresford, 2001).

Limited participation

It could be argued that all three approaches have achieved some success in involving people and in promoting social change. However, despite the fact that the concept of 'participation' has also been a core ingredient of the practice since the 1970s (Kelleher and Whelan, 1992; Miller and Rein, 1975) it could be argued that it has mainly been the case of involvement for the few rather than the many. Despite the rhetoric and the best intentions of many, the participation of residents is often seen as a means to an end rather than as central to the approach. The goals of 'development', 'action' and 'planning' seem always to take precedence over 'involvement'. Consequently, 'community participation' is confined to core groupings of the 'usual suspects' – the existing 'community leaders', paid workers and those with the loudest voices. Over the past ten years, and particularly as part of the development and planning approaches, partnership has replaced participation and the authentic voices of poor and excluded people are lost within new community structures that continue to serve the most powerful (Hoban, 2002a). As Meade (2005) argues in her analysis of Irish social partnerships:

> Although contemporary Irish community development is rooted in the oppositional social movements of the nineteenth century... within the last 30 years, values such as voluntarism and autonomous struggle have been superseded by an emphasis on professional standards, a movement towards regularized organizational structures and a willingness to engage in partnership. (p.360)

Learning from practice and research

This critique raises a number of important questions for me about community work:

- What is the essential value that underpins the practice?
- What are the key roles of the worker?
- What do we mean when we talk about the community work process?

It is important to raise these questions at this time. If we seriously want to extend the potential of community work to promote service user involvement then we need to take a critical look at the practice. I sometimes think that the practice seems trapped between the realms of theoretical abstraction on the one hand and current new management methods on the other. For me community work is a relatively straightforward process of workers helping people to get together around their issues and assisting them to plan their own actions.

In the next section, I will attempt to address these questions. In doing so, I will draw on my learning from my practice and research in Rhondda Cynon Taff in South Wales. Rhondda Cynon Taff is a local authority area comprised largely of former coalmining communities. From 1995 to 1998, I worked as a community worker for Save the Children on the Perthcelyn estate in the Cynon Valley (Hoban, 2002b). From 1998 to 2004, and as part of a PhD, I conducted participatory research on new approaches to community regeneration in Rhondda Cynon Taff (Hoban, 2005). In 2009, I returned to the area and carried out short studies of the participation of excluded groups in the Welsh Assembly's Communities First programme (Hoban, 2009a, 2009b).

Reclaiming community work
The value of participation

> We need to move from a situation of asking what you and they are going to do about the problem to one which asks, 'what are we going to do about it?' (Village activist cited in Hoban, 2005)

What is the essential value that underpins the practice? The central message from participants in the research I conducted is that the participation of people is central to improving *their* lives and *their* communities. From my work with residents on the Perthcelyn estate, I learned that it was only when local people took control of the campaign that things began to change. The local authority and existing voluntary agencies had failed to involve local activists, to any significant extent, in local projects or initiatives. The aims of my employer Save the Children were laudable but I soon realised that local activists (mainly women) did not just want local childcare services. They had their own concerns that were to do with the provision of a new school and the regeneration of their estate. As they formed a group for this purpose and began to take action, they became more confident. After a year and a half of campaigning, they achieved a new community school and a regeneration plan that included new play areas, new playing fields, new fencing, traffic calming and funding for new workers.

From my learning, the essential value of community work is participation. It is the participation of people in a collective process of *their* making that can create the necessary conditions for the changes *they* want to bring about. Moreover, this form of engagement implies a human connection with the issues and their motivations, activities and actions.

The key roles of the worker

What are the key roles of the worker? A key question is the nature of the support required for people to achieve what they want. They may already have support they can call upon and can sometimes generate the resources to help themselves. Increasingly, however, people rely on external support in the form of paid community workers. In the research I conducted, participants were very grateful to workers who give support and guidance. At the same time, many of those I spoke with were also critical of workers. These were some of the issues raised:

- They ask the wrong questions.
- They spend too much time in the office and not enough time doing face-to-face work.
- They lack certain skills.
- They lack commitment and professionalism.
- They do not stay long.
- Their work is too localised.
- There is not enough of them.
- They get burnout, lack support and feel isolated.
- They are part of the poverty industry – they follow the money.

(Hoban, 2005)

Most participants had a very clear idea of the nature of the support they required. They wanted help from workers based on *commitment, respect and trust.* As one activist stated:

> People in these communities can see through people in a minute. You have got to be someone who they can trust. (Activist cited in Hoban, 2005)

They want workers who will listen, who are open to learning from people who live in Valley communities, have no pre-conceived ideas about what is best for people and who will allow them to set their own agendas:

> A community development worker must have the agenda of the community as opposed to a pre-conceived agenda that is set by somebody who doesn't live in the community or doesn't know what the community needs. (Estate activist cited in Hoban, 2005)

They stress the need for more 'enablers' rather than 'doers'. One estate activist describes the kinds of questions community workers should be asking:

> The questions that should be asked are not: 'what do you want?' But what do you want to achieve? The next question is, 'what level of support do you want? …the attitude of the people coming in has got to be that we are not coming in to change the world. We are coming in to help YOU to change your area… You want help but you don't want interference. (Estate activist cited in Hoban, 2005)

A key element of the role is about challenge. As a worker, I spent as much time challenging the people I worked with as I did in a supportive role. Community work is a human process and the dialogical relationship between the worker and the people is critical (Freire, 1993). The nature of this relationship can be complex. On the one hand, it can be based on solidarity and trust. However, on the other hand it can often be fraught with tensions and difficulties. The worker also has a responsibility to raise issues such as inequality and power and to confront internal and external oppression. However, this does not mean that the worker imposes his or her own worldview on the people. For instance, on issues such as equality it may often require the worker to challenge existing thinking and to locate it within a wider context to facilitate a more critical analysis. My work with the Communities First programme reveals that equality issues need to be embedded into existing experiences on the ground. They should not be viewed as an externally imposed set of ideas or policy which bears no relationship with people's lived experiences.

In short, workers are needed who help support and challenge but who will not seek to dominate and control. They will need knowledge and skills to enable people to focus their concerns, anger and commitment into various forms of collective action. The particular knowledge and skills identified by participants in my research were in relation to people skills, communication, counselling and group development. In addition, people also recognise that community workers do not have all the knowledge and skills they require. They also need people with organisational expertise particularly with the current preoccupation with project development, complex funding arrangements and management of staff.

The process clarified

What is the community work process? In other words, how does the process of collective action occur? Can we explain the process in simple terms and show what the worker needs to do to facilitate collective action? My approach (when not constrained by agency pressures) has been to start with and between people and to facilitate a process where they can create their own vision and values. I believe that values should not be imposed (in terms of the issues identified or the methods used) but must be generated within the participatory process and from the dialogical relationship between the worker and the group. These are some of my thoughts on the process based on critical reflections on my own practice and from discussions with colleagues in both Britain and Ireland. For explanation, it implies a series of stages which in my experience rarely follow a logical sequence.

STARTING WITH PEOPLE

As noted above, it is an important first step that the dialogue should first happen within communities and between people themselves. It is necessary to start with the issues of direct concern and importance to people in their daily lives. This stage is about identifying issues of common concern and creating a process where people can meet to discuss these collectively. A key element of this stage is creating the necessary trusting environment for listening and to allow for the open expression of experiences, feelings, thoughts and concerns. It is at this stage that issues of equality and diversity need to be considered as the loudest voices in the community may merely reflect the dominant power holders.

ANALYSIS OF THE ISSUE

This might involve a small group sharing personal experiences of the issue. Group members may need access to external knowledge and the opportunity to discuss and critique various explanations of their concerns. Crucially, it means having the opportunity to talk to other people, discuss and explore the issue as part of a bigger picture before people are ready to take action. This stage will influence at what level (local, national, global) the group chooses to take action and the form of approaches to be deployed.

AIMS AND STRATEGY

This is when the group decides its aims and how it is going to achieve them. In doing this, it is important to sustain the goodwill and achievements that already exist and start to take actions around small initiatives. At this stage, groups should not be sidetracked with chasing funding pots but should be supported to set their own agendas.

SUPPORTING AND CHALLENGING

Supporting and challenging each other through the often painful journey of personal and collective change is crucial. In my own practice, I have seen people change dramatically through the process of being involved. Indeed, in many contexts it is sometimes difficult and dangerous to get involved, for example, residents in certain areas who stand up to criminals and drug gangs. People will need to be supported by both the worker and other group members.

ORGANISATION, LEADERSHIP AND ACCOUNTABILITY

This is when the group seeks to identify the most appropriate form of leadership, organisation and accountability for its purpose. Traditional understandings of leadership may need to be challenged and more democratic forms introduced.

A BASE

At some stage, the group may establish a local base or network of organisation. This would provide a focus for autonomous and manageable activity that attracts the active participation and support of people. People could develop a sense of ownership to a place or network that would have a friendly and welcoming culture.

SKILLS AND KNOWLEDGE

This is when the group decides what knowledge, skills and personal resources it requires to achieve its aims. This may include an evaluation of its own actions and processes, understanding of how the local council or health authority works, how to work in groups, how to speak effectively in public, chairing meetings, letter writing, taking minutes, doing research, use of computers, managing finance/premises, publicity, fundraising, campaigning and so on. The important issue here is that the group has an input into both the design of the training and who delivers it.

MAINTAINING THE PASSION

The group may go through both high and low periods of emotion. Group members will need to support each other, deal with disappointments and celebrate achievements.

DEALING WITH TENSIONS AND CONFLICTS

In community work there is potential for conflict within the group, between the group and the community and with dominant power holders (Hoban, 2002a). The group will need to understand and address these tensions and conflicts and agree ways to deal with these. This is often a difficult stage and activists can come under personal and external agency pressures (Owen, 2002).

BUILDING CO-OPERATION WITH OTHER ORGANISATIONS

This is an important element particularly in relation to the limitations identified earlier in the locality approach to community work. Small isolated projects while well intentioned have many limitations. In my research, participants stated that while community workers are often well intentioned, they do not make any long-term impression on the scale and extent of poverty and exclusion in areas such as the South Wales Valleys. For these reasons, it is necessary to build co-operation with other groups *within* and *between* communities and to build common approaches to influence wider policy and political changes.

DIALOGUE AND NEGOTIATION WITH THE STATE

This is about challenging relations of power and achieving concrete gains. It is not about engaging in relations that seek to retain the status quo. It seeks to redress inequitable power relations through dialogue and negotiation with power holders.

BUILDING AN HONEST AND OPEN RELATIONSHIP WITH THE WORKER

The group will need some kind of working agreement between the worker/s and the group. This may be formal or informal. It may include some clarification of the role/s and the approximate timescale for eventual withdrawal from the group.

Conclusion

Community work approaches offer potential opportunities for improving the lives of poor and excluded people and have achieved limited forms of involvement. If we are to propose community work approaches to service users as a strategy for liberation then we need to reclaim the essential elements of the practice. I have argued that community work has lost its essential message of promoting participation for social change and that it has become more an instrument of managerialism and control. This is of particular concern at a time when increasing numbers of service users are experiencing unemployment, poverty and cutbacks in benefits and services. There is an urgent need for user-led collective forms of power to challenge those who want to transfer the responsibility of the financial crisis onto those who are least organised and who are already experiencing inequalities.

A reclaimed community work can have an important role to play in supporting this movement. From my learning in Rhondda Cynon Taff, the key value is involvement. Things will only change when people who are affected by the issues get involved. The primary roles of the worker are to enable, support and challenge. People need community workers who they respect and trust and who are committed to dialogue with the people who need their help. Finally we need to simplify and clarify the community work process. If we can rise to this challenge, then community work can offer service users a genuine participatory practice that can support their struggles for improving their own lives.

References

Anti-Poverty Network Cymru (2006) *Walking the Talk: Communities on Communities First*. Anti-Poverty Network Cymru.

Bennington, J. (1970) 'Community development project.' In *Social Work Today*, August, 5–17.

Blair, T. (1998) *The Third Way: New Politics for the New Century*. London: Fabian Society.

Blair, T. (2000) 'The Blair Interview.' *The Observer*, 9 April.

Calouste Gulbenkian Foundation (1968) *Community Work and Social Change: A Report on Training*. London: Longman.

Campbell, J. and Oliver, M. (1996) *Disability Politics*, London: Routledge.

Cooke, I. and Shaw, M. (1996) (eds) *Introduction in Radical Community Work: Perspectives from Practice in Scotland*. Edinburgh: Moray House.

Cunningham, J. (2001) 'University of life.' *The Guardian*, Society, 11 April, p.2.

Curno, P. (ed.) (1978) *Political Issues and Community Work*. London: Routledge & Kegan Paul.

Freire, P. (1993) *Pedagogy of the Oppressed*. London: Penguin.

Gilligan, R. (2011) *Tony Gregory*. Dublin: The O'Brien Press.

Henderson, P. and Thomas, D. (1987) *Skills in Neighbourhood Work*. London: Allen and Unwin.

Hoban, M. (2002a) 'The Same Old Story: Implications of Current Government Policy for the Involvement of Residents in Neighbourhood Regeneration.' In S. Clarke, A. Byatt, M. Hoban and D. Powell (eds) *Community Development in South Wales.* Cardiff: Wales University Press.

Hoban, M. (2002b) 'Local Action for Participation and Change.' In S. Clarke, A. Byatt, M. Hoban and D. Powell (eds) *Community Development in South Wales.* Cardiff: Wales University Press.

Hoban, M. (2005) *Humanising Development and Regeneration: A Dialogical Enquiry with Grassroots Activists and Community Workers in Rhondda Cynon Taff.* Unpublished thesis, Brunel University.

Hoban, M. (2009a) *Supporting Resident Led Regeneration in Rhondda Cynon Taff: A Participatory Report for Discussion and Action.* Rhondda Cynon Taff: Interlink.

Hoban, M. (2009b) *Older People's Involvement in Rhondda Cynon Taff: A Participatory Report for Discussion and Action.* Rhondda Cynon Taff: Age Concern Morgannwg.

Hoban, M. and Beresford, P. (2001) 'Regenerating regeneration.' In *Community Development Journal* 36, 4, 312–320.

Holman, B. (2000) 'Pride of Place.' *The Guardian*, 9 February.

Holman, B. (2002) '"Doubly Deprive" Society', *The Guardian*, 23 January, p.11.

Jones, D. (1981) 'Community Work in the United Kingdom.' In P. Henderson and D. Thomas (eds) *Readings in Community Work.* London: George Allen & Unwin.

Kelleher, P. and Whelan, M. (1992) *Dublin Communities in Action.* Dublin: Combat Poverty Agency, Ireland.

Ledwith, M. (2005) *Community Development: A Critical Approach.* Bristol: Policy Press.

Meade, R. (2005) 'We hate it here, please let us stay! Irish social partnership and the community/voluntary sector's conflicted experiences of recognition.'*Critical Social Policy 25*, 3, 349–373.

Miller, S.M. and Rein, M. (1975) 'Community Participation: Past and Future.' In D. Jones and M. Mayo (eds) *Community Work Two.* London: Routledge & Kegan Paul.

NOS (2010) *National Occupational Standards for Community Development.* Federation of Community Development Learning.

O'Malley, J. (1977) *The Politics of Community Action: A Decade of Struggle in Notting Hill.* Nottingham: Spokesman.

Owen, J. (2002) 'My Story of the "Lost City".' In S. Clarke, A. Byatt, M. Hoban and D. Powell (eds) (2002) *Community Development in South Wales.* Cardiff: Wales University Press.

Popple, K. (1995) *Analyzing Community Work: Its Theory and Practice.* Buckingham: Open University.

Powell, F. and Geoghegan, M. (2004) *The Politics of Community Development: Reclaiming Civil Society or Reinventing Governance.* Dublin: A. & A. Farmar.

Rothman, J. (1970) 'Three Models of Community Organisation Practice.' In F. Cox, J. Erlich, J. Rothman and J. Tropman (eds) *Strategies of Community Organisation.* Itaska, Illinois: Peacock Publishing.

SEU (Social Exclusion Unit) (1998) *Bringing Britain Together: A National Strategy for Neighbourhood Renewal.* London: Stationery Office.

SEU (Social Exclusion Unit) (2001) *A New Commitment to Neighbourhood Renewal: National Strategy Action Plan.* London: Cabinet Office.

Smith, J. (1981) 'Possibilities for a Socialist Community Work Practice.' In P. Henderson and D. Thomas (eds) *Readings in Community Work.* London: George Allen & Unwin.

Smith, T. (1980) 'Community Work: Profession or Social Movement.' In P. Henderson *et al.* (1980) *The Boundaries of Change in Community Work.* London: George Allen & Unwin.

Thomas, D.N.T. (1978) 'Community Work, Social Change and Social Planning.' In P. Curno (ed.) *Political Issues and Community Work.* London: Routledge & Kegan Paul.

Twelvetrees, A. (2002) *Community Work.* Basingstoke: Palgrave (Third edition).

CHAPTER 5

Rainbow Quality System
User-led Innovation in
Quality Assurance

Arne Kristiansen

Introduction

This chapter deals with user-led organizations which provide services for drug addiction and how these organizations can develop forms of quality assurance from a user perspective. Quality assurance and method development are issues that have increased in importance in recent years. The increasing demands on efficiency in care and treatment are part of the background to this development. The efficiency demands, in turn, are results of the impact of New Public Management which, among other things, has led many public sector activities to adopt organizational forms adjusted to the conditions on the market (Blom, 1998; Blomberg, 2004; Blomberg and Petersson, 2011).

All activities dealing with care and treatment under the social services in Sweden, and in accordance with the Swedish Social Services Act (2001), are obliged to have a system for quality assurance. In Sweden it is the social services in the municipalities which are responsible for the treatment of drug addiction, both in institutional and out-patient settings. Although the social services and the municipalities often are carrying out treatment, they also often engage external organizations which provide treatment for drug addiction (i.e. private care companies and non-profit organizations such as service users organizations). This means that user organizations carrying out treatment for drug addiction by order of social services are also responsible for and subject to quality assurance. The implementation of quality assurance differs, but supervision and education of staff are common elements as well as application of different kinds of documentation systems and evaluations. How to quality assure treatment for drug addiction run by user organizations is an essential question, since user organizations to a quite large extent are responsible for the institutional treatment for drug addiction in Sweden. State and local authorities have an interest in collaborating with user organizations and other non-profit organizations in this matter (Johansson, 2005).

It is problematic however to make the same demands on quality assurance in activities for non-profit organizations as on municipal or state activities (Lundström, 2004). One problem is due to the fact that the dominant forms of quality assurance in treatment for drug addiction are adjusted to services run by professionals (such as social workers and psychologists). People who are active in user organizations sometimes lack formal education on care and treatment. It is also difficult to maintain advanced quality assurance systems in user organizations because of the high turnover of people. It can also be problematic to engage outside experts, often because it makes it difficult to ensure continuity in quality assessment. This is an important background to the development of Rainbow Quality System (RQS), an innovative quality assurance system for user organizations providing treatment for drug use and addiction and developed by users with personal experiences of abuse (Kristiansen, 2006, 2011a).

The organizations using RQS belong to Rainbow Sweden, an umbrella organization for user organizations in the Swedish drug abuse field. At present five organizations under Rainbow Sweden are using RQS. Presently there are about 300 individuals undergoing rehabilitation for drug addiction within these five organizations.

RQS consists of peer review, education and documentation. RQS does not have any counterparts in Sweden. There are however examples in other countries of non-profit organizations that have created alternative quality assurance systems. One example is the Charities Evaluation Service in the UK which has developed the Practical Quality Assurance System for Small Organizations (PQASSO).

Apart from the fact that many of the quality assurance systems used in the treatment of drug addiction are difficult to apply to user-led rehabilitation work, the development of RQS also should be viewed in the light of the differences in ideology and approach between Rainbow

Sweden and the public treatment of drug addiction. Rainbow Sweden aims to be an alternative to the public treatment of drug addiction. The term 'empowerment' represents an ideological starting point of great importance. Rainbow Sweden wants to avoid terms like 'treatment' and 'client.' Other terms used instead are 'rehabilitation' and 'user' or 'comrades' as markers against approaches that are based on deficit models and those which objectify people who have addiction problems. Rainbow Sweden is of the opinion that drug addiction depends not on individual flaws or illnesses, but rather on the economic and social conditions of human life. Another ideological mark is the emphasis on 'help to self-help', meaning that participation in rehabilitation should be voluntary and implies a genuine wish to quit using drugs.

Furthermore the personal experiences of social exclusion are regarded as important knowledge and experience bases in the rehabilitation process. People working in the member organizations of Rainbow Sweden mostly have personal experiences of abuse and social exclusion. The concrete everyday work within Rainbow Sweden also differs from the ways of traditional treatment of drug addiction. There is for example no application of psychotherapy, neither on an individual level nor on a group basis. The everyday business focuses on engagement in meaningful activity, and occupation. In several of Rainbow Sweden's services there is the opportunity to engage in construction, furniture manufacturing and farming activities.

I have been project leader and responsible for the building up of RQS, but the work has been done in close co-operation with representatives of Rainbow Sweden. All parts and developments of RQS have been discussed in, tried out and approved by the member organizations of Rainbow Sweden. The development of RQS is inspired by the principles applicable to user-controlled research (Beresford, 2002) and social mobilizing research (Kristiansen, 2011b). Today RQS is relatively established and the work has been going on for seven years. My part in RQS now is to be scientific advisor for people who put RQS into practice at the same time as I watch and study the project as a researcher. From a scientific point of view RQS among other things is interesting because of the resource mobilization (see McAdam, 2008; Tilly, 1978) and the implementation perspective (Fosse, 1999; Robinson *et al.*, 2006).

Development of Rainbow Quality System

At the beginning of 2004, some representatives of Rainbow Sweden contacted me to discuss the possibility of developing a system for quality assurance based on a service user perspective. For several years they had used various strategies to meet the quality assurance requirements from municipalities and other stakeholders. However, they had found it difficult to get continuity and structure in this work, which was due to the fact that the various forms of quality assurance they had tried were developed and adapted for treatment by professional social workers and psychologists. They told me that they wanted to develop a system for quality assurance based on a service user perspective. It is important to clarify that RQS not only emerged as an adaptation to the requirements from the municipalities they co-operated with, but is primarily a project for generating knowledge about treatment and social change within Rainbow Sweden. It also focuses on creating better conditions for supporting the people who seek help from Rainbow Sweden's member organizations. Rainbow Sweden made contact with me because my research is mainly based on a service user perspective and I am familiar with several members in Rainbow Sweden because of my involvement in some service user organizations in the field of drug addiction. This is a commitment that began when I studied social work at university in the late 1970s.

In the spring of 2004 we worked out an application to finance a project for development of a service user-led system for quality assurance. The application was submitted to *Mobilisering mot narkotika* (Mobilisation Against Drugs), a committee linked to the Swedish government, and at that time an important funder of different projects about prevention and treatment in the field of drug addiction.[1] We were granted funds to develop a system for quality assurance over one year and we started this work in the autumn of 2004. The project plan stated that the goal was to create a system for quality assurance which:

- would be simple to use in practice
- would be easily accepted by both practitioners and service users
- would be applicable in practical rehabilitation work
- would function in organizations with high staff turnover.

---

1 In 2004 Sweden had a Social Democratic government. After the Conservatives won the elections in 2006 it did not take a long time before they shut down Mobilisation Against Drugs.

In the autumn of 2004 I began to do an inventory of needs and resources to build a service user-controlled quality assurance within the six organizations in Rainbow Sweden to be included in the project. I visited the organizations and during the visits I interviewed several of the members. I interviewed both people who worked in the organizations and people who had recently come there for support with drug use and addiction. The purpose of the interviews was to initiate a dialogue and get a picture of the needs and interests that existed for quality assurance in the organizations.

The interviews gave a patchy picture of both the quality assurance activities and how the members perceived it. All organizations were engaged in some kind of quality assurance. Some of the organizations had engaged external evaluators. Some of the organizations used ASI,[2] to obtain a basis for recording and monitoring of the people who came there to get help. Some of the organizations had worked out their own questionnaires to maintain a record. Most of the people I spoke to felt that they could get help in their daily work with a system for quality assurance, which was based on their specific conditions and experiences. There were also members in the organizations who were skeptical and questioned whether quality assurance really was something that Rainbow Sweden should put energy into.

One observation that emerged from the interviews was that daily discussions between the members often focused on work and production, but not often on the conditions for rehabilitation. One question I asked everyone I interviewed was: 'How can people with substance abuse problems be supported to change their lives?' The question was answered in many different ways, which strengthened the image of an absence of a common 'rehabilitation language,' both within and between the member organizations in Rainbow Sweden. The lack of discussion about rehabilitation and the lack of a shared understanding of how to support people to stop using drugs is obviously a barrier to building a common system for quality assurance.

In December 2004 we organized a two-day conference in Stockholm for the participating organizations. The aim of the conference was to deepen the understanding of the importance of quality assurance within the member organizations and to create a commonly agreed basis for a system for quality assurance that could be used in Rainbow Sweden.

---

2   ASI stands for Addiction Severity Index. ASI is a standardized interview form which is used in drug abuse treatment and research. In Sweden it is commonly used in drug abuse treatment.

At the conference I gave a few brief talks on social change, treatment of drug addiction and quality assurance, but above all, we had group discussions. In various group constellations the participants on the conference discussed issues such as: 'What is required to support people with substance use problems to develop and change their lives in a positive direction?', 'What does good rehabilitation for drug addiction look like?', 'How does your rehabilitation work today?' and 'How do you want to develop it?' There was a positive response to the conference and it provided an important starting point for further work. Several of those who attended the conference said that it was very rewarding to meet members from other organizations, working with the same things, and have time to talk about rehabilitation and social change. We agreed that these kinds of discussion should be an element in the system of quality assurance we were going to develop during the project.

In the spring of 2005 I visited all organizations again to discuss a proposed system for quality assurance which I had formulated on the basis of the interviews and the discussions at the conference in Stockholm. The proposal meant that the common system of quality assurance for Rainbow Sweden should be based on peer review, documentation and training. The purpose of peer review was to create transparency in organizations, but also to maintain and develop the dialogue, co-operation and learning between the organizations. The purpose of the documentation was that we should develop a number of questionnaires to use when people came to and left the organizations. The questionnaires could also be used for monitoring and evaluation of the organizations and their rehabilitation work. When it came to education, the focus was on interview techniques, management of statistical programs and confidentiality. The proposal was well received and we agreed that I would present a more detailed proposal at a conference in June.

At the conference in Stockholm in June 2005 I presented the first version of Rainbow Sweden's system for quality assurance to representatives from all participating organizations. For peer review, I proposed that it should be based on an agreed set of standards to serve as criteria for user-led treatment activities and which the organizations working with RQS should sign up to. The proposal also contained questionnaires for different types of monitoring and evaluation. At the conference I also proposed that our system for quality assurance should get the English name Rainbow Quality System (RQS). We also discussed the contents of the questionnaires and how the standards for the peer review should be agreed. Those who attended the conference were positive about the proposal as a whole, however, one of the things criticized in the proposal was the extent of the questionnaires. Participants wanted to know how to get a clearer perspective of empowerment in the questionnaires. When it came to the name proposal, Rainbow Quality System (RQS), everyone was in agreement and the importance of unifying names or symbols should not be under-estimated. It can be an important element of a resource mobilization work (Tilly and Wood, 2009). I remember how one of the conference participants said: "We have RQS! They have ASI!' At the conference, we agreed that I should work out a new proposal to be brought back at a new conference in early autumn.

In September we had a one-day conference in Stockholm. At this conference I got new comments and criticism on the questionnaires and the standards, which I redrafted and presented at another conference in Stockholm a few weeks later. We met on five more occasions during the autumn of 2005 to discuss and adjust the final contents of the questionnaires and the standards before the version of the RQS, which became operational in January 2006, was ready.

Rainbow Quality System (RQS)

Central elements of RQS are peer review, documentation and training. The peer review means that each organization in Rainbow Sweden that carries out rehabilitation is visited and reviewed approximately once a year by representatives from the other organizations in Rainbow Sweden.

The peer review is based on seven agreed standards for drug addiction rehabilitation for Rainbow Sweden member organizations. According to Rainbow Sweden these seven standards constitute quality criteria for service user-led rehabilitation. The standards are the following:

- empowerment
- positive role models
- absence of drugs
- work
- social integration
- development
- transparency.

Empowerment

The first standard is underpinned by the belief that all people have the potential and the right to have power over their own lives. It focuses on the importance of service users' participation and influence. It requires member organizations of Rainbow Sweden to offer real opportunities for their members to develop and have influence on their own lives.

Positive role models

This standard is based on the fact that the majority of people who work for the members organizations of Rainbow Sweden have personal experience of drug addiction and social exclusion. They bring an important asset, partly because they know what it means to get out of a difficult life situation and build a new life and can be role models who give hope to people who are in vulnerable situations. Therefore it is desirable that the majority of those who work for Rainbow Sweden are people with personal experiences of drug addiction and social exclusion.

Absence of drugs

Absence of drugs and alcohol is an important prerequisite for drug rehabilitation and daily life in the member organizations. It is therefore important that the organizations ensure that the absence of drugs and alcohol is maintained.

Work

Practical work is an important part of the daily life of Rainbow Sweden's member organizations. All work which is performed within Rainbow Sweden should be meaningful and instructive. Work should not just be about giving people tasks to do. All work should be both meaningful and beneficial to the person and to the organization.

Social integration

Social integration refers to the social inclusion of the people who come to Rainbow Sweden. It also refers to the ambition for member organizations to have a continuous interaction with the surrounding local community.

Development

This standard involves striving for the member organizations to continuously develop and improve. It also means that the organizations will have a self-reflective and self-critical approach to challenge any stagnation and complacency.

Transparency

The member organizations of Rainbow Sweden should be characterized by transparency, both within and between their organizations and externally to the community. Transparency refers to decision-making within Rainbow Sweden, but also transparency in how the organizations work.

The requirement that the organizations using RQS must fulfil these seven standards is genuine and enforceable and one of the organizations that was involved in RQS from the beginning was later excluded from RQS in 2007. This was due to the fact that the organization did not use the RQS in practice, although they said they did, and importantly they seldom participated in the peer review activities. Other organizations working with RQS said that there was a risk that the organization has used RQS for marketing purposes, but did not implement it. Their lack of participation in the peer review significantly reduced the degree of transparency in their activities. Although it was not an easy decision, the exclusion made clear that it is challenging to be a part of the RQS co-operative.

The basis for the documentation in the RQS are eight questionnaires:

- RQS01: Registration form
- RQS02: Follow-up form
- RQS03: Organization questionnaire
- RQS04a: Check-out form with user interview
- RQS04b: Check-out form without user interview
- RQS05: Questions to the commissioning body
- RQS06: After treatment check-out
- RQS07: Basis for colleague evaluation.

RQS01 is to be used when a user arrives at Rainbow Sweden. RQS02 is designed to serve as a basis for a conversation about what the user would like from rehabilitation. RQS03 is used as an anonymous survey to get an idea of what the users think about the rehabilitation and the organization. RQS04a and RQS04b are used when a person has completed the rehabilitation and leaves the organization. RQS05 is a questionnaire for the organization's managers, to get an idea of what they think about the rehabilitation and to co-operate with Rainbow Sweden. RQS06 is a questionnaire for use after teatment to see what life looks like for those who received rehabilitation services from Rainbow Sweden. RQS07 is a questionnaire used for different types of performance appraisal.

Importantly, RQS aims to offer support in the rehabilitation work for those who work with RQS, so that they can better understand and support the users' rehabilitation process. The peer reviews also contribute to this. The questionnaires offer a framework for those who work in rehabilitation for talking to the users about important issues related to the development of their lives. The RQS questionnaires are different from how questions in questionnaires in drug treatment are usually formulated. The RQS questionnaires focus on the users' resources and prospects, not on their weaknesses and shortcomings.

Training and education is also an important part of RQS. Four times a year we arrange training days where participants have opportunities to develop themselves in, for example, interview methodology and treatment, but also in more factual knowledge about substance use and social change. Some of the courses have offered training on the statistical program used to process and compile data from the questionnaires. Another topic of the training is confidentiality regulations.

RQS in practice – results and experiences

It is over seven years since we started to develop RQS and it has been used continuously in Rainbow Sweden for five years. It turned out that RQS was not just another pilot project limited by funding, but an activity that has developed into an important and integral part of Rainbow Sweden's rehabilitation work. Peer review and training days are held every third month, with many people participating. The documentation system is used within the organizations to a great extent. RQS has been accepted by municipalities and the organizations have agreements with them to continue providing services. In 2008 RQS was brought out as an interesting example in a government inquiry (SOU, 2008, p.18) of a quality assurance system developed by service users. In recent years other organizations have shown interest in getting to use RQS, a fact that made Rainbow Sweden trademark protect the RQS two years ago.

Many people working in Rainbow Sweden believe that RQS supports their work by providing them with a basis for discussing and planning rehabilitation with the users. The co-operation between the organizations has been strengthened by the continuous peer review process. Such co-operation includes helping each other with detoxification when users have relapses and staff exchanges between services. Every year we provide a statistical report of the material received by the questionnaire data which has taught us more about the rehabilitation work in the organizations. The information about people turning to Rainbow Sweden organizations for support is now of good quality.

So why has RQS been so successful in being sustained in the long term? One important reason is that RQS plays a vitally useful role in the work of Rainbow Sweden. RQS functions well and facilitates the people working in Rainbow Sweden rehabilitation services.

Another reason for the success of the RQS is that people using it feel that they participate in its development. In other words, you can say that RQS has been developed by the users in both the development and implementation phases.

RQS also functions well because even though there has been quite a large turnover of people working with RQS – as we had anticipated at the planning stage – there have been a core number of key figures engaged from the very start, working patiently and continuously developing RQS. In implementation research the importance of the dedication of influential actors for innovations to succeed has been emphasized elsewhere (see Fosse, 1999; Guldbrandsson, Bremberg and Bäck, 2005; Robinson *et al.*, 2006).

Finally, by being accepted by the organizations' managers, RQS strengthens the legitimacy of Rainbow Sweden's rehabilitation services in relation to addiction treatment activity run by professionals. RQS can be regarded as an important part of a resource mobilization (McAdam, 2008; Tilly, 1978) facilitated by Rainbow Sweden at a time when demands on quality assurance and efficiency are increasing.

Acknowledgements

Many thanks to Eva Schmitz, Library and IT at Malmö University, who translated this text into English.

References

Beresford, P. (2002) 'User involvement in research and evaluation: liberation or regulation?' *Social Policy and Society 1*, 2, April, 95–105.

Blom, B. (1998) *Marknadsorientering av socialtjänstens individ- och familjeomsorg. Om villkor, processer och konsekvenser.* Umeå: Umeå universitet, Institutionen för socialt arbete.

Blomberg, S. (2004) *Specialiserad biståndshandläggning inom den kommunala äldreomsorgen Genomförandet av organisationsreform och dess praktik.* Lund: Lunds universitet, Socialhögskolan.

Blomberg, S. and Petersson, J. (2011) När en ny organisationsmodell blir vardag – spridningen av specialiserad biståndshandläggning inom den kommunala äldreomsorgen och vad som hände sedan. *Socionomens forskningssupplement* nr 29/2011.

Fosse, E. (1999) *Implementering av helsefremmende og forebygande arbeid.* Bergen: Universitet i Bergen, Institutt for adminstrasjon og organisasjonsvittenskap/Hemilsentret.

Guldbrandsson, K., Bremberg, S. and Bäck, H. (2005) 'What makes things happen? An analysis of the development of nine health-promoting measures aimed at children and adolescents in three Swedish municipalities.' *Social Science and Medicine 61*, 11, 2331–44.

Johansson, S. (2005) *Kommunalt stöd till sociala ideella organisationer. Omfattning, utveckling och former.* Stockholm: Socialstyrelsen.

Kristiansen, A. (2006) RQS – kvalitetssäkring på brukarnas villkor. *Socionomen* nr 4/2006.

Kristiansen, A. (2011a) Utvärdering av brukarstyrd rehabilitering. *Alkohol och Narkotika* nr 4/2011.

Kristiansen, A. (2011b) Forskning som resurs i social mobilisering. V. Denvall, C. Heule and A. Kristiansen (red) *Social mobilisering. En utmaning för socialt arbete.* Lund: Gleerups.

Lundström, T. (2004) *Teorier om frivilligt socialt arbete – En diskussion om forskningens läge och organisationernas framtid.* Sköndalsinstitutets skriftserie nr 22. Stockholm: Ersta Sköndal Högskola.

McAdam, D. (2008) 'Conceptual Origins, Current Problems, Future Directions.' In D. McAdam, J. McCarthy and Z. Mayer (ed.) (1996) *Comparative Perspectives on Social Movements: Political Opportunities, Mobilizing Structures, and Cultural Framings.* New York: Cambridge University Press.

Robinson, K.L., Driedger, M.S., Elliot, S.J and Eyles, J. (2006) 'Understanding facilitators of and barriers to health promotion practice.' *Health Promotion Practice 7*, 4, 467–476.

SOU (2008) *Evidensbaserad praktik inom socialtjänsten – till nytta för brukaren.* Betänkande av Utredningen för en kunskapsbaserad socialtjänst. Stockholm: Socialdepartementet.

Tilly, C. (1978) *From Mobilization to Revolution.* New York: Random House.

Tilly, C. and Wood, L.J. (2009) *Social Movements 1768–2008.* London: Paradigm Publishers.

CHAPTER 6

Co-production in Evaluation and Outcomes

Lessons from Working with Older People in Designing and Undertaking Research Initiatives on Older People's Lives, Independence and Wellbeing

Helen Bowers and Anita Wilkins

Overview

This chapter shares experiences and lessons from working with older people and other key stakeholders in three initiatives spanning five years, each concerned with improving older people's outcomes and life chances through the design and delivery of inclusive and responsive public services. There is a particular focus within these examples on older people who need support in their lives; and on the processes designed and outcomes achieved as a result of working in partnership with them to influence, deliver and evaluate those services. It also reflects on the literature on co-production and user-defined outcomes, with specific attention paid to the recent history and examples of how older people's views, opinions, experiences and expertise have influenced policy and practice at a national and local level.

Context

A review of the last ten years of older people's participation in decision making and the literature on co-production in public services reveals numerous examples of older people influencing the shaping of policy and practice at a national, regional and local level.

There are many definitions of 'co-production', which will be discussed in more detail later in this chapter. The definition of co-production adopted by the Older People and Ageing Programme at the National Development Team for Inclusion (NDTi) (www.ndti.org.uk/who-were-concerned-with/older-people-and-ageing) has been influenced by the diverse older people with whom the authors have worked (Bowers *et al.*, 2010):

> Coproduction is a simple idea: it's about individuals, communities and organisations having the skills, knowledge and ability to work together, create opportunities and solve problems. Putting this into practice is not so simple, and for older people who need support in their lives is a relatively new phenomenon.

The Joseph Rowntree Foundation funded programme of research about the lives of older people (2004), draws out the lessons from 18 projects that took place over a four-year period to help understand the critical issues involved in shifting the focus of attention from policy makers' and planners' priorities and modes of measuring effectiveness, to those aspects of service delivery that matter most to older people and local communities.

This important programme highlighted five key themes, or dimensions of effective participation, which are as relevant today as they were seven years ago:

- Strategies should start with older people's lives, taking full account of their diversity and definitions of 'a life worth living'.

- Services – thought important – are only a part of the picture of support that older people value and the experience of growing older.

- Citizenship, community and family are fundamental to older people's wellbeing and quality of life.

- The meaningful involvement of older people – individually and collectively – is under-developed and needs clear standards to ensure it happens.

- Learn from 'what works' from older people's perspectives, and from their leadership and contributions in setting local agendas for change.

Despite a recent and current emphasis on co-production within national policy developments and programmes such as those associated with personalisation and the transformation of adult social care (Department of Health, 2010a), it is striking to observe how pertinent and relevant these messages remain today. It is also interesting to note that, in spite of the obvious contributions that older people have made to shaping policy and practice, most of the developments associated with the transformation of social care are connected to the disability and independent living movements – which themselves are most often associated with and involve younger adults who need support in their lives (Morris, 2011; Office for Disability Issues, 2008):

> Many policies and initiatives exist which seek to improve quality of later life and older people's experiences of public services generally. However, it is still health and social care services that dominate discussions about support and assistance; and there is little focus on choice and control as defined in 'Improving the Life Chances of Disabled People'... A key issue for older disabled people is how their voices are heard and experiences captured, given that they are amongst the most excluded groups in society. Further attention needs to be given to how user led initiatives and disability organisations take account of the diverse needs, experiences, voices and contributions of older people. Older people's forums, advisory groups and other influencing mechanisms also need to pay attention to how older disabled people are enabled to participate. (Office for Disability Issues, 2008, pp.21–2)

This may be because the main focus of older people's participation and influencing activities have related to public services and issues that extend far beyond health and social care, such as: housing, town planning, transport, the democratic processes of decision making and so on. This level of engagement is reflected in the (now defunct) Comprehensive Area Assessment Process (CAA) which examined the involvement and wellbeing of older people in shaping public service delivery at a local level (Audit Commission, 2009). Examples of older people's involvement in setting standards or designing services based on their priorities in health and social care still tend to be focused on fairly limited developments based on models of 'user compliance' (Needham and Carr, 2009) rather than as equal partners in transforming local services. Examples include developments such as the NHS Expert Patient and the care regulators' Experts by Experience programmes, local implementation teams set up following the publication of the *National Service Framework for Older People* (Department of Health, 2001) and developments associated with the implementation of the National Dementia Strategy (Department of Health, 2010b).

This chapter, therefore, shares three examples of older people's involvement in and leadership of developments based on their definitions of quality of life and priorities for improving the outcomes and life chances of older people who need support in their lives.

These examples include:

1. the development of eight outcome areas driving the work of the Dorset Age Partnership and POPP programme – now in its fifth year of delivery and evaluation in partnership with older people and local communities across the county

2. working with older people with high support needs to identify their definition and priorities for 'a good life' including six principles of independent living for older people which have been shaped with a range of other stakeholders (including government departments, commissioners and providers) to develop a 'readiness check' which can be used to assess whether these things are happening or not

3. the co-design of a guide on co-production with older people, as part of a suite of materials focusing on personalisation and the implementation of personal budgets for older people.

Lessons from the literature on co-production and user-defined outcomes

Co-production is of central importance to the transformation of adult social care services, and is relevant to all sectors in adult social care (including voluntary and independent sector providers) and for all kinds of people who use social care services (Needham and Carr, 2009; Coote, 2010). There is an increasing drive for co-production to be adopted as a standard, mainstream approach whereby people who use services are recognised as having expertise and assets which are essential to creating effective services, and thus are involved in an 'equal and reciprocal relationship' with professionals and other stakeholders (Boyle *et al.*, 2010).

As a concept, co-production is also renowned for its 'excessive elasticity' in terms of the ways in which it has been defined and interpreted. Needham and Carr (2009) provide a helpful overview of the most common interpretations, categorising co-production into three levels:

1. user compliance (i.e. all services relying on some input of users, even if that is simply compliance with social norms such as doing homework, or not dropping litter)

2. increased user recognition and involvement (where service users are invited – required – often on an ad hoc basis – to make a greater contribution towards shaping the service)

3. transformation (where there is a shift in power and control brought about by a change in mechanisms for planning, delivery, management and governance).

They argue that it is the third, transformational level that is most likely to bring about better outcomes for people who use social care.

In their work together in building a network of co-production practitioners, the New Economics Foundation and NESTA (Boyle *et al.*, 2010) have written about the key drivers for and barriers to 'mainstreaming' co-production, highlighting four big challenges which need to be crucially addressed at a time of increasing economic constraints and debates about the future security, purpose and role of public services. The four challenges are:

1. embedding co-production within commissioning activity

2. generating evidence of the value of co-production

3. scaling up successful approaches

4. developing professionals' skills.

The following case studies provide illustrations of different approaches taken to addressing these and other challenges with a particular focus on the first two: working with older people and commissioners, as well as 'providers' and wider members of local communities (i.e. not using local services) to improve the design and commissioning of local services; and working with older people, commissioners, providers, researchers, and policy makers to generate evidence and methods of evaluating outcomes achieved as a result of co-producing local services.

A key message across each of these examples is that outcomes and outcome measures are only meaningful if they focus on what's important to older people and the changes that they want to see, feel and experience in their lives. Services and organisations are secondary considerations. This message resonates with findings from earlier studies, most notably a Joseph Rowntree Foundation study (Shaping Our Lives, 2003) on user-defined outcomes, which found that:

- It is impossible to separate ideas of user-defined outcomes from actions to define and achieve them.

- Involvement to support user-defined outcomes takes more time and resources than usually envisaged.

- Users felt that services continued to show a lack of respect, and the value of their own outcomes was not acknowledged nor valued.

- Users value the everyday things in life such as cleaning, shopping and support at home – yet they found it very difficult to get services to prioritise support in these areas.

- Other services were very important to people beyond ideas of social care, in particular, housing and information.

- It was important for users to meet together to strengthen their own voice in achieving the outcomes they valued.

A key challenge, therefore, is to achieve a shift whereby outcomes are defined by and reflect older people's lives and priorities, and the changes they want to see or make; and are measured in terms of what (and how) contributes to these goals, including specific services and support such as health and social care. In our experience, this shift can only happen when strategies and services are designed, developed, commissioned, delivered and evaluated with older people's full engagement as equal partners with commissioners, providers, researchers and policy makers within these services. A second important message is the need to illuminate the vast literature and range of older people's influence in the design and delivery of public services, so that their examples of effective co-production achieve a much greater profile – and are more likely to become embedded in service commissioning, delivery and day-to-day practice.

Case study 1: influencing and measuring the outcomes of early intervention and prevention work in Dorset

The experiences of and learning from working with diverse partners and stakeholders in Dorset highlights the benefits of working in partnership and building close working relationships with diverse older people, paid officers and community leaders in developing, testing, refining, capturing, measuring and reporting on eight outcome areas of the county's impressive range of early intervention and preventative work.

Dorset Age Partnership (DAP) is a network of older people drawn from forums and groups across the county; strategic leads from Dorset County Council, district councils and NHS organisations; police, fire and rescue services; and a range of voluntary and community organisations. It acts as the theme group for the Dorset Strategic Partnership, and was established as a partnership body where older people are in the majority and an older person is always the chair. It is supported and fed into by six locality partnerships (based on district council areas), each with a similar make-up to DAP. This intricate infrastructure is designed to ensure that outcomes and overall direction established at a county level is informed by people's priorities at a local, neighbourhood level. These two levels of engagement and co-production shape the direction, focus and content of Dorset-wide strategies and investment plans.

DAP was initially established to secure older people's engagement and leadership in the county's successful POPP pilot[1] from 2005–06 to 2007–08. In addition to DAP and the network of local partnership groups, 100 older people were recruited, trained and supported to work as community leaders, 'wayfinders' (local navigators providing information, advice and signposting activities) and evaluators in order to develop and embed locally based approaches and interventions to promote healthy, active ageing and avoid hospital and care home admissions. A key goal of all of this work was to ensure older people's contributions, assets and talents were harnessed, valued and used to improve public services.

These partnerships have resulted in over 4000 older people being directly involved in the development of strategies that impact on their lives, and outcome measures that reflect their priorities. They have been

---

1   Partnerships for Older People Project, a Department of Health sponsored programme focusing on shifting the focus of investment and activity away from secondary health and social care to early intervention and preventative approaches.

instrumental in defining and using a set of eight outcome areas to evaluate the impact of Dorset's Ageing Well Strategy and the ongoing work of the POPP programme (the pilot initiative having been embedded within local planning and service delivery mechanisms).

The eight outcome areas were agreed through working with members of all of these partnerships and Board members of the local POPP programme (which includes older people engaged through DAP) in a series of interactive workshops, meetings, surveys and intensive analysis co-ordinated and facilitated by an evaluation team working with DAP and local partnerships.[2] The eight outcome areas are:

Older people in local communities...

1. have housing suitable for individual needs

2. are socially integrated and not isolated

3. are making positive contributions and experiencing fulfilment as a result

4. feel secure and safe

5. feel free from discrimination

6. feel financially secure

7. are in good health in mind and body

8. have dignity, choice and control throughout their life, especially towards the end.

In addition to agreeing these outcome areas, the same network of partners has been involved in establishing the method by which these outcomes are captured, measured and analysed to determine whether progress is being made in improving older people's outcomes and quality of life. This method is based on the Most Significant Change technique (MSC), a participatory process for collecting and identifying 'Outcome stories to demonstrate impact and change' (Davies and Dart, 2005). This method is similar to the Delphi Panel technique used in a qualitative study and consensus development exercise to establish user-defined outcomes in mental health (Perry and Simon, 2009). This study analysed the views of two service user focus groups to gauge their understanding of the concept of 'outcomes', and used a Delphi Panel to prioritise these outcome domains and formulate consensus between participants. With

---

2   The evaluation team is led by staff and older people working as local evaluators from NDTi.

MSC, a small, defined group of local people (in this case, members of the Evaluation and Data Steering Group referred to above) follow a systematic process for recording, collecting, sifting and selecting, and then analysing personal stories of change (i.e. outcomes). The emphasis is on agreeing and then distilling the *most significant changes* experienced (in this case by older people) in relation to agreed outcome areas or domains.

The diagram shown in Figure 6.1 summarises the key steps and processes involved to identify and analyse outcome stories in Dorset – using POPP funded projects and services as the key source for generating and recording personal stories and examples of change.

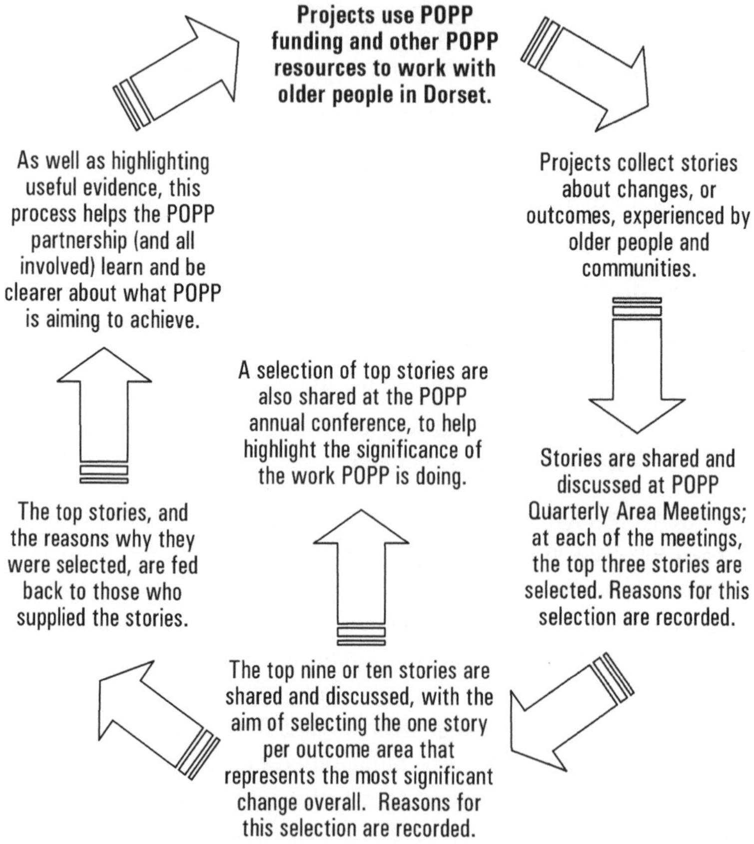

Projects use POPP funding and other POPP resources to work with older people in Dorset.

As well as highlighting useful evidence, this process helps the POPP partnership (and all involved) learn and be clearer about what POPP is aiming to achieve.

Projects collect stories about changes, or outcomes, experienced by older people and communities.

A selection of top stories are also shared at the POPP annual conference, to help highlight the significance of the work POPP is doing.

Stories are shared and discussed at POPP Quarterly Area Meetings; at each of the meetings, the top three stories are selected. Reasons for this selection are recorded.

The top stories, and the reasons why they were selected, are fed back to those who supplied the stories.

The top nine or ten stories are shared and discussed, with the aim of selecting the one story per outcome area that represents the most significant change overall. Reasons for this selection are recorded.

FIGURE 6.1 USING THE 'MOST SIGNIFICANT CHANGE' PROCESS IN DORSET

The final selection of outcome stories are analysed by members of the Evaluation Data Steering (EDS) Group, as follows:

- All members are given copies of the stories to be discussed at a specially convened EDS Group meeting. Members of the group read and consider each story in turn, discussing their impact on the eight outcome areas before recording the outcome areas where they agree the story demonstrates impact. This process is deliberately led by observed themes within the stories, rather than other 'service' sub-categorisations (i.e. what the older people are saying is different for them, and not what the service usually measures or thinks is important).

- Positive and negative impacts are recorded, and a record is kept of:

    o the outcome numbers where impact is demonstrated within each story

    o a brief note giving the key theme of the impact/story, and justification for the decision made by the group

    o any wider issues, questions or observations resulting from the discussion around each story.

- The group aims to reach consensus about each story before moving on to the next.

    By analysing the stories together, we are constantly testing out our analysis against one another's knowledge and views, and that's leading to greater consistency – and avoiding personal bias – in the evaluation. The older people involved in the group have direct experience and understanding of the realities of life for older people in Britain and in Dorset, and this helps in interpreting the outcome stories. It's only a contributing factor, but it's an extra dimension by which we can make the whole process more real and effective. (Sylvia Barker – POPP Local Evaluator representative on the EDS Group)

Lively discussions often ensue, especially around the less easily identified or less tangible outcome areas, such as 'discrimination'. The group uses the following ground-rules to maintain a consistency of approach, which helps participants to examine areas of disagreement, tension and conflict:

- The wording of the story has to demonstrate an impact. For example: it is not enough to say that because someone has been given information about a lunch club, they are more socially integrated. That (and other information supplied) would be recorded under 'increased choice and control'. It would only be counted under 'socially integrated' if there is some evidence in the story that the person was previously isolated, or that their social networks have widened as a result of attending the lunch club.

- Group members try to pick out the most direct outcome areas for each story, recognising that there are implicit connections between the different outcome areas. For example, having access to specific benefits may impact positively on someone's mental health, which may in turn benefit social integration; or by accessing a community transport scheme someone is saving money they would have had to have spent on taxis etc. These 'programme level' connections and observations arising from the discussion/deliberation process are recorded and listed, but, as above, only the direct outcome areas where the impact is clearly evidenced within the story are recorded.

The system that has been devised over the past few years to evaluate the POPP outcome stories is based on the bottom-up approach used by Dorset POPP. We have found by looking at the outcomes of POPP how direct help and advice can have far-reaching implications. The methods used have been honed over time to enable every positive/negative outcome to be recorded. It has been useful in seeing what is working well and why and also what is not working so well and how POPP can put this right. The system also allows the Leaders[3] to see where there are gaps in provision locally, enabling them to fill them. (Dawn Jones – POPP Community Leadership programme representative on the EDS Group)

Detailed notes are taken throughout this process, and written up into a spreadsheet where they can be further quantified, for example, by totalling the number and percentage of stories demonstrating impact in each outcome area. More in-depth statistical analysis can also be undertaken on these datasets, for example, to identify trends in the grouping of multiple outcome areas or the types of outcomes that appear *within* the outcome stories. There is also potential for carrying out detailed cost–benefit analyses on the outcome stories, both as individual

---

3   Community Leaders are older people recruited and employed for seven hours a week to act as local leaders for change in developing healthy and supportive neighbourhoods across Dorset.

case studies and to model 'assumed' savings across health and social care services in a given area.

The analysis of findings and lessons generated from this process are fed back into local decision making forums and Boards, facilitated by the fact that commissioners and providers are represented on the EDS Group undertaking the selection and analysis of outcome stories.

> We want to know how people are better off as a result of the services that we put in place. Outcome stories are used by Dorset County Council and NHS Dorset, to help us learn more about how to develop and deliver early intervention and prevention opportunities through Dorset POPP in support of people ageing well. (Andrew Archibald, Head of Adult Services, Dorset County Council)

The process of bringing partners together to analyse stories in this way has served a number of important and valuable functions:

- It has brought different partners and stakeholders together to reflect on, learn about and agree what is meant by 'outcomes' and 'priorities' and how to capture and measure these in a way which is meaningful and consistent across all interest groups.

- It has provided direct learning for partners about the impact local strategies, services and options for support are having.

- It has involved a rigorous and robust approach to distilling, analysing and discussing different sources of information and data in order to achieve consensus – giving a robustness to what could easily otherwise have become a very subjective and contested process.

- As well as asking for stories, we have also asked funded projects and providers to report their own outcome 'numbers' as part of the six-monthly monitoring process. However the data from this was patchy and unreliable in that some projects were claiming outputs as outcomes etc. And we think some projects were struggling to relate their everyday achievements to the broad and sometimes more conceptual outcome areas. The story analysis process has enabled the partnership to take a more consistent approach to determining when a difference has been made for a person through POPP, and therefore provides a more reliable body of outcome data, to accompany the powerful detail of the individual stories.

Although time intensive, this iterative process of exploring, defining, testing and refining clear statements that reflect older people's priorities and ways of measuring these, has been an important part of the process of co-production with older people in Dorset, across services, agencies and sectors who do not normally sit down together to examine outcome measures and data in this way. As one participant said:

> This process has been a good outcome in itself. (Dorset EDS Group member)

Case study 2: 'Keys to a good life' – identifying the outcomes of increased choice and control by older people with high support needs

A qualitative research study funded by the Joseph Rowntree Foundation (Bowers *et al.*, 2009) examined and identified a vision of what a 'good life' looks and feels like to diverse older people with high support needs, as a means of shifting the debate on long-term care from its focus on funding and demand for care home places, to what is important to and for older people themselves. A team of researchers from the National Development Team for Inclusion met with over 200 people using face-to-face interviews, focus group discussions and local stakeholder discussions in four study sites (three in England and one in Scotland) in order to learn from the experiences and aspirations of older people living in care homes, extra care housing and supported family placements (now part of Shared Lives arrangements). A call for information and examples of best practice provided further evidence of different approaches and knowledge about 'what works' in this area. The study also included a review of existing literature on the subject of the voice, choice and control of older people with high support needs.

Researchers and older people worked side by side in designing the study, undertaking the fieldwork, call for information and literature review; and analysing the findings and producing the final report. The team met on a regular basis throughout the study, and meetings were used to share findings and experiences of undertaking the work; checking the results of the subsequent analyses of different sources of data; triangulating these data sources and findings; and distilling key themes and messages that were then used to inform and structure the final report. In the final stages of the analysis, members of the research team also co-designed a framework for capturing the key messages that came from the older people they had interviewed about what, for them, constitutes a 'good life' if/when you need a lot of support in your life, and in this case if you live away from your personal, home environment. This framework was then tested again with local stakeholders in facilitated discussion forums, and through a one-day sounding board event involving a wider group of national as well as local stakeholders from the study site.

The resulting 'Keys to a good life (for older people with high support needs)' are summarised below:

1. personal identity and self-esteem

2. meaningful relationships

3. personal control and autonomy

4. home and personal surroundings

5. a meaningful daily and community life

6. personalised support and care.

Six principles and associated actions for ensuring this vision is achieved were identified by working in partnership with older people with a diverse range of support needs, carers, government departments, commissioners and provider organisations through a follow-up initiative funded by the Office for Disability Issues (Office for Disability Issues and NDTi, 2010; Office for Disability Issues, 2011).

During this subsequent piece of work, an expert panel was established involving older people; policy leads on personalisation, co-production, independent living and an ageing society; local authority leads on ageing, wellbeing and adult social care; and independent analysts and commentators working in relevant fields. Older people were in the majority of this panel, which worked together with the help of a lead facilitator (one of the chapter's authors) over a period of six months to agree a set of guiding principles for achieving independent living with and for older people with high support needs. Outcome statements that would reflect whether these things were happening were also developed during this time. Examples of great practice illustrating how these outcomes can be achieved were then sourced, as were a range of practical and conceptual tools to help move the independent living agenda forward with and for older people.

Table 6.1 summarises the six principles and outcome statements developed through this process.

TABLE 6.1 A READINESS CHECK FOR ACHIEVING INDEPENDENT
LIVING WITH AND FOR OLDER PEOPLE

Six principles of independent living	What older people experience or say
Increase voice Older people need a much stronger voice than at present in order to exercise choice and control in their own support, in local services and wider developments. 'Voice' is the ability to express oneself, be listened to and to have one's views and experiences taken into account. It is part of a continuum that spans consultation, involvement, inclusion, influence and co-production.	'I am in the driving seat of my own support.' 'I am involved in the local developments and decisions that I want to be a part of.'
Ensure equal access Commissioners, providers and local communities need to ensure equal access to: information, advice, advocacy and brokerage support; a range of early intervention and preventative services; specialist and diagnostic services; community-based support including housing-related support, aids and adaptations; different ways of managing long-term conditions at home, in the community and in supported accommodation including extra care and care homes.	'I know what's available locally and can access the kinds of support that make sense to me and my lifestyle.' Older people are accessing: • information, advice, advocacy and brokerage support through a range of places, people, organisations, formats and media • a range of early intervention and preventative approaches/support • hospital and other specialist/diagnostic services in a timely and professional manner • community-based support (including housing-related aids and adaptations) from a range of sources to avoid admission and facilitate smooth and timely discharge home • a range of supports to manage long-term conditions at home and in supported accommodation including care homes.

Enable choice and control

Enabling choice and control is a key goal for those seeking to embed independent living for older people at a strategic level. This means older people having choice and control over the support they need to live their everyday lives across the six 'Keys to a good life'.

'I know what I'm entitled to, and how to access it.'

'I know where to go to for assistance if I need it.'

Older people report increased choice and control in six key domains:

- personal identity and self-esteem
- personalised support and care
- housing and home
- meaningful daily and community life
- relationships with others
- getting out and about.

'I am living where I want to, and with the people I want to live with.'

'I am able to take risks, am respected, know my rights and am treated as an equal and valued member of my family and local community.'

Enable participation

Participation in family, community and civic life is a key aspect of independent living and is inextricably linked to people's roles, activities, interests and relationships – i.e. what people do and who they see in their everyday lives.

'I am part of family and community life.'

Join it up strategically

Professionals and agencies still work in silos. Joining it all up is a central feature of independent living. A strategic approach that looks across *all* areas of action, funding and needs is required to join up different kinds of support that reflect the whole of people's lives.

'The support I have helps me to lead my life across all aspects (i.e. the six keys above).'

cont.

TABLE 6.1 A READINESS CHECK FOR ACHIEVING INDEPENDENT
LIVING WITH AND FOR OLDER PEOPLE *CONT.*

Six principles of independent living	What older people experience or say
Promote a new way of thinking By 2020, half the adult population in the UK will be over 50. The way we think about ageing, older people and disability needs to change to catch up with this demographic reality. This means moving away from negative attitudes that implicitly or explicitly portray older people as a drain on public resources. A new way of thinking will lead to new ways of organising resources and financing models of support that make voice, choice and control a reality for everyone, which benefits all generations.	'I am part of the big decisions going on around me.' 'I am inspired by the images of older people I see in local and regional media.' 'I am part of a vibrant, multi-generational community.' 'I am not discriminated against because of my age, gender, ethnicity, sexuality, disability, income (etc.).'

These principles and outcome statements form part of a detailed 'Readiness Check' to enable local systems and communities to better understand what's involved in increasing older people's voice, choice and control, especially when they need a lot of support in their lives. It helps to highlight priorities where further, joint action and possibly reallocation of resources may be required in order to achieve older people's vision (the 'Keys to a good life') and to ensure that the six principles of independent living are embedded within local systems and public services.

The Readiness Check is designed as a self-assessment tool using a simple Red, Amber, Green (RAG) traffic light system rather than weighted scores, to enable participation in this process from as broad a range of local stakeholders as possible.

The intention is for local authorities to use the tool with local older people's organisations, groups and networks, disability organisations and networks including user-led organisations (ULOs) and peer support groups, local NHS organisations and provider organisations from all sectors – as well as broader community networks and groups with an interest in shaping local provision. The tool asks: which traffic light colour most closely reflects the current local situation, Red, Amber or Green?

Red

- Traditional forms of support dominate.

- No awareness of voice, choice and control, or how they apply to older people – including those with high support needs.

- No visible leadership at any level, although there may be some commitment from a small number of enthusiastic individuals.

Amber

- Senior leads committed to working towards the independent living vision and six principles.

- Some plans and early signs of progress in commissioning and delivery.

- A few examples of good practice emerging and some stories of older people exercising voice, choice and control over their support.

Green

- Older people visibly engaged in local developments and exercising choice and control.

- Older people using different ways to manage personal budgets to achieve their goals and meet their needs.

- Older people choosing where they live, and what support they access from a wide range of options and opportunities.

- Problems are addressed in partnership with older people and flexible solutions are sought.

The six principles and the detailed 'Readiness Check' are available via a web-based Resource on Independent Living and Older People (RILOP), available at www.independentlivingresource.org.uk.

Case study 3: defining 'co-production' with older people

Various contemporary policy frameworks designed to improve public services for and the life chances of older people have aspects of co-production at their core, or cannot be fully and effectively implemented unless a genuine partnership is developed with older people including those using the services in question. One example is personalisation and the introduction of personal budgets. The Government's guide to making personal budgets work well with and for older people (Department of Health, 2010c, p.9) states: 'Change will not succeed unless providers and commissioners work together with older people throughout.'

The Department of Health commissioned the authors of this chapter to co-design and develop a practical guide to help councils to work in partnership with older people at a local level. A small co-production team was established to work together to identify 'what co-production with older people means', what it involves, and what it looks and feels like when it really happens at a local level. The published guide written as part of this process (Bowers *et al.*, 2010), has been used to help local authorities and their partners work together and with local communities to transform the way that older people's opportunities for participation, services and support are planned, delivered and monitored through working in partnership *with* older people.

The co-production team involved older people, strategic leads and paid officers from three diverse areas of the country, who worked together with a small design and publication team from the National Development Team for Inclusion (NDTi) and Helen Sanderson Associates (HSA). Members were recruited for their experience and expertise in influencing local service delivery, development and design particularly in relation to personalised services for older people; designing participation methods; person-centred thinking and person-centred practice with older people; graphic design and product development. Overall numbers were kept small and focused to enable strong positive relationships to develop between participants, and an open, honest and mutually supportive working style to become established. There were equal numbers of older people and other members of the group.

The work was undertaken largely through and during a series of four, day-long meetings that took place over a four-month period. These monthly meetings were designed to be interactive, and to harness the contributions of each group member. The aims and outcomes of each meeting as well as the overall task were set out clearly, checked and agreed by all participants; and each meeting was chaired and facilitated by an experienced 'co-production facilitator' who ensured both that these aims were achieved and that the experience of doing this had been inclusive and positive.

Between meetings, further work was undertaken by participants, delivering on agreed tasks and actions that had been identified during the course of each meeting, for example with each member taking a lead area of interest or section of the publication to develop and share with co-production colleagues in the group. This ensured a momentum was developed and work was produced between the monthly meetings that took place. The graphic designer working with the group developed drafts of the publication for each meeting, so that members could see the tangible outcomes of their work over time, comment on and either approve or reject drafts in order to develop the final, co-produced guide.

Through this process, the group identified the following definition of co-production with older people:

> Local authorities [and their partners], older people and older people's organisations working together to design and deliver opportunities, support and services that improve wellbeing and quality of life.

The guide contains a number of stories that describe how individuals and communities have worked in partnership with public services to co-produce services and change lives. These stories illustrate how co-production releases the knowledge and skills of individuals for the benefit of the community; reconnects individuals to their communities; and connects local authorities to the people that they serve.

Eight underpinning principles and associated actions were identified, which local organisations, older people and communities can use to determine whether local people really are influencing local services, as illustrated in Figure 6.2 on the next page.

Conclusions – key themes to aid the future development and use of older people's outcomes and co-production processes

The following themes have been identified by looking across these three examples and previous studies of older people's involvement in defining the priorities for developing and measuring the effectiveness of local services. They are presented both as conclusions to this chapter on older people defined outcomes, and as pointers for the future development outcome measures and of co-production with older people more generally.

- It takes time to build effective working relationships based on trust and a shared understanding of what services should be seeking to achieve (and how), and the methods of determining whether these things are happening.

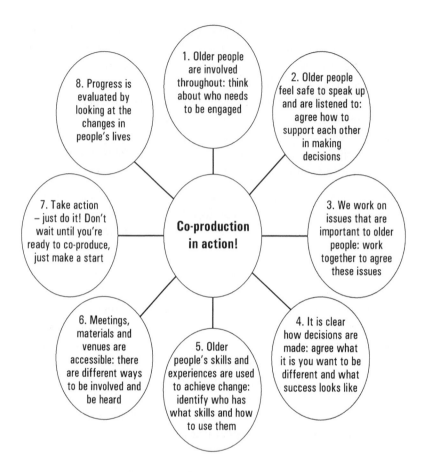

FIGURE 6.2 EIGHT CORE PRINCIPLES AND PRACTICES OF CO-PRODUCTION WITH OLDER PEOPLE

- Thinking about outcomes is still new and unfamiliar territory, especially on a cross-sector/agency and community basis. It is still very rare to find service-related data and measures that focus on changes in people's lives, health and wellbeing. Most data is volume-based information relating to inputs and outputs of current service provision.

- It is this combination of genuine partnership working (co-production) and this focus on people's lives that indicates whether a transformation of local services has really occurred or is happening.

- Older people and other stakeholders involved in participatory processes such as those described in this chapter, need to be informed, educated and 'street wise' about the kinds of information/data/measures that 'hold water' with commissioners and influencers (who are increasingly concerned with measures of cost effectiveness) as well as local stakeholders such as users and carers (who remain focused on quality, inclusion and wellbeing measures).

- Working in partnership to define outcomes and then measure them is not a one-off exercise, and it takes time to develop and hone a method that works for those involved at a local and individual level. The dynamics of who is involved and mechanisms for engaging and working with different partners/ stakeholders will necessarily need to evolve and change shape over time. Everyone involved needs to be prepared to go with the flow whilst staying focused on what they are there to do.

- At the same time, there remains a need to pay close attention to whose voices are heard and how, and whose voices are not heard and why – and to think through and embrace a range of methods for engaging and working with people in this way. There is still a tendency to focus on face-to-face methods such as meetings and workshops which may not be feasible or suit everyone who has a contribution to make and a perspective to share. Social media and networking techniques are still relatively undeveloped in this respect.

- It really helps to have one person or organisation holding the ring on co-ordinating activities and key stages of the iterative processes described in this chapter, and for ensuring that information is captured, data is analysed, and progress on developing and embedding shared priorities and outcome measures is maintained between specific events or meetings. This person or organisation needs to be able to demonstrate and role model their commitment to co-production, for example by ensuring that data analysis, presentation and reporting/ presenting findings is as equally co-produced as the definition of priorities, principles and outcomes.

- There is a need for more effective dissemination and ongoing evaluation to ensure such approaches are profiled and embedded within local services and in national frameworks and policies, and that older people's experiences and impacts in influencing change are recognised, valued and used on an ongoing basis.

Co-production is as much about the bringing together of different and diverse perspectives as it is about the principles of partnership, power shifting and mutuality. As the examples shared in this chapter have shown, co-production is more likely to lead to significant change which is embedded and sustained over time whether it is at a local or national level. The authors believe this is because the evidence of successful outcomes and processes generated through these co-produced developments has been driven, tested and ratified by older people *and* other key stakeholders. There is no doubt that older people have driven these developments, but other stakeholders (commissioners, providers, policy makers, researchers and other members of local communities) have also been involved at the same time and at every stage. No one voice has been more important than another, although the perspective of older people has been central throughout.

These developments and initiatives do take time, and each of these examples was funded through dedicated resources, either additional to or ring-fenced above those routinely available to commissioners, providers and communities as part of their substantive budgets/resources. The authors believe this investment has been essential, given the lack of emphasis and evidence of co-production with older people (especially those with high support needs) in health and social care policy since 2007. However, this brings with it certain challenges, not least a financial one with the severe cuts to public sector funding following the 2008 economic crisis.

Two key priorities, therefore, that the authors believe need to be addressed if this agenda is to be taken forward as the (intended) corner-piece of contemporary policy, service delivery and research practice are:

1. The need to distil and widely distribute the practical learning from initiatives outlined in this chapter and others, such as those shared via the co-production practitioner's network (New Economics Foundation and NESTA, 2010) to ensure that small-scale, localised innovation is 'scaled up and spread out. A key part of this priority involves further developing and increasing the skills and confidence of commissioners, providers, practitioners and older people in working together in ways most closely associated with co-production approaches.

2. The need to pull together the economic case for co-production, with a view to changing current commissioning, provision and delivery so that, as the New Economics Foundation state (Boyle *et al.*, 2010), the key features of co-production are embedded within and drive local commissioning practice and service delivery with and for older people.

References

Audit Commission (2009) 'How good is the well being of older people?' London: Audit Commission. Available at http://oneplace.audit-commission.gov.uk/aboutthissite/contents/pages/aboutthemes.aspx#wellbeingolderpeople, accessed on 4 April 2012.

Bowers *et al.* (2009) *Older People's Vision for Long Term Care.* Joseph Rowntree Foundation. Available at www.jrf.org.uk, accessed on 4 April 2012.

Bowers *et al.* (2010) *Personalisation: Don't Just Do It, Coproduce It and Live It! A Guide to Coproduction with Older People.* Stockport: HSA Press.

Boyle, D. *et al.* (2010) *Right Here, Right Now: Taking Co-production into the Mainstream.* London: NESTA.

Coote, A. (2010) *Ten Big Questions about the Big Society – and Ten Ways to Make the Best of It.* London: New Economics Foundation.

Davies, R. and Dart, J. (2005) *The 'Most Significant Change' (MSC) Technique: A Guide to its Use.* Available at www.mande.co.uk/docs/MSCGuide.pdf, accessed on 26 June 2012.

Department of Health (2001) *National Service Framework for Older People.* London: Department of Health.

Department of Health (2010a) *A Vision for Adult Social Care: Capable Communities and Active Citizens.* London: Department of Health.

Department of Health (2010b) *Quality Outcomes for People with Dementia: Building on the Work of the National Dementia Strategy.* London: Department of Health.

Department of Health (2010c) *Putting People First: Personal budgets for older people – making it happen.* Londond: Department of Health.

Joseph Rowntree Foundation (2004) *Older People Shaping Policy and Practice.* York: Joseph Rowntree Foundation.

Morris, J. (2011) *Rethinking Disability Policy.* York: Viewpoint for the Joseph Rowntree Foundation.

Needham, C. and Carr, S. (2009) *Co-production: An Emerging Evidence Base for Adult Social Care Transformation.* SCIE Research Briefing 31. London: SCIE.

New Economics Foundation and NESTA (2010). Available at www.coproductionnetwork.com, accessed on 21 June 2012.

Office for Disability Issues (2008) *Independent Living Strategy: A Cross Government Strategy about Independent Living for Disabled People.* London: Office for Disability Issues.

Office for Disability Issues (2011) *The SERI Story: Increasing the Voice, Choice and Control of Older People with High Support Needs in the South East of England.* London: Office for Disability Issues.

Office for Disability Issues and NDTi (2010) A Resource on Independent Living and Older People. London: Office for Disability Issues. Available at www.independentlivingresource.org.uk, accessed on 4 April 2012.

Perry, A. and Simon, G. (2009) 'User-defined outcomes in mental health: a qualitative study and consensus development exercise.' *Journal of Mental Health 18*, 5, 415–423.

Prime Minister's Strategy Unit (2005) *Improving the Life Chances of Disabled People.* Available at www.cabinetoffice.gov.uk/strategy/work_areas/disability.aspx, accessed on 21 June 2012.

Shaping Our Lives (2003) *Shaping Our Lives – From Outset to Outcome: What People Think of the Social Care Services They Use.* York: Joseph Rowntree Foundation.

CHAPTER 7

Involving Ethnically Diverse Service Users in the Research Process
Alliances and Action

Karen Newbigging, Alastair Roy, Mick McKeown, Beverley French and Zemikael Habte-Mariam

Introduction

Involving service users in research is widely promoted as good practice (Frankham, 2009). Relatively little, however, has been written about involvement of black and minority ethnic (BME) mental health service users in the research process or the involvement of service users in the technical intricacies of projects such as systematic reviews. What commentary there is suggests that the relationships between academics and black and minority ethnic peer researchers, universities and communities, can present a difficult terrain for forging authentic and productive research alliances. In this chapter we discuss some of the practical and conceptual challenges arising from aspirations to be more inclusive of minority ethnic individuals in the research process. We then go on to describe one particular project of our own as an example of building alliances in the research enterprise. This specific study involved efforts to include African and Caribbean men as members of a research team conducting a commissioned knowledge review of mental health advocacy serving their communities (Newbigging *et al.*, 2007). The notion of a knowledge review, combining a formal systematic literature review and primary fieldwork in the practice domain, illustrates some choices for peer researchers in terms of preferred forms of involvement, and some particular challenges which relate to the scholarly practicalities and demands of undertaking systematic reviews.

African and Caribbean men living in the UK, particularly those experiencing mental health problems, are at risk of social exclusion and are not well represented in the service user movement. We employed a range of methods to maximise the involvement of African and Caribbean men in our review (funded by the Social Care Institute of Excellence). We reflect on the process of involvement in the review, steps taken to ensure this involvement was meaningful, and difficulties encountered. The experience of undertaking a systematic review in the context of a broader approach to establishing the evidence is considered and it is argued that this provides a platform for involvement in aspects of systematic reviews that might otherwise be inaccessible for particular groups. The implications for strengthening service user involvement in the research process are considered together with critical reflections upon academic and lay identity.

A note on terminology

We have used the term 'peer researchers' to refer to people with an identity shared with research participants, the term 'co-researcher' to refer to service user members of the research team and the terms 'service user', 'survivor' and 'experts by experience' to refer to the wider group of people with experience of mental distress. The terms 'black' and 'white' are in common use to reflect a social identify defined by ethnic group and we have followed this tradition, whilst recognising the potentially problematic adoption of these terms as categories. Indeed this is discussed in more detail in this chapter.

Valuing different forms of knowledge

The increasing emphasis on involving service users and survivors in research in the UK arguably reflects a growth in service user involvement in the planning and provision of services, particularly where there has been a change from institutional service provision to community-oriented care, as with mental health service provision in the UK (Thornicroft and Tansella, 2005). Service user involvement in the research process is commonly required by funders and organisations and is widely promoted as good practice, yet service users themselves can be sceptical about degrees of authenticity and have levelled accusations of tokenism (Beresford, 2003, 2005; Frankham, 2009). Critical commentators have noted the influence of complex and sometimes contradictory drivers in all of this, notably the rise of consumerism and an emergent service user movement, the former with undertones of conservatism, the latter more implicitly radical and concerned ultimately with transformative change in services and wider society (Crossley, 2006; McKeown *et al.*, 2010).

Participation can range from involvement on a project advisory group to leading the research. Cowden and Singh (2007, pp.15–16) suggest that contemporary user involvement initiatives in health and social care services are typically top-down, rather than bottom-up, exercises and that the notion of user voice has been fetishised: 'held up as a representative of authenticity and truth' but lacking any 'real influence over decision making'. Furthermore, they claim, the fact that user involvement shares some of the characteristics and aspirations of new social movements has not significantly altered the social, cultural and political context in which participation takes place. Similarly, Beresford (2003) has argued that user involvement in mental health research is more often than not conceived of as a technique for data collection rather than constituting an essentially political act.

The theoretical and political basis for involving service users and survivors in research hinges on the nature of the knowledge produced and views experiential knowledge as generating a different and sometimes deeper understanding of the phenomena under investigation. Beresford (2003, p.5) argues:

> ...one of the particular and fundamental issues raised by user involvement is the nature of the origin of knowledge...we need to challenge the assumptions that the greater the distance between direct experience and its interpretation, the more reliable it is, and explore the evidence and the theoretical framework for testing out whether the shorter the distance there is between direct experience and its interpretation then the less distorted, inaccurate and damaging the resulting knowledge is likely to be.

Such a state of affairs has clear implications for both knowledge production and for involvement in research. The desirability of deploying more appropriate research methods such as participatory approaches to community involvement has been argued persuasively for a range of ethnic minority communities (Okereke *et al.*, 2007). The underpinning rationale is that this involvement enhances the validity and credibility of any research findings by virtue of accessing an authentic community voice.

It is argued that the more genuinely participatory the research design is, the more there is a shift in focus away from communities being the subject of research undertaken by outsider academics, towards experts by experience being the co-producers of knowledge (Fountain, Patel and Buffin, 2007). The extent to which such ideals are lived up to has been assessed in practice by a variety of appraisal tools that delineate a hierarchy of authentic participation. Arnstein's (1969) ladder of involvement, which can be applied to rating the extensiveness of participation in research studies, describes eight levels of involvement ranging from tokenistic involvement to complete control (Hanley, 2005; McGlauglin, 2010). We feel it is important to move beyond the notion that all that is required to solve the problems of participation in research is more involvement in fieldwork. This is in line with critics who contend that overly simplistic adoption of the rhetoric of participation without careful attention to a detailed analysis of its structures (who holds the power) can lead to a performance of involvement (Roy, 2012). Roy suggests, in these cases where the structures of participation are controlled by academics or statutory bodies, lay researchers can feel like agents within outside controlled research agendas in which their communities remain the *objects* of study despite their own involvement.

Involving ethnically diverse participants in the research process

Service users and survivors are a hugely diverse group with various skills, experiences and backgrounds and there are both practical and theoretical considerations concerning the involvement of ethnically diverse service users in the research process. Some people from BME communities have had little engagement with mental health services or particularly negative experiences and these may shape their attitude and motivation to research in this area. African and Caribbean men living in the UK, particularly those living with mental health problems, experience particular social disadvantage in general and in their relationship with mental health services. The anomalous experiences of African and Caribbean men in relation to mental health services have been well documented (Bhui *et al.*, 2003; Care Quality Commission, 2010; Healthcare Commission, 2008; Keating, 2007; Keating *et al.*, 2002). Research has shown that they are under-represented as users of the enabling services and over-represented in the population of patients who are admitted to, compulsorily detained in and treated by mental health services (Care Quality Commission, 2010; Healthcare Commission, 2008).

One of the explanations for this pattern of disadvantage is that the frameworks and assumptions that underpin psychiatry and mental health service provision are implicitly ethno-centric, being based on western concepts of distress and illness. These implicit biases can be viewed as reflecting wider social processes of exclusion and marginalisation (Mclean *et al.*, 2003), including an interaction between stigma attached to popular understandings of mental health, racism in society, and the social construction of difference and otherness (Stowell-Smith and McKeown, 2001).

There have been relatively few accounts that have focused on the involvement of BME service users or African and Caribbean men in the research process. Previous studies have highlighted difficulties in engaging African and Caribbean men as participants in studies of advocacy (Bowes *et al.*, 2002). Further accounts have rarely considered the involvement of service users in systematic reviews, which involves identifying and synthesising the research evidence relevant to a particular research question. Service users are less likely to be involved in this approach to knowledge production than in empirical research and a 2007 review was only able to identify three examples (Carr and Coren, 2007).

Service user involvement in research: does ethnicity matter?

Alexander (2004) contends that the question of how race and ethnicity should be researched and by whom is a seemingly unmanageable problem. The terminology itself is difficult to agree on and various scholars have pointed out inadequacies of commonly used terminology. For example, 'race', 'ethnicity' and 'community' are all terms which are hard to define clearly. Some question whether 'race' is a useful or acceptable term to use in social science in the twenty-first century. Commentators like Lewis (2000) and Fanshawe and Sriskandarajah (2010) suggest that race or ethnicity should not be used as independent categories of difference which primarily order personhood or identity. Rather, other forms of difference, for example gender, sexual orientation, disability, age, faith etc. have a dynamic interaction with ethnicity and race resulting in a variety of effects at an individual and collective level.

There is a long tradition, particularly in the context of qualitative research, to be concerned with issues of reflexivity. Reflexivity refers to the researcher(s) being deliberately aware of how s/he may have influenced the various elements of the research process, from defining the questions to be asked to interpreting the data. This has raised interesting debates regarding the subjectivity of the person in the researcher role and the inter-subjectivity between the researcher and research participant. Researchers' affinity for the notion of giving a voice to oppressed groups has been severely problematised. Feminist researchers have argued persuasively for the value of women researching women (Wilkinson and Kitzinger, 1996) or, in sensitive settings, for instance inside the criminal justice system, prisoners as interviewers of other prisoners (Carlen *et al.*, 1985).

Such considerations lend weight to the idea that researchers who share ethnicity with those being researched should figure prominently within research teams. Whilst various researchers and commentators have noted the value and insights afforded in having a shared or similar ethnicity with the group being studied, this can also be a mixed blessing. A common ethnicity and insider knowledge may render certain situations and meanings more accessible, however it should not be assumed that membership of certain groups (for example 'mental health service user', 'minority ethnic service user', 'academic researcher') offers simple access to shared experiences, shared meanings of those experiences or shared understandings about them (Callender, 1997). Many have sought to question the homogenous nature and assumed effects of categories such as 'ethnicity', 'service user status' or 'academic'. One such concern has focused upon a tendency to assume the homogeneity of ethnic categories which can serve to erase important differences within ethnic groups on the basis of other categories such as age, gender, sexuality, country or region of birth, class, or religion. For Hammersley (1995) we should not privilege someone's knowledge claims due to their membership or non-membership of a particular social category but on the basis of the strength of the evidence they present; to do otherwise is to assume that one group has superior insight into reality whilst another is blinded by ideology.

Therefore, we argue that the involvement of service user researchers may be necessary but not sufficient for knowledge production. We also suggest that an analysis of research structures (including issues of power) and researcher reflexivity is also vital, whoever conducts the research. This is because the involvement of so called 'insiders' does not unproblematically guarantee better data, improved understandings, democratising processes within research or power-free relations between academics, communities and statutory bodies (Roy, 2012). As Edwards (1993) argues, it is most important that all parties to the research endeavour are able to locate themselves in relation to the wider social structure and the different ways in which they may be different (or not) from each other.

The debate is further complicated by assertions, from 'black community researchers', that research projects dominated by academics tend towards lip service rather than genuine action (Hanley, 2005). For such commentators, objectionable research projects subject non-white 'others', and their communities, to the inquiring gaze of the supposedly objective, unbiased, dispassionate, and usually white outsider. Despite increases in numbers of black researchers (Bulmer and Solomos, 2004), the overwhelming majority are white. Hence the calls for greater levels of authentic community participation in all aspects of the research process which have come from academics, statutory bodies and different communities of interest.

Involvement in research may be interesting, engaging and possibly emancipatory. For example black community groups or activists can be attracted to research projects because they feel they provide avenues to initiate change. However such involvement can become a double-edged sword (Alexander, 2004). This is especially the case when research seems to reproduce normative or stereotyped thinking about those involved. For example, female khat users have sometimes failed to register on the radar of research programmes that include Somali, Eritrean and Yemeni researchers, a point which emphasises the many layers of difference that exist within and across ethnicity based groupings (Roy, 2011). Such research findings can reinforce instead of deconstruct traditional accounts of the differences within and between certain groups. However problems can also arise because service users are primarily involved as researchers with the power of other elements of the work (such as funding, decisions over research design, dissemination and subsequent action) held by other groups. It is these characteristics that can lead service user researchers to report that the practices of involvement are sometimes experienced by those who take part as having both regulatory as well as emancipatory potential (Roy, 2012 forthcoming, cites Baistow, 1994).

These are difficult issues for researchers to wrestle with. Our view is that a critical focus on the structures of involvement (i.e. who holds the power to make decisions) and the relational context of projects are two important foci. Those who design research which seeks involvement of service user researchers should define *process, reflection and critical scrutiny* as central to project and data validity (Alam and Husband, 2006). In addressing issues of reflexivity critically, Alexander (2004, p.145) describes a research setting in which she was both an 'insider' – of sorts – and an academic. She emphasises that in this research space she was neither insider nor outsider but in a space between the two. Alexander observes that neither status offered a golden ticket to insight or truth. Rather the richness of her understandings emerged through time spent in the field and the energy and emotion invested in building complex and trusting relationships as the following quotation highlights:

> While I would acknowledge that my identification as 'Asian' facilitated my access initially, it was neither a sufficient nor simple foundation for the relationships that emerged later. Nor were these relationships based on ideas of shared 'culture', but on a less tangible set of alliances and hard-won mutual trust and affection. (Alexander, 2004, p.145)

Reflection on a knowledge review: approach to involvement

Our review built upon firm foundations of community engagement and service user and carer involvement in the International School for Communities, Rights and Inclusion (ISCRI) and the School of Nursing and Caring Sciences at the University of Central Lancashire (UCLan) (now reorganised into a School of Health). ISCRI had a lengthy and well-respected track record in engaging with BME communities and black voluntary sector organisations, underpinned by a model of community engagement (Fountain et al., 2007) and a comprehensive network of contacts with BME community groups. In this programme individuals from target communities were recruited by the university, trained in research methods and given regular support by a university staff member throughout the research process. The projects were commissioned by statutory bodies and academics administered and managed them. Each project produced a research report which was given to local commissioners. The reports from the individual projects tended to articulate the specific needs of each ethnically based community. A critical perspective might suggest that despite the broadly positive intent of this programme which delivered many useful findings, ethnicity was sometimes over-used as a primary characteristic of difference and the powerful positions held by statutory bodies and academics within the programme were not sufficiently analysed. The Comensus initiative, in the School of Health, has been funded since late 2003 to develop, under the aegis of participatory action research, an infrastructure to support the authentic involvement of health and social care service users and carers in all aspects of the university's work including, teaching, research and strategic decision making (Downe et al., 2007). Comensus supports an extensive network of community and voluntary sector groups and interested individuals. These developments enabled us to identify and bring together the partners on our project.

The review was undertaken in partnership with the African and Caribbean Mental Health Service, Manchester (ACMHS-Manchester), Equalities – the National Council for Disabled People and their Carers from Black and Minority Ethnic Communities, London, and Lancashire Advocacy (LA), Preston. Equalities and LA are user-led organisations with Equalities having specific expertise and established networks in relation to African and Caribbean communities and both having expertise in the development of advocacy. ACMHS-Manchester provides a range of mental health services to the African and Caribbean communities in Manchester and also has expertise with advocacy and an extensive knowledge of service provision.

Together these partners represented the major stakeholders in this review and crucially they brought knowledge and experience of the issues and expertise and networks for engaging with African and Caribbean men. The partnership with the university clearly provided opportunities for capacity-building, particularly the development of research skills. At the same time it enabled the project to be delivered so that it was grounded in the experience of African and Caribbean service users and their communities, whilst at the same time aiming to be methodologically robust.

The knowledge review was made up of two elements, a systematic review of the literature relating to mental health advocacy and African and Caribbean men and a practice survey of advocacy, which included a survey of advocacy services, focus groups with African and

Caribbean men using mental health services and interviews with a range of stakeholders, also including service users, service providers, and commissioners.

A project team led by university research staff and including two people (i.e. co-researchers who were either service users or advocates) from each of the partner organisations was established and met on a regular basis (every 6–8 weeks depending on the phase of the research) to shape the direction of the review; develop the methodology; share experience of collecting and analysing data; discuss the emergent findings and comment on drafts of the report. The team was comprised of nine researchers, who were roughly equally split in terms of gender and ethnicity. Team members, as well as other service users from the partner organisations, were subsequently involved in disseminating the findings from the review, through conference presentations and through writing. The full report (Newbigging *et al.*, 2007) and a Resource Guide subsequently developed with some members of the original project team (Newbigging *et al.*, 2008) are available on the SCIE website.

Process of involvement
Developing the proposal

The partners were identified through existing relationships and experience of working together previously. Building on an existing relationship is clearly important not only in developing trust between research partners but also in capacity-building. The individuals and their organisations were all paid for their involvement and between them received just over 40 per cent of the research budget. This enabled these organisations to identify potential co-researchers and recruit service users as research participants, particularly as members of focus groups.

One of the constraints on the involvement both of the organisations and service users was the limited opportunity for input into developing the initial proposal, because of the short time needed to apply within the set deadlines. The project team did not meet at this stage – in part because it took time to identify who might want to be involved and because until the research monies were identified there was no budget for involvement. This was viewed by the partners as a significant limitation and service user involvement in research design, as we noted earlier, has been identified as important in defining the type of data and how it is to be collected which are important aspects of knowledge production. Facilitating genuine involvement from the outset clearly has implications for universities and for funders to ensure both adequate resources and appropriate timescales.

Involvement in the systematic literature review

The systematic review was undertaken in accordance with SCIE guidelines (Coren and Fisher, 2006). In terms of the systematic research review the co-researchers were directly involved in:

DEFINING THE SCOPE AND PARAMETERS OF THE REVIEW

The scope and parameters for the systematic review were outlined in the original commission. In the process of developing the protocol the project team debated the search terms and picked up issues that might have either gone unquestioned by the university research staff or have been missed. For example, there was much debate about the definition of the client group. The commission used the term 'African-Caribbean', which was immediately criticised for masking the heterogeneity of the research population. Whilst the commission reflected the use of terminology in the literature and was probably referring to Black Caribbean men, the co-researchers argued that there were potentially at least four populations: Black African, Black Caribbean, White/African mixed and White/Caribbean mixed that should be the focus of the review. This was adopted and agreed with the commissioners and supported by evidence from the Healthcare Commission census of inpatient admissions that found increased rates of admission and detention for all four populations. Clarifying the definition of the target population in this way also meant that the exclusion of asylum seekers and refugees from the original commission was challenged. This was debated by the research team and the conclusion, not necessarily accepted by all, reached that advocacy for this client group is substantially different from that of mental health advocacy.

IDENTIFYING LITERATURE

The literature search was undertaken by academic researchers. One of the partner organisations (LA) developed a database of organisations building on and extending its own database. They took the lead in contacting organisations for the practice survey element of the review and as part of this process requested information from organisations about their services. These service descriptions formed an important body of primary literature.

IDENTIFYING RELEVANT OUTCOMES

The analysis of the literature involved distilling information about advocacy outcomes, which were developed in discussion with the co-researchers. Decision-mapping software (Banxia) was used to derive outcomes from an initial scoping of key reports and from the direct quotations from men during focus groups and interviews in the practice survey element of the review.

Involvement in the practice survey

The drive to improve the quality of life for men experiencing mental health problems from these communities was evident during the regular meetings of the project team. Involvement in the practice survey element of the knowledge review was therefore perceived as more relevant. It was also more accessible because team members had experience to build on and it was relatively straightforward to design participatory training to build the research capacity of service users. The experience and networks of co-researchers and their organisations (ACMHS and Equalities) undoubtedly facilitated engagement with African and Caribbean men with mental health problems in this element of the review. The practice survey involved individuals from all the partner organisations, taking on different roles in the different aspects of the survey. This included:

CONSTRUCTION OF THE DATABASE OF GROUPS

This was a major task and involved collecting and collating information from a number of sources and marshalling it into an easily navigable database. The LA members were solely responsible for the technical aspects of building the database and were supported by academic input in populating it.

CONSTRUCTION AND REFINEMENT OF THE SURVEY QUESTIONNAIRE

The development of the survey questionnaire was straightforward and had immediate face validity having been assembled and refined by service users and practising advocates. The conduct of the telephone interviews was more complicated, with efforts made to boost confidence of co-researchers and undertake a number of shadowing interviews for purposes of preparation. Despite these efforts, a small number of the eventual service user completed interviews were relatively less successful at gathering the relevant information, and depth of information, as those undertaken by academic/professional researchers. Nonetheless, the project served to bolster enthusiasm of individuals to take part in this and future research projects, whilst suggesting that more thorough and comprehensive training for service user researchers would be appropriate given more time and resources.

DESIGNING AND DELIVERING TRAINING TO UNDERTAKE FOCUS GROUP FACILITATION AND INTERVIEWS

The topic guides for the focus groups and interviews were developed by academic staff and refined by the wider project team. A member of academic staff worked with a service user/survivor researcher to develop training for men who might be interested in facilitating focus groups or undertaking interviews. These sessions were highly participative and two separate groups of between eight and 15 participants ran over five weeks. The workshops always began with warm-up exercises to enable everyone to feel at ease. Role play exercises with interview techniques and facilitation skills were undertaken. Time was allowed in each session for the participants to share their experiences and explore issues around advocacy and experience of advocacy services. Although designed as training, these workshops clearly had other benefits, with a number of participants commenting on how helpful they had been in increasing their confidence. The informality of the sessions and the fact that the facilitators shared a language and an understanding of the participants' culture was identified as critical. Interestingly, none of the men wanted to go on to take on the role of co-researchers, for example to facilitate focus groups or interviews, but were involved in disseminating the findings.

Synthesising the findings from the systematic review and the practice survey

The method for synthesising the findings from the research review and the practice survey also directly drew on the views expressed by African and Caribbean men during the focus groups and interviews.

Possibly the most innovative aspect of this review was the development of the conceptual framework for analysis of the material from the different data sources. One of the research team, who was only involved in the systematic review element of the knowledge review, mapped the discussion at one of our team meetings when we were discussing the emergent findings. This informed conceptual maps that were developed from the focus group and interview data and these were subsequently used to develop a framework for synthesising and interpreting the findings from the systematic review with those from the practice survey – as illustrated in Table 7.1. The framework was further developed and modified through discussion at one of the team meetings.

TABLE 7.1 FRAMEWORK FOR SYNTHESIS OF THE FINDINGS FROM DIFFERENT SOURCES: DERIVED FROM DISCOURSE OF SERVICE USERS AND CO-RESEARCHERS AND THEMATIC REVIEW OF SECONDARY LITERATURE

What is the evidence? (Practice survey data)			CONCEPTUAL FRAMEWORK	What is the evidence? (Systematic review data)	
Case studies	Survey	Focus groups	Needs/ experiences of advocacy services	Literature	Service descriptions
			Outcomes from advocacy services		
			Characteristics of advocates		
			Characteristics of advocacy services		
			Organisational arrangements for advocacy		
			Barriers/ facilitators		

Ensuring that involvement is meaningful

From the outset, the team adopted a number of practical strategies to facilitate meaningful user involvement. This was inevitably an iterative process, learning through action and strengthening the process and building on the strengths and interests of the co-researchers as the project proceeded. The practical steps that were taken and are transferable to other projects included:

- building on existing relationships that endure beyond this specific project

- regular team meetings and discussions supported by briefings, held in an accessible venue used by African and Caribbean service users

- access to individual support from university research staff

- resourcing the partner organisations to enable them to pay service user researchers, service user participants and reimburse expenses

- clarifying roles and investment in capacity-building

- using a broad range of methods to engage men in the research process, facilitated through community organisations

- providing feedback in accessible formats.

Involvement in the review could have been further strengthened by induction and training in systematic reviews and clarifying skills and interest in being involved in this element of the review.

Discussion

The involvement of African and Caribbean men in this project was built on a foundation of partnership and experience of working with diverse service users, including the development of innovative methods for engaging service users, whose voices are seldom heard. The approach was distinctive in working with community organisations to identify potential researchers and providing support and capacity-building. This involved adequately resourcing partner organisations so that they could identify and support service user involvement in the process and pairing each organisation with a member of academic staff. The project team meetings were a central mechanism for involvement as they provided a forum for tasks to be identified and allocated and for emergent findings to be discussed and exposed to scrutiny by the wider group. They also provided a forum for exploration and reflections on the research process and engagement with some of the challenges identified earlier in this chapter. Reflections on the process at the end of the project indicated that these meetings had been highly valued, with comments suggesting that the process was, in and of itself, valuable and there was a sense that involvement felt like being part of a movement for change. The process of workshops, training and focus groups were also identified as crucial. Finding ways of engaging with people on their own terms laid a foundation for real and meaningful involvement. Although the method of training did not lead to any of the men involved becoming co-researchers, there were other benefits and the facilitators described seeing 'people growing in confidence'. The role and skills of the facilitators, and their shared ethnic identity, was seen as an important contribution to this process. However reflection on the research process with a separate group of men, involved in one of the focus groups, indicated that the process had stimulated an interest in research and its potential contribution to social change, with this group going on to develop their own research. Support for this was provided by one of the original facilitators in a voluntary capacity.

Although the review relied on a foundation of partnership for its delivery, this was not always an easy process, with issues regarding power and credibility often surfacing, as noted by other authors in this field (Carr, 2004). There were a number of dimensions to this but commitment to genuine involvement and empowerment of African and Caribbean men using mental health services was often raised. Further, tensions around race and authority have the potential to undermine alliances, solidarity and consensus in partnership and these were exposed during some of the team debates. This overall research question tied in with government policy agendas; in effect the government set the research question without the involvement of service users. The limited involvement of service users in defining the review question, however, was perceived as a struggle between executive authority (the university/ academics/SCIE) and service users and indeed reflects how service users are often excluded from setting research questions. It resonated psychologically and socially, with the history of black oppression, and black experience in mental health services, to the point that a latent potential for mistrust within the partnership was given space to emerge. This raised questions about the legitimacy and/or credentials or credibility of white researchers undertaking inquiry into BME people. Such concerns reflect wider debates around alliances in the pursuance of black political objectives and the issues covered earlier in this chapter.

It was also apparent from the outset that the peer researchers were most interested in the utility of the project, that is, the use and purpose it can be put to in terms of changing practice, introducing more fairness into the allocation of resources into communities in general and around mental health and advocacy in particular. This raised questions about the value of knowledge production and dissemination as opposed to more direct campaigning and the role of academic researchers and their relationships with the partner organisations beyond the life of the review.

Further, the high level of service user involvement in the review was subject to external criticism for compromising objectivity and introducing bias into the process when the method was presented at the Campbell Colloquium in May 2007 (Newbigging, 2007). Such a response raises important questions about the nature of knowledge. Service users have a clear claim to experiential knowledge but this is not the only type of knowledge and the systematic review element introduced a different type of knowledge: research-based, theoretical and empirical; driven by method with the aim of producing a robust systematic review. It was clear from the outset that service users wanted their involvement to give voice to the experiences of African and Caribbean men and therefore were primarily, and some possibly exclusively, keen to be involved in accessing this directly. They were much less interested in taking part in locating, sifting and synthesising research papers and reports. This was compounded by the systematic review element being perceived as overly technical, academic and removed from people's direct experience. Conversely, involvement of peer researchers in interviews and focus groups had an immediacy of real contact with people and first-hand data, with all the obvious opportunities for valued relational experiences in the process.

Arguably, combining a systematic review with a practice survey introduced an element of choice for our co-researchers with regard to which aspects of the project to engage in most thoroughly. The incorporation of a systematic review, usually seen as the desk-based province of professional academics, however, does offer an opportunity for a wider group of service users to become involved in this aspect of the overall knowledge review and provides a basis for involvement in subsequent reviews.

Our experience has highlighted the value of developing partnerships with community organisations to involve service users, who may have little experience or opportunity to become involved in research. The importance of recognising the complexity of identity and the risks in privileging ethnicity, in the context of oppression and racism, provided an important strand of this research and one which the team frequently wrestled with both internally and also in presenting the work externally. These discussions, although at times difficult and personally challenging, strengthened the reflexivity of the research process. The discussions we had as a team thus actively sought to increase our awareness of personal views and standpoints and how these interacted with the views of others and the subject matter of the research. Ultimately, becoming more conscious of such matters can contribute to the validity of the findings. For these discussions to take place there needs to be a foundation of resources and capacity to support genuine collaboration and partnerships and suggestions based on our experience are summarised in Box 7.1.

Further, the use of conceptual mapping provided a method for enabling service users to influence the interpretation and organisation of data. This suggests the need to explore innovative methods to realise the contribution of service user views and experience to knowledge production. This may be of particular value in ensuring the broad diversity of service user views and experience are brought into the research process and contribute to knowledge production.

BOX 7.1 SUGGESTED STEPS TO FACILITATE SERVICE USER INVOLVEMENT IN SYSTEMATIC REVIEWS

1. Involving service users in the commissioning process for research.

2. Ensuring appropriate timescales and resources to support service user involvement in research.

3. Training and information for service users about systematic reviews, why they are done and what they involve.

4. Clarifying skills and development needs of service users and identifying mechanisms to ensure that involvement supports individual ambitions.

5. Formal acknowledgement by academic bodies (such as the Campbell Colloquium) of the added value of service user involvement in systematic reviews.

6. The development of an infrastructure by universities to support service user involvement, including access to university resources, to facilitate service user involvement in systematic reviews.

7. Considering ways in which service users can contribute their experience and knowledge to systematic reviews and the merits of combining a systematic review element with a more practical focus.

8. Dissemination of review findings in highly accessible formats.

Conclusions

This chapter started with a critical review of the challenges in involving ethnically diverse service users in the research process and identified some of the tensions that researchers, academics and service users, face in building genuine participatory approaches. The knowledge review described used a range of methods to maximise service user involvement, including African and Caribbean men, who often have negative experiences of mental health services. Our approach was grounded in previous experiences of participatory approaches and community engagement and crucially relationships with partner organisations that facilitated service user engagement and involvement. This included involvement in a systematic review and led to an exploration of methods and the question of how best to achieve authentic involvement in this field of research activity. This involved both practical steps to facilitate involvement and address barriers through the use of participative methods and conceptual mapping to enable the experiences of African and Caribbean men who use mental health services to shape the interpretation. Reflection on the research process and the socio-political context was identified by the theoretical review as a critical aspect of the process for the research team. The diversity within the research team has led to interesting forms of partnership and alliance, which connect with wider issues in the politics of the service user movement, black communities and voluntary expression, and their voice within mental health services.

Notwithstanding the clear benefits of such alliances, there were also some difficulties in the partnership, connecting with wider histories of oppression and mistrust that we also need to learn from. The validity and quality of the review was enhanced by service user involvement, despite this view clearly not being universally held by the wider research community. This suggests a need for further developments in systematic review methodology to support service user involvement and ensure, as Beresford (2005) proposes, that the mechanisms and experience of involvement supports and indeed enhances a systematic approach to knowledge production.

Strategies to ensure authentic and meaningful service user involvement in the research process have to be informed by an appreciation of some of the complexities of doing research alongside black and minority ethnic participants, which will, it is hoped, avoid some of the practical and conceptual pitfalls associated with overly simplistic analyses of context, methodology and politics. Researchers in this field have both the chance to help shape society and viewpoints, tackle racism, and redress 'the perpetuation of constructions of black identity which maintain the oppressed position of black and other disadvantaged people' (Boushel, 2000, p.85).

Acknowledgements

We are particularly grateful to Evette Hunkins-Hutchinson for the method for facilitating the focus groups and to other members of the Project Team, Dennis Mullings, Anthony Stephens, Keith Holt and Linda Coleman-Hill and also Julie Jaye-Charles and Sheffield African Caribbean Mental Health Association, for their role in the original research and reflections on the process.

References

Alam, M.Y. and Husband, C. (2006) *British-Pakistani Men from Bradford: Linking Narratives to Policy.* York: Joseph Rowntree Foundation.

Alexander, C. (2004) 'Writing Race – Ethnography and the Imagination of the Asian Gang.' In M. Bulmer and J. Solomos (eds) *Researching Race and Racism.* London: Routledge.

Arnstein, S.R. (1969) 'A ladder of citizen participation.' *Journal of the American Institute of Planners* 35, 4, 216–224.

Baistow, K. (1994) 'Liberation of regulation? Some of the paradoxes of empowerment.' *Critical Social Policy 14*, 34–46.

Beresford, P. (2003) *It's Our Lives: A Short Theory of Knowledge, Distance and Experience.* London: Citizen Press in association with Shaping Our Lives.

Beresford, P. (2005) 'Developing the theoretical basis for service user/survivor-led research and equal involvement in research.' *Epidemiologia e Psichiatrica Sociale 14,* 1, 4–8.

Bhui, K., Stansfeld, S., Hull, S., Priebe, S., Mole, F. and Feder, K. (2003) 'Ethnic variations in pathways to and use of specialist mental health services in the UK: systematic review.' *British Journal of Psychiatry 182,* 105–116.

Boushel, M. (2000) 'What kind of people are we? "Race", anti-racism, and social welfare research.' *British Journal of Social Work 30,* 1, 71–89.

Bowes, A.M., Valenti, M., Sim, D. (2002) 'Delivering advocacy services to Glasgow's Black and minority ethnic communities: report to Glasgow City Council and Greater Glasgow Health Board.' University of Stirling, Department of Applied Social Science, Glasgow: Greater Glasgow Health Board.

Bulmer, M. and Solomos, J. (2004) *Researching Race and Racism.* London: Routledge.

Callender, C. (1997) *Education for Empowerment – the Practice and Philosophies of Black Teachers.* London: Trentham.

Care Quality Commission (2010) *Count Me In Census.* London: Care Quality Commission. Available at www.cqc.org.uk/sites/default/files/media/documents/count_me_in_2010_final_tagged. pdf, accessed on 4 April 2012.

Carlen, P., Hicks, J., O'Dwyer, J., Christina, D. and Tchaikovsky, C. (1985) *Criminal Women.* Cambridge: Polity Press.

Carr, S. (2004) *Has Service User Participation made a Difference to Social Care Services?* London: SCIE.

Carr, S. and Coren, E. (2007) *Collection of Examples of Service User and Carer Participation in Systematic Reviews.* London: SCIE.

Coren, E. and Fisher, M. (2006) *The Conduct of Systematic Research Reviews for SCIE Knowledge Reviews.* London: SCIE.

Cowden, S. and Singh, G. (2007) 'The "user": friend, foe of fetish? A critical exploration of user involvement in health and social care.' *Critical Social Policy 27*, 5, 5–21.

Crossley, N. (2006) *Contesting Psychiatry: Social Movements in Mental Health.* London: Routledge.

Downe, S., McKeown, M., Johnson, E., Comensus Community Involvement Team, Comensus Advisory Group, Koloczek, L., Grunwald, A. and Malihi-Shoja, L. (2007) 'The UCLan Community Engagement and Service User Support (Comensus) project: valuing authenticity making space for emergence.' *Health Expectations 10*, 4, 392–406.

Edwards, R. (1993) 'An Education in Interviewing: Placing the Researcher and the Researched.' In C. Renzetti and R. Lee (eds) *Researching Sensitive Topics.* London: Sage.

Fanshawe, S. and Sriskandarajah, D. (2010) '"You can't put me in a box": super-diversity and the end of identity politics in Britain.' London: Institute for Public Policy Research.

Fountain, J., Patel, K. and Buffin, J. (2007) 'Community Engagement: The Centre for Ethnicity and Health Model.' In D. Domenig *et al.* (eds) *Migration, Marginalisation and Access to Health and Social Services.* Amsterdam: Foundation Regenboog AMOC.

Frankham, J. (2009) 'Partnership research: a review of approaches and challenges in conducting research in partnership with service users.' ESRC National Centre for Research Methods Review Paper. NCRM/013. London: ESRC.

Hammersley, M. (1995) *The Politics of Social Research.* London: Sage.

Hanley, B. (2005) *User Involvement in Research: Building on Experience and Developing Standards.* Joseph Rowntree Foundation Findings (Ref 0175). Available at www.jrf.org.uk/publications/user-involvement-research-building-experience-and-developing-standards, accessed 4 April 2012.

Healthcare Commission, Mental Health Act Commission, and National Institute for Mental Health England (2008) *Count Me In 2008: Results of the 2008 National Census of Inpatients in Mental Health and Learning Disability Services in England and Wales.* London: Commission for Healthcare Audit and Inspection.

Keating, F. (2007) *African and Caribbean Men and Mental Health.* Race Equality Foundation Briefing Paper 5. Available at www.nmhdu.org.uk/silo/files/african-and-caribbean-men-mental-health.pdf, accessed on 21 June 2012.

Keating, F., Robertson, D., McCulloch, A. and Francis, E. (2002) *Breaking the Circles of Fear: A Review of the Relationship Between Mental Health Services and African and Caribbean Communities.* London: Sainsbury Centre for Mental Health.

Lewis, G. (2000) *'Race', Gender, and Social Welfare: Encounters in a Postcolonial Society.* Cambridge: Polity Press.

Mclean, C., Campbell, C. and Cornish, F. (2003) 'African-Caribbean interactions with mental health services in the UK: experiences and expectations of exclusion as (re)productive of health inequalities.' *Social Science and Medicine 56*, 3, 657–669.

McGlauglin, H. (2010) 'Keeping service user involvement in research honest.' *British Journal of Social Work 40*, 5, 1591–1608.

McKeown, M., Downe, S., Malihi-Shoja, L., supporting The Comensus Writing Collective (2010) *Service Users and Carer Involvement in Education for Health and Social Care.* Oxford: Wiley-Blackwell.

Newbigging, K. (2007) 'Involving diverse service users in knowledge reviews.' Presentation to the Campbell Colloquium: Quality, Utility and Credibility: The Relevance of Systematic Reviews.

Newbigging, K., McKeown, M., Hunkins-Hutchinson, E. and French, B. (2007) *Mtetezi: Mental Health Advocacy with African and Caribbean Men.* London: Social Care Institute for Excellence (SCIE). Available at www.scie.org.uk/publications/knowledgereviews/kr15.pdf, accessed 4 April 2012. DOI:10.177/0261018312439362.

Newbigging, K., McKeown, M., Habte-Mariam, Z., Mullings, D., Jaye-Charles, J. Holt, K. (2008) *Commissioning and Providing Mental Health Advocacy for African and Caribbean Men: A Resource Guide.* London: Social Care Institute for Excellence. (Web-based resource.) Available at www. scie.org.uk/publications/guides/guide21/index.asp, accessed 4 April 2012.

Okereke, E., Archibong, U., Chiemeka, M., Baxter, C.E. and Davis, S. (2007) 'Participatory approaches to assessing the health needs of African and African-Caribbean communities.' *Diversity in Health and Social Care 4,* 4, 287–301.

Roy, A. (2011) 'Thinking and doing: "race" and ethnicity in drug research and policy development in England.' *Critical Policy Studies 5,* 1, 17–31.

Roy, A. (2012) 'Avoiding the involvement overdose? Drugs, race, ethnicity and participatory research practice.' *Critical Social Policy.*

Stowell-Smith, M. and McKeown, M. (2001) 'Race, Stigma and Stereotyping: The Construction of Difference in Forensic Care.' In C. Carlisle, M. Mason and C. Watkins (eds) *Stigma and Social Exclusion in Health.* London: Routledge.

Thornicroft, G. and Tansella, M. (2005) 'Growing recognition of the importance of service user involvement in mental health service planning and evaluation.' *Epidemiologia e Psichiatria Sociale 14,* 1, 1–3.

Wilkinson, S. and Kitzinger, C. (1996) 'Theorizing Representing the Other.' In S. Wilkinson and C. Kitzinger (eds) *Representing the Other – A Feminism and Psychology Reader.* London: Sage.

CHAPTER 8

Researching Continuity of Care in Mental Health

What Difference Does Holding a Survivor Researcher Identity Make?

Angela Sweeney

Introduction

This chapter is based on my experiences of conducting PhD research as a mental health survivor. This means that I have a 'double identity', that of survivor and researcher (Rose, 2003). A simple definition of a survivor researcher is someone with personal experience of mental distress or service use who also researches mental distress and psychiatric services and treatments. However, this definition means more than the sum of its parts; many researchers have experienced mental distress and psychiatric services without being survivor researchers. Instead, a survivor researcher explicitly draws on her or his personal experiences to inform their understanding. Moreover, being a survivor researcher affects the decisions that are made and the actions that are taken throughout the research, both knowingly and unknowingly. This is because all researchers have something called a research identity. Ponterotto and Grieger (1999) defined a research identity as being how one perceives oneself as a researcher. They argue that this will then have strong implications for the researcher's choice of topics and methods.

This means that being a survivor researcher affects the topics you choose to study. It affects the processes, or how you conduct the research. And it also affects the outcomes, or the results of the research. In this chapter I am going to describe how my research identity of survivor researcher affected the topics I chose to study, the process I used and the results that I found for my doctoral research. I will also consider the factors that make survivor research successful, and will conclude by considering some of the implications of this research.

The background
Conducting a PhD as a survivor researcher

The PhD described in this chapter was conducted part time at the Service User Research Enterprise, Institute of Psychiatry, King's College London whilst I was also employed as a researcher in the department. It was supervised by a survivor researcher, Diana Rose, and a clinical academic, Til Wykes. The research was part of a larger programme of research exploring 'Experiences of Continuity of Care and Health and Social Outcomes' (ECHO) (Burns et al., 2007). The ECHO research programme was comprised of a number of strands: a developmental phase which generated a user- and a carer-defined measure of continuity; a main strand which explored users' and carers' continuity experiences and the links with health and social outcomes; an organisational strand which investigated the staff and services within two NHS trusts; and a qualitative strand which interviewed a sub-sample of main phase participants to explore users' and carers' experiences in more depth. My thesis was based on the developmental phase research with service users.

The Service User Research Enterprise is a unique academic unit, almost exclusively employing people who have experienced significant mental distress or have used mental health services. Researchers in the unit draw on these experiences to inform the research they conduct, much as clinical academics draw on their experiences of clinical practice to inform their research.

The ethical framework of survivor research

One of the factors that distinguishes survivor research from clinical academic research is that survivor researchers subscribe to a unique and shared set of ethical principles. These principles have been described by Faulkner (2004) as:

- *Clarity and transparency:* being clear and open with all involved.

- *Empowerment:* challenging stigma and ensuring participants' voices are heard.

- *Identity:* disclosing a shared identity with participants during the research.

- *Commitment to change:* conducting research that in some way contributes to change.

- *Respect:* respecting and listening to participants' views.

- *Equal opportunities:* ensuring people from diverse or marginal communities are heard.

- *Theoretical approach:* being open about the theoretical underpinnings of the research.

- *Accountability:* clarifying the relationship between the research and wider society, and taking a sophisticated approach to accountability to other users.

A number of these principles are fundamental to all good research (though this doesn't mean that they routinely occur in mainstream research). Examples include being clear and transparent, respecting participants and ensuring equality of opportunity. Similarly, all researchers – survivors and clinical academics alike – share a commitment to conducting high quality, rigorous research. However, three of the ethical principles described by Faulkner are particularly relevant when considering how survivor research differs from mainstream research: these are identity, empowerment and commitment to change. The role of these ethical principles in this research will be considered later in the chapter.

The topic
Why study continuity of care as a survivor researcher?

My doctoral research focused on mental health service users' perspectives on and experiences of continuity of care. Continuity is widely considered a central goal of mental health services (Crawford *et al.*, 2004; Farrell, Koch and Blank, 1996; Greenberg and Rosenheck, 2003; Percudani *et al.*, 2002). This is largely because of the closure of the old asylums and their replacement with care in the community – known as deinstitutionalisation. In the old asylums, psychiatric treatments were delivered under one roof. Patients were provided with food, shelter and psychiatric treatment. In the community, mental health services are delivered in many different locations, often leading to a lack of joined-up services. There have also been concerns that people can 'fall through the gap' of care when they leave psychiatric wards. Consequently, ensuring that people receive continuity of care has become a central challenge of contemporary service provision (Tessler and Mason, 1979). In addition to this, a number of official inquiries have (rightly or wrongly) implicated poor continuity of care in suicides and homicides by people who use psychiatric services (see Crawford *et al.*, 2004). This has led to a focus on the dangers of *dis*continuity of care.

Although continuity and discontinuity of care have had a major impact on policy and research, there is no agreed definition: 'Policy reports and charters worldwide urge a concerted effort to enhance continuity, but efforts to describe the problem or formulate solutions are complicated by the lack of consensus on the definition' (Haggerty *et al.*, 2003, p.1219).

Furthermore, most definitions of continuity come firmly from clinical academic perspectives. Little is known about how service users understand continuity, and how this might differ from academic definitions. This has made it impossible to understand or assess continuity from service users' perspectives.

To me, researching continuity as a survivor researcher meant exploring how service users define and prioritise continuity. Without this understanding, we cannot know when service users want continuity of care, when we want discontinuity, how we believe continuity should be shaped, and whether we are receiving the continuity we need. Having this knowledge supplements – and at times challenges – what is already known from clinical academic perspectives. This helps researchers to access a fuller picture about continuity of care. Thus, my doctoral research aimed to be the missing piece of the jigsaw in our understanding of continuity of care by exploring the concept through survivor research.

Why develop a service user-defined measure of continuity of care?

As part of this research, I generated a service user-defined measure of continuity of care, called CONTINU-UM (CONTINUity of care – Users' Measure).

Historically, most attempts to measure continuity of care in mental health research have been limited. Few studies define what they mean by continuity of care: for example, Freeman and colleagues found that only five of 28 studies exploring continuity offered a clear definition (2000). The majority of studies look at a single aspect of continuity of care (such as discharge from hospital to the community) rather than exploring a coherent model of continuity that reflects all that continuity of care can entail (examples of this include Berghofer *et al.*, 2002 and Warner *et al.*, 2000). Although most researchers now agree that service users' experiences should lie at the heart of continuity of care research, this rarely occurs in practice. This means that continuity is usually measured from service provider and academic perspectives, with service users' views rarely considered (for examples see Farrell *et al.*, 1996; Fu Chien *et al.*, 2000; Kopelowicz, Wallace and Zarate, 1998; Saarento *et al.*, 1998; Sytema, Micciolo and Tansella, 1997). Indeed, where research has explored service users' views of continuity, results have been merged with provider perspectives, making it impossible to know whether definitions and experiences do indeed differ. However, there is a small grey literature exploring users' experiences of services or community living, often authored by or with service users. Whilst continuity is not explored specifically, the findings often reveal that aspects of continuity are highly important to service users. Common themes include:

- gaps in care, particularly the need for someone to talk to (Faulkner and Layzell, 2000; Rogers, Pilgrim and Lacey, 1993)

- poor crisis support, particularly difficulty accessing services swiftly (e.g. Care Quality Commission, 2009; Davies *et al.*, 2009) and the lack of someone to talk to in a crisis (Faulkner and Layzell, 2000; Rogers *et al.*, 1993)

- the need for information to navigate complex care systems (Rose, 2001)

- the importance of ongoing, supportive relationships with peers and staff (Kai and Crossland, 2001; Noble and Douglas, 2004)

- inadequate hospital discharge (e.g. Beeforth, Conlan and Graley, 1994; Noble and Douglas, 2004)

- lack of knowledge of and involvement in Care programme Approach (CPA) planning (Rose, 2001; Phillips, 1998; Webb *et al.*, 2000).

Since the late 1990s, three research teams have developed continuity measures that attempt to address the limitations of previous continuity of care research. These are the Maudsley team in the UK (Bindman *et al.*, 1997, 2000; Johnson *et al.*, 1997); Ware and colleagues in the United States who generated CONNECT (1999, 2003); and the Canadian Alberta team who generated the ACSS-MH (Adair *et al.*, 2005; Durbin *et al.*, 2004; Joyce *et al.*, 2004). All three teams produced measures that assess a complex definition of continuity of care, although each assesses continuity in a different way:

- The Maudsley team assess continuity through the way that the mental health system works.

- CONNECT assesses continuity through the relationships between service users and providers.

- The ACSS-MH assesses a definition of continuity that is shared by service users and providers.

Each measure has strengths and limitations. Whilst the Maudsley measure is a useful way of understanding and assessing how systems are functioning, it has no published psychometric properties and therefore its reliability and validity is unknown. Furthermore, it does not claim to include service users' perspectives. Conversely, CONNECT does claim to represent service users' perspectives but this does not withstand scrutiny. This is because the team focused almost exclusively on the mechanisms that staff were seen to employ to increase continuity (such as 'pinch hitting', defined as staff stepping outside a prescribed role to perform someone else's tasks and so close a gap in care). Therefore, it is best seen as a measure of how providers attempt to construct continuity of care for service users. Similarly, the ACSS-MH claims to measure continuity from a service user perspective. Whilst service users and families were included in some stages of the development of the ACSS-MH (as were clinicians), mainstream researchers took the decisions relating to the content of the measure, relying heavily on mainstream literature to do so.

Therefore, whilst researchers can employ a measure that has the best fit with the goals of their research – whether that be understanding continuity through systems, relationships or shared definitions – they cannot measure continuity as it is uniquely understood by service users. Yet because service users' perspectives are – to a degree – included in two of the measures, there is a danger that researchers can claim that they are assessing continuity from service users' perspectives. This means that researchers can appear to be researching continuity as it is understood by service users, whilst excluding service users' unique definitions. This perpetuates clinical academic dominated understandings of mental health services, whilst appearing to do the opposite.

Service user-defined outcome measures are an important way of redressing the imbalance between survivor and service provider knowledge. Having a service user-defined outcome measure of continuity of care based on service users' own definitions and priorities should help to place service users' perspectives at the heart of mental health services evaluation.

The process
What did I do? The research methods
The research was conducted in a number of phases, using both qualitative and quantitative methods. In the first phase, focus groups were used to explore service users' perspectives on and experiences of continuity. Four focus groups were held with service users from South London. Groups began with participants telling their stories of their first crises and contacts with mental health services. Exploring 'personal narratives' in this way is a common way of understanding survivors' individual and collective experiences. Kalathil (2007), a survivor researcher, has defined a personal narrative as:

> our story as told by us. Traditionally our stories have been told by other people – psychiatrists, researchers who do not understand or share our lived experiences, professionals who write up our case files, anthropologists who define our races and attribute characteristics to us. A personal narrative attempts to counter these various representations. It offers a different point of view – our point of view – about our life.

Kalathil believes that, used in the right way, personal narratives have the power to change mental health service provision for black women. In this research, telling one's own story at the beginning of the first group was seen as vital. This is because it helped participants ease into the setting, share their experiences on their own terms and coalesce as a group by building connections with one another through shared experiences. Most crucially of all, having the space to tell your story in your own words helped participants feel a sense of ownership over the research.

Data were analysed thematically (Braun and Clarke, 2006) and the results presented at a repeat group held one or two weeks later. During this repeat group, participants also discussed and ranked elements of continuity. Therefore, over the course of the focus groups, participants were supported to move from storytelling to defining a complex model of continuity to ranking individual elements by their importance.

In the second phase, two waves of expert panels were held to examine the definition of continuity generated by the focus groups.

In Phase 3, a consultation exercise was held with three continuity experts in order to establish whether any important elements had been overlooked (face and content validity). This led to a final draft of a service-user defined outcome measure, CONTINU-UM.

In Phase 4, CONTINU-UM was used as part of the main phase of the ECHO research programme. The data this generated were analysed in two ways. Firstly, the psychometric proprerties of CONTINU-UM were assessed using both qualitative and quantitative methods. This meant exploring whether CONTINU-UM was reliable, valid, feasible, interpretable, appropriate and so on. Secondly, service users' priorities for, experiences of and satisfaction with continuity of care were assessed.

Finally, the focus group data were subject to an in-depth analysis. This generated a model of the role of fear in the lives of mental health service users.

For a discussion of this method of generating service user-defined outcome measures see Rose *et al.* (2011).

How did this differ from mainstream research?
A survivor-led research process

In the opening background section I described eight fundamental principles of survivor research as clarity and transparency; empowerment; identity; commitment to change; respect; equal opportunities; theoretical approach; and accountability. A consideration of identity and empowerment can help demonstrate how survivor research differs from mainstream research. Commitment to change will be considered in the section on success.

IDENTITY

In the introduction, I explained that survivor researchers have a double identity, that of survivor and researcher (Rose, 2003). Whilst this is rewarding, it also brings challenges. For example, although the focus group facilitators (myself and Diana Rose) disclosed our survivor status, one participant felt that his views of services would shock us. This seemed to suggest that the survivor aspect of our identities was not always recognised. Thus, service users participating in research sometimes see survivor researchers as professionals, with all the power of a traditional researcher. Likewise, mainstream researchers often see the survivor before the researcher, dismissing research expertise. Encouraging each group to recognise both identities can be a significant challenge.

EMPOWERMENT

Many researchers now recognise that there is a significant power imbalance between researchers and participants. This can mean that participants feel disempowered by their involvement in research. Because of this, research models have been developed that attempt to dissolve these differences. A clear example is participatory research, where participants and researchers act together as 'co-researchers' throughout the process (see, for example, Minkler and Wallerstein, 2003).

The issue of power within survivor research can be open to misinterpretation. The most obvious example of this is where it is believed that disclosing your identity as a survivor to participants means that power differences have been addressed. This is because the 'double identity challenge' (described above) means that participants often see the researcher before the survivor. Thus, survivor researchers can retain all the power of a traditional researcher. Consequently, like all researchers, survivor researchers must carefully consider and address issues of power throughout the research, making deliberate and concerted efforts to address imbalances.

Because of this, I was constantly mindful of the need to transfer power to participants throughout the research. This did not mean that all power was handed to participants; Baker and Hinton have cautioned that this can mean relinquishing responsibility, and is not necessarily empowering for participants (1999). Instead, adopting the framework of the ethics of survivor research meant that participants were viewed as active partners in a process of mutual discovery. This meant creating a safe, open and understanding space facilitated by peers in which to discuss shared experiences. Having the groups facilitated by survivor researchers meant that the research could gain expertise and cohesion whilst centralising the perspectives of participants.

The results

What did I find? Select research results

CONTINU-UM contains a service user-defined model of continuity of care. It consists of 16 separate elements of continuity (see Table 8.1 for an overview and description of the elements). Many of these elements are found in service provider-led definitions of continuity. For example, all three measures described above (the Maudsley measure, CONNECT and the ACCS-MH) include questions that relate in some way to some of CONTINU-UM's elements. However, in CONTINU-UM, the elements have been described from the perspective of using services, rather than providing services. This means that the elements are sometimes understood differently.

The clearest example of this is information. Service providers and clinical academics tend to define continuity of information as staff sharing information between themselves about service users. However, in the focus groups the idea that information is shared between staff was not always welcomed. This was because some people felt that personal information ought to be confidential. Instead, what focus group participants prioritised was being able to access information from staff. Participants wanted information on issues such as health and social services, self-help groups, medication and its side-effects, diagnosis (although this was debated), the content of care plans, what to do in a crisis, and what to expect in the future. Participants believed that staff should provide information that is clear, relevant, appropriate and accessible. Having the right information at the right time often gave participants more choice over the services they received, which made people feel more empowered. However, very few participants were provided with or signposted to information by staff. Instead, participants proactively sought information from self-help groups, national charities and, most commonly, other users.

TABLE 8.1 OVERVIEW AND DESCRIPTION OF THE ELEMENTS
OF USER-DEFINED CONTINUITY OF CARE

Elements of user-defined continuity of care	Description
Access	Getting the services you feel you need at the time that you need them
Range	Getting the whole range of services you feel would help you, regardless of whether anyone else agrees or those services are available
Waiting	How long you have to wait to receive the services you need
Out-of-hours support	Getting support from services outside of normal office hours (such as evenings and weekends)
Hospital discharge	Receiving the support you need when you come out of psychiatric hospitals
Staff changes	Seeing the same member of staff every visit
Information	Getting the information that you want or need from staff
Flexibility	If you change or your mental health changes, what you get from services changes as well
Individual progress	Having services that help you to progress, rather than keeping you where you are
Day centres	Having the option to go to a day centre that would help you, if you wanted to
Care plans	Having a care plan, which is a written agreement between yourself and staff/services about what is going to happen in your care
Crisis	Having an agreement about what will happen if you go into crisis, and being happy with this
Staff communication	Having the staff involved in your care tell each other what is happening
Peer support	Having support from other people who have experienced mental distress
Life histories	Not repeating your life history to members of staff that you are seeing for the first time
Avoiding services	Being able to choose when you see staff, including not having contact if you do not want to

Participants also identified three elements of continuity that are not found anywhere else in the literature. These elements are day centres, peer support and avoiding services. Experiences and views of day centres were mixed. To some people, they were an important source of social contact and support, particularly for people who often felt lonely. However, many people felt that day centres should help people to re-enter their communities, thereby reducing social exclusion.

Similarly, peer support was extremely important to the majority of participants. It was important because other service users have very similar experiences, and the empathy and understanding this brings can be invaluable. However, a small number of participants felt that their peers sometimes made them feel more distressed or 'brought them down'.

The final element of continuity that is unique to service users is avoiding mainstream services. When service users avoid services (for example, missing appointments or stopping treatment) it is often seen as a sign that their mental health is deteriorating (e.g. Killaspy *et al.*, 2000). There are also concerns that avoiding services could lead to adverse events (e.g. Crawford *et al.*, 2004; Durbin *et al.*, 2004). Whilst a small number of participants shared these views, being able to avoid services was also valued by some people. This was often where people had been forced to receive treatments or services that they did not want in the past, and were afraid that this would happen again in the future. Because of this, avoiding services is an important aspect of user-defined continuity.

What difference did having a survivor researcher identity make?

As described above, service user-defined continuity contains elements that have not previously been identified (day centres, peer support and avoiding services). It is possible that these elements were identified because service users' perspectives and experiences were explored through survivor research. Clearly, the values and histories of survivor researchers have an impact on the way that data is interpreted: 'Interpretation is at the heart of all research practices. That we drive research projects with our values, histories and interests is central to this' (Koch and Harrington, 1998, p.82).

Beresford believes that sharing experiences (of mental distress and/ or service use) with participants leads to more accurate and reliable interpretations of the data (2003). This means that it can be argued that having the research identity of survivor researcher led to trustworthy and credible interpretations of participants' perspectives on continuity. However, this does not mean that survivor researchers are complacent. Instead, reflexivity is an important way of understanding the relationship between personal values, the data and their interpretation (e.g. Malterud, 2001; Merrick, 1999). This occurs through critical and honest reflection on one's beliefs and biases and their impact on the research. Throughout data collection, analysis and interpretation, reflexivity was aided by memo writing (personal reflection) and supervision (formal reflection).

As a survivor researcher, I came to the topic with few identifiable preconceptions about what continuity of care should mean. Indeed, I was deeply sceptical about the importance of continuity, and would have preferred to have researched alternatives to the psychiatric system. Despite this scepticism, through listening to people's stories I came to see that continuity of care is deeply valued by service users, and is consequently a vital topic for study by survivor researchers.

There were also examples of my prior beliefs being challenged. For example, before coming to this research I had believed that once in the mental health system, service users were typically trapped there, through, for example, labelling and compulsion. Whilst this view was expressed by a minority of participants, the overwhelming concern was in fact how to access services. This was a surprise to me, and led me to re-evaluate my views.

Inevitably, the values and histories that researchers bring to research are not fixed, but are shaped by the process of data collection and analysis itself. By conducting this research, my understanding of what it means to be both a service user and a survivor researcher has developed and grown. This in turn will affect the way that I understand data in the future, which will in its turn affect my research identity. Thus, the relationship between research identities and data interpretation is a fluid and dynamic one.

The success?

How can the success of any survivor research be judged? Returning to Faulkner's principles of survivor research, two of the defining criteria must be empowerment and commitment to change. This means that we try to conduct research that in some way has a positive impact on the lives of service users and survivors, and that tries to make a difference.

EMPOWERMENT

During this research, expert panels had the task of generating the final draft of CONTINU-UM. One of these panels was made up of people who had also taken part in the focus groups. At the end of the panel, these participants said that they felt pride in and ownership of CONTINU-UM. These participants had gone on a journey from telling their stories, to generating a complex model of continuity of care, to identifying the most important elements for an outcome measure, to commenting on the first draft of that measure. The sense of pride and ownership suggested that the efforts to transfer power to participants, and so enable people to create an outcome measure from their perspective, had been – at least to a degree – a success.

After the research, participants were encouraged to get involved in further research activity and training. As a result of this, four participants went on to conduct their own research on a self-identified topic with support from researchers at the Service User Research Enterprise (see Rose et al., 2010). Of course, not everyone wanted to get more involved in research. Indeed, one woman wanted to move on with her life and leave everything connected with mental health behind her. Yet for some people, taking part in this research opened the door to research involvement much more broadly.

COMMITMENT TO CHANGE

As well as having a positive impact on participants' lives, survivor research aims to effect change more broadly. In this research, this meant generating knowledge from a service user/survivor perspective, increasing understanding of service users' experiences and creating a service user-defined outcome measure. It is hoped that this will redress the imbalance between knowledge about continuity of care generated from clinical academic perspectives, and knowledge and measurement from service user perspectives.

However, there is no guarantee that service user-defined outcome measures like CONTINU-UM will be used. Translating research findings into practical change is perhaps one of the most difficult aspects of any research. This difficulty is amplified when research is conducted from a survivor perspective. This is because, as Beresford has argued, mainstream research prioritises neutrality, objectivity and distance, and typically sees the knowledge that is generated from an explicitly survivor perspective as subjective and partial (Beresford, 2003). Thus, it is easy for mainstream researchers and service providers to dismiss uncomfortable – or indeed any – survivor research findings as biased.

Furthermore, Perkins has argued that there are numerous stakeholders in mental health, each holding different perspectives (2001). Perkins agrees that service user-defined outcome measures are an important way of placing service users' views at the centre of mental health services evaluation. However, she goes on to argue that service users have little power within the mental health system and this powerlessness must be challenged for service user-defined measures to make any difference.

Conclusion

Defining continuity of care from a service user perspective has created a new understanding of how continuity is prioritised and experienced by service users. It has also generated a new understanding of how mental health services can encourage continuity on terms that service users find acceptable and helpful. It is notable that service user-defined continuity of care places service users at the heart of mental health services. It centres on service users having the information needed to make choices, having access to services, being involved in care planning, determining what crisis support is needed, having support to move forward with our lives, and even being able to avoid services. Thus, rather than passively receiving care, service user-defined continuity is about *active* engagement with services.

Over the past 15 years, survivor researchers have consistently identified the importance of peer support to service users (e.g. Beeforth and Wood, 2001; Faulkner and Layzell, 2000; Rose, 2001). This research has added to this body of evidence. Despite this, mental health services consistently underestimate the value of peer support. This is evidenced by the fact that survivor researchers and allies have called for services to facilitate peer support for many years, to little effect. There is also little recognition amongst service providers that service users can help people leaving psychiatric hospital to make the transition to the community (Rogers *et al.*, 1993). Some participants recommended that services formally encourage peer support, by providing meeting spaces, for example, or training service users to support others on hospital discharge. Whilst we are now seeing the advent of peer support workers (e.g. Woodhouse and Vincent, 2006), the idea has still not been widely adopted in the mainstream.

This underscores the fact that the knowledge generated by service users often challenges mainstream understanding. Yet where such differences occur, service users' views are often disregarded. Pilgrim and Rogers (1999) have outlined four main ways in which service users' voices are silenced in mainstream research:

1. Users' views are disregarded where they do not coincide with professionals' views.

2. Users are seen as consistently irrational and therefore unable to give valid views.

3. Professionals assume that users and relatives share opinions, and where they conflict, users' views are ignored.

4. Users' views are reframed to coincide with professionals' views.

Thus, where the knowledge generated by survivor research and by mainstream research contradicts one another, user-generated knowledge is marginalised and dismissed. As described above, this can make it difficult for service user research to affect change. Service users must challenge this silencing through the user movement, and through political and rights-based arguments. But we can also challenge this exclusion by demonstrating the success of survivor research. The research I have described demonstrates that mental health service users and survivors can generate both our own knowledge, and our own outcome measures. This is based entirely on expertise by experience.

This research was part of the wider mental health user movement. This movement is a broad church that houses a wide variety of perspectives (e.g. Rogers and Pilgrim, 1991; Sweeney, 2009; Wallcraft, Read and Sweeney, 2003). Yet it is characterised by the persistent struggle to be recognised as having a legitimate voice, and to have that voice heard. There is a strong relationship between the user movement and survivor research (Sweeney, 2009), with both underpinned by values of empowerment, emancipation, participation, equality and anti-discrimination (Turner and Beresford, 2005). Members of the user movement pioneered survivor research through their frustration at the failures of mainstream research to represent them. Survivor research is an important means of hearing users' collective voices and creating a body of knowledge from a service user/survivor standpoint. This doctoral research was a deliberate and conscious part of this project.

References

Adair, C., McDougall, G., Mitton, C., Joyce, A., Wild, C., Gordon, A., Costigan, N., Kowalsky, L., Pasmeny, G. and Beckie, A. (2005) 'Continuity of care and health outcomes among persons with severe mental illness.' *Psychiatric Services 56*, 9, 1061–1069.

Baker, R. and Hinton, R. (1999) 'Do Focus Groups Facilitate Meaningful Participation in Social Research?' In R. Barbour and J. Kitzinger (eds) *Developing Focus Group Research: Politics, Theory and Practice.* London: Sage.

Beeforth, M., Conlan, E. and Graley, R. (1994) *Have We Got Views For You: User Evaluation of Case Management.* London: Sainsbury Centre for Mental Health.

Beeforth, M. and Wood, H. (2001) 'Needs from a User Perspective.' In G. Thornicroft (ed.) *Measuring Mental Health Needs.* London: Gaskell, Royal College of Psychiatrists (Second Edition).

Beresford, P. (2003) *It's Our Lives: A Short Theory of Knowledge, Distance and Experience.* London: OSP for Citizens Press in Association with Shaping Our Lives.

Berghofer, G., Schmidl, F., Rudas, S., Steiner, E. and Schmitz, M. (2002) 'Predictors of treatment discontinuity in outpatient mental health care.' *Social Psychiatry and Psychiatric Epidemiology 37*, 6, 276–282.

Bindman, J., Johnson, S., Szmukler, G., Wright, S., Kuipers, E., Thornicroft, G., Bebbington, P. and Leese, M. (2000) 'Continuity of care and clinical outcome: a prospective cohort study.' *Social Psychiatry and Psychiatric Epidemiology 35*, 6, 242–247.

Bindman, J., Johnson, S., Wright, S., Szmukler, G., Bebbington, P., Kuipers, E. and Thornicroft, G. (1997) 'Integration between primary and secondary services in the care of the severely mentally ill: patients' and general practitioners' views.' *British Journal of Psychiatry 171*, 169–174.

Braun, V. and Clarke, V. (2006) 'Using thematic analysis in psychology.' *Qualitative Research in Psychology 3*, 2, 77–101.

Burns, T., Catty, J., Clement, S., Harvey, K., Rees Jones, I., McLaren, S., Rose, D., White, S. and Wykes, T. (2007) *Experiences of Continuity of Care and Health and Social Outcomes: The ECHO Study.* London: National Coordinating Centre for Service Delivery and Organisation.

Care Quality Commission (2009) *The 2008 Survey of Community Mental Health Services.* London: Care Quality Commission.

Crawford, M., de Jonge, E., Freeman, G. and Weaver, T. (2004) 'Providing continuity of care for people with severe mental illness.' *Social Psychiatry and Psychiatric Epidemiology 39*, 4, 265–272.

Davies, R., Shocolinsky-Dwyer, R., Mowat, J., Evans, J., Heslop, P., Onyett, S. and Soteriou, T. (2009) *Effective Involvement in Mental Health Services: The Role of Assertive Outreach and the Voluntary Sector.* Bristol: Mind.

Durbin, J., Goering, P., Streiner, D. and Pink, G. (2004) 'Continuity of care: validation of a new self-report measure for individuals using mental health services.' *Journal of Behavioral Health Services and Research 31*, 3, 279–296.

Farrell, S., Koch, J. and Blank, M. (1996) 'Rural and urban differences in continuity of care after state hospital discharge.' *Psychiatric Services 47*, 7, 652–654.

Faulkner, A. (2004) *The Ethics of Survivor Research: Guidelines for the Ethical Conduct of Research Carried Out by Mental Health Service Users and Survivors.* Bristol: Policy Press on behalf of the Joseph Rowntree Foundation.

Faulkner, A. and Layzell, S. (2000) *Strategies for Living: A Report of User-Led Research into People's Strategies for Living with Mental Distress.* London: Mental Health Foundation.

Freeman, G., Shepperd, S., Robinson, I., Ehrich, K., Richards, S. and Pitman, P. (2000) *Continuity of Care: Report of a Scoping Exercise for the SDO Programme of NHS R&D.* London: National Coordinating Centre for Service Delivery and Organisation.

Fu Chien, C., Steinwachs, D., Lehman, A., Fahey, M. and Skinner, E. (2000) 'Provider continuity and outcomes of care for persons with schizophrenia.' *Mental Health Services Research 2*, 4, 201–211.

Greenberg, G. and Rosenheck, R. (2003) 'Managerial and environmental factors in the continuity of mental health care across institutions.' *Psychiatric Services 54*, 4, 529–534.

Haggerty, J., Reid, R., Freeman, G., Starfield, B., Adair, C. and McKendry, R. (2003) 'Continuity of care: a multidisciplinary review.' *British Medical Journal 327*, 1219–1221.

Johnson, S., Prosser, D., Bindman, J. and Szmukler, G. (1997) 'Continuity of care for the severely mentally ill: concepts and measures.' *Social Psychiatry and Psychiatric Epidemiology 32*, 3, 137–142.

Joyce, A., Wild, C., Adair, C., McDougall, G., Gordon, A., Costigan, N., Beckie, A., Kowalsky, L., Pasmeny, G. and Barnes, F. (2004) 'Continuity of care in mental health services: toward clarifying the construct.' *Canadian Journal of Psychiatry 49*, 8, 539–549.

Kai, J. and Crossland, A. (2001) 'Perspectives of people with enduring mental ill health from a community-based qualitative study.' *British Journal of General Practice 51*, 470, 730–737.

Kalathil, J. (2007) *Let's Tell Our Stories: Looking for Black Women's Personal Narratives.* Available at www.survivor-research.com/index.php/publications/4-lets-tell-our-stories-looking-for-black-womens-personal-narratives, accessed 4 April 2012.

Killaspy, H., Banerjee, S., King, M. and Lloyd, M. (2000) 'Prospective controlled study of psychiatric out-patient non-attendance: characteristics and outcome.' *British Journal of Psychiatry 176*, 160–165.

Koch, T. and Harrington, A. (1998) 'Reconceptualizing Rigour: the case for reflexivity.' *Journal of Advanced Nursing 28*, 4, 882–890.

Kopelowicz, A., Wallace, C. and Zarate, R. (1998) 'Teaching psychiatric inpatients to re-enter the community: a brief method of improving the continuity of care.' *Psychiatric Services 49*, 10, 1313–1316.

Malterud, K. (2001) 'Qualitative research: standards, challenges, and guidelines.' *The Lancet 358*, 483–488.

Merrick, E. (1999) 'An Exploration of Quality in Qualitative Research: Are "Reliability" and "Validity" Relevant?' In M. Kopala and L. Suzuki (eds) *Using Qualitative Methods in Psychology.* Thousand Oaks, CA, London and New Delhi: Sage.

Minkler, M. and Wallerstein, N. (2003) *Community-Based Participatory Research for Health.* San Fransisco: Jossey-Bass.

Noble, L. and Douglas, C. (2004) 'What users and relatives want from mental health services.' *Current Opinion in Psychiatry 17*, 289–296.

Percudani, M., Belloni, G., Contini, A. and Barbui, C. (2002) 'Monitoring community psychiatric services in Italy: differences between patients who leave care and those who stay in treatment.' *British Journal of Psychiatry 180*, 3, 254–259.

Perkins, R. (2001) 'What constitutes success? The relative priority of service users' and clinicians' views of mental health services.' *British Journal of Psychiatry 179*, 9–10.

Phillips, P. (1998) 'The Care Programme Approach: the views and experiences of service users.' *Mental Health Care 1*, 5, 165–168.

Pilgrim, D. and Rogers, A. (1999) *A Sociology of Mental Health and Illness.* Buckingham and Philadelphia: Open University Press (Second edition).

Ponterotto, J. and Grieger, I. (1999) 'Merging Qualitative and Quantitative Perspectives in a Research Identity.' In M. Kopala and L. Suzuki (eds) *Using Qualitative Methods in Psychology.* Thousand Oaks, CA, London and New Delhi: Sage.

Rogers, A. and Pilgrim, D. (1991) '"Pulling down churches": accounting for the British mental health users' movement.' *Sociology of Health and Illness 13*, 2, 129–148.

Rogers, A., Pilgrim, D. and Lacey, R. (1993) *Experiencing Psychiatry: Users' Views of Services.* Basingstoke: Macmillan and MIND.

Rose, D. (2001) *Users' Voices: The Perspectives of Mental Health Service Users on Community and Hospital Care.* London: Sainsbury Centre for Mental Health.

Rose, D. (2003) 'Having a diagnosis is a qualification for the job.' *British Medical Journal 326*, 1331.

Rose, D., Fleischmann, P. and Schofield, P. (2010) 'Perceptions of user involvement: a user-led study.' *International Journal of Social Psychiatry 56*, 4, 389–401.

Rose, D., Evans, J., Sweeney, A., Wykes, T. (2011) 'A model for developing outcome measures from the perspectives of mental health service users.' *International Review of Psychiatry 23*, 1, 41–6.

Saarento, O., Olafsdottir, S., Gostas, G., Kastrup, M., Lonnerberg, O., Muus, S., Sandlund, M. and Hansson, L. (1998) 'The Nordic comparative study on sectorized psychiatry: continuity of care related to characteristics of the psychiatric services and the patients.' *Social Psychiatry and Psychiatric Epidemiology 33*, 521–527.

Sweeney, A. (2009) 'So What is Survivor Research?' In A. Sweeney *et al.* (eds) *This is Survivor Research.* Ross-on-Wye: PCCS.

Sytema, S., Micciolo, R. and Tansella, M. (1997) 'Continuity of care for patients with schizophrenia and related disorders: a comparative South Verona and Groningen case-register study.' *Psychological Medicine 27*, 6, 1355–1362.

Tessler, R. and Mason, J. (1979) Continuity of care in the delivery of mental health services.' *American Journal of Psychiatry 136*, 10, 1297–1301.

Turner, M. and Beresford, P. (2005) *User Controlled Research: Its Meaning and Potential.* Eastleigh: INVOLVE Support Unit.

Wallcraft, J., Read, J. and Sweeney, A. (2003) *On Our Own Terms: Users and Survivors of Mental Health Services Working Together for Support and Change* London: Sainsbury Centre for Mental Health.

Ware, N., Tugenberg, T., Dickey, B. and McHorney, C. (1999) 'An ethnographic study of the meaning of continuity of care in mental health services.' *Psychiatric Services 50*, 3, 395–400.

Ware, N., Dickey, B., Tugenberg, T. and McHorney, C. (2003) 'CONNECT: a measure of continuity of care in mental health services.' *Mental Health Services Research 5*, 4, 209–221.

Warner, J., King, M., Blizard, R., McClenahan, Z. and Tang, S. (2000) 'Patient-held shared care records for individuals with mental illness.' *British Journal of Psychiatry 177*, 319–324.

Webb, Y., Clifford, P., Fowler, V., Morgan, C. and Hanson, M. (2000) 'Comparing patients' experience of mental health services in England: a five-Trust survey.' *International Journal of Health Care Quality Assurance 13*, 6–7, 273–281.

Woodhouse, A. and Vincent, A. (2006) *Delivery Plan: Development of Peer Specialist Roles: A Literature Scoping Exercise.* Edinburgh: Scottish Recovery Network and the Scottish Development Centre for Mental Health.

CHAPTER 9

Involving a Marginalized Group in Research and Analysis – People with Life Limiting Conditions

Issues and Gains

Phil Cotterell and Mandy Paine

Introduction

There has been an increasing emphasis and priority on involving service users in research in the UK, particularly since the health and social care modernization policies of the New Labour government (Department of Health, 2005, 2006), with the Department of Health funding an organization since 2000 to promote and advise on all aspects of involvement in public, health and social care research (Hanley *et al.*, 2000). In this chapter we reflect on our particular experience and knowledge of service user involvement in research that involved people with life limiting conditions and explore key issues that required attention. We have written this as a collaborative exercise with each of us writing and editing the chapter. We come to this writing with differing perspectives. Phil has a background in the health professions which developed into a research career for some time. Mandy is a music teacher and lives with a life limiting condition, Chronic Obstructive Pulmonary Disease (COPD). We met when Phil was undertaking his doctoral research and

Mandy became a member of the Advisory Group that worked on the research with Phil. We mainly focus here on our experiences of this and on our learning.

At the outset we want to make clear what we mean by some of the terms we use in this writing. We are using the term 'service user' here to describe those people who make use of health and social care services (including carers and family members) but do so recognizing that it is far from universally acceptable. We use it because it is a term that is widely understood. We have considered the use of the term 'marginalized' here as well and are aware that there are many ways to describe individuals or groups who are less likely to become involved in research, for example, hard to reach, under-represented, seldom heard, socially excluded, hidden group, vulnerable. We use the term 'marginalized' to illustrate the sense of exclusion or social invisibility that people with life limiting conditions, and those with other conditions or in other circumstances, can experience (Small and Rhodes, 2000).

Thinking generally about service user involvement in research it is clear that service users can be usefully involved. It is however often challenging to achieve (Oliver et al., 2004); there is evidence that active involvement only occurs in a small proportion of studies (Barber, Boote and Cooper, 2007), and researchers remain 'uncomfortable' and critical of the 'value' of involving service users in research (Becker, Sempik and Bryman, 2010; Thompson et al., 2009). Many of the major health and social care research funding organizations in the UK expect studies they fund to have provision for service user involvement described and incorporated into research activities both within grant applications and within ongoing research work. Such expectations and consequent involvement activities have been increasing exponentially since 2000 despite reservations such as those highlighted above.

There are many claims made for the involvement of service users in research. It has been argued that involvement in research concerns contributing a unique perspective that can change research design and/ or conduct, and can lead to the generation of new knowledge (Small and Rhodes, 2000). Active involvement is argued to produce research that is considered to be more relevant to people's needs, is more reliable, collects more useful information, and is more ethical (Hanley, 1999; Staley and Minogue, 2006; Staniszewska et al., 2007). Further to this, what service users want from research has moved far from a passive notion of involvement and it has been said that service users now expect '…to offer their own analyses, interpretations and plans for action' (Beresford,

2001, p.508). It also needs to be noted however that involvement can have unwanted effects that make the involvement experience a negative one (Cotterell *et al.*, 2011; Staniszewska *et al.*, 2011). Involvement can appear to be a straightforward undertaking that is easily achieved. In fact it is complex with many opportunities for unintended consequences to arise. Such complexities across a range of settings are described in a recent volume by Barnes and Cotterell (2011).

Service user involvement in research has been particularly developed in health and social care within the UK in the settings of mental health, disability, and clinical trials research. It is acknowledged though that certain communities or settings remain particularly marginalized from involvement in research (Hanley, 2005). People with life limiting conditions are said to be one such group that is difficult to involve in research (Steel, 2005). It is argued that those who are marginalized from having a voice in health and social services or research are likely to be those who are highly reliant on services or excluded from services (Anderson *et al.*, 2002). In terms of those with a life limiting condition that is clearly the case. For example, Mandy has high support needs in terms of both health and social care services and has experience of being denied access to a local hospice. The need to include a diverse range of 'voices' in research, including those who may be referred to as marginalized, has been identified by service users themselves (Branfield and Beresford, 2006) and inclusion of such groups needs to be achieved in respectful ways and on equal terms (Beresford, 2007).

There are examples of research that involve people from marginalized groups (see, for example, Blackburn, Hanley and Staley, 2010; O'Keefe and Hogg, 1999) and these reinforce that issues of respect and trust are key factors that assist with making this relationship, between researchers and service users, work. The other key factor is striving for a collaborative relationship. It is to the nature of relationships we turn to next in relation to our own experience.

Developing relationships

The research that we are referring to in this chapter was a doctoral research study (Cotterell, 2006). Specifically it was a qualitative participatory study that aimed to explore what service users with a range of life limiting conditions identified as their key experiences and needs generally and, specifically, from health and social care services. It was participatory in that the meaningful involvement of service users, involvement that could impact upon the research process and outcomes, was strived for and, we feel, achieved. We will describe this below. The research utilized an exploratory cross-sectional design whereby a diverse range of research participants (n. 25) were interviewed on one occasion. Interviews were audio recorded, transcribed verbatim and analysed thematically. We have described this research (Cotterell *et al.*, 2007a), its key findings (Cotterell, 2008a), and some related methodological issues previously (Cotterell, 2008b). Here we want to focus on some key issues we feel need to be addressed in order for people from marginalized groups to be effectively involved on equal terms.

Prior to commencing the research a meeting with representatives from various local service user groups was organized to discuss the research aims and questions. At this meeting the research idea was proposed and it was widely welcomed as a project that was potentially of use to people with life limiting conditions. During this period Phil made contact with many individuals in health and social care to advertise the research, to secure support, and to convince these people to inform clients about the research. These individuals were for example hospital consultants, specialist nurses, social workers, community district nurses, and general practitioners, as well as local social service and mental health organizations and individuals. The intention here was to let a wide range of people know about the research and to prompt these people to discuss the research with service users they knew.

The Service User Research Advisory Group (SURAG) was also being developed in this period and it was through this group that the participatory method was delivered. This group's objective was to work together, with Phil, keeping the research clearly in mind and focused on a common purpose. The group was conceived so that members could draw upon the knowledge and experiences of living with life limiting conditions to influence the research at all stages. The aim was to ensure that the research remained in tune with service user concerns and needs. It aimed to be a democratic group whereby the service user members could genuinely shape and influence the research in a collaborative way. Access to people with life limiting conditions and subsequent recruitment to the SURAG was a process that took time and effort. Potential group members were contacted in two ways: by introductory letter and by meeting with condition-specific groups such as 'breatheasy' groups which offer support and advice for people with breathing difficulties.

Upon an expression of interest from the person with a life limiting condition or a professional involved in their care the person was contacted by phone and then met in person to discuss the research and outline plans for the SURAG. This meeting was seen as very important and as an opportunity to set the scene both in terms of the research and its possibilities, and in terms of the relationship strived for between Phil and SURAG member. This initial face-to-face contact took time. Phil introduced himself and the study, and the potential SURAG member had time to describe their current situation and ask any questions about the research and their possible role in it. Phil was honest about a number of uncertainties: the outcomes of the research and the level of influence possible from the SURAG. These uncertainties were a necessary aspect of the research in that there was an expectation that the group when formed would direct its own remit and role to a significant level. There was however a clear initial commitment to enable the group to develop and make a significant contribution to the research. This commitment was openly discussed and, although no promises could be made as success of the research and the SURAG depended on many things, all were aware of the presence of much genuine good will.

Eight service users joined the SURAG and met 32 times over a three-year period. It is important to note that group members were severely affected by their various conditions. For example, one group member had been in intensive care on a ventilator for over a month in the previous year as her breathing was so poor and others had advanced cancer and experienced associated problems such as fatigue, pain and nausea. The impact of marginalization had been wide ranging, for example, under-confidence, social withdrawal, neglected 'social skills', challenged identity, economic disadvantage, low self-esteem and passivity. To illustrate more thoroughly the type of experiences and needs group members had, in the next section Mandy describes her situation in more detail.

Being marginalized: Mandy's experiences

I was 40 years old when I became involved with the research we are referring to here and I had just, one year previously, been told that my breathing condition was 'end stage'. This news was given to me and my family in order that we prepare for the fact that my condition had neared its end – I was facing the fact that my life was approaching its end.

Over my lifetime I have had to negotiate many different identities and roles that might be themed as relationship identities (wife, mother, daughter, carer), and as health identities (asthmatic, bronchitis and bronchiectesis 'patient', COPD diagnosis, hypertension, liver and kidney disease). Even though I had breathing problems when I was young I did what I could to help myself such as swimming, running, and playing wind instruments. I also avoided smoking. Despite my actions my breathing difficulties progressed and I had to leave university prior to graduating ending up in hospital to regain adequate lung functioning and energy. I tried to resume 'normal' life and trained as a jeweller and taught the flute and piano. I also kept up with my exercise regime swimming, running and cycling.

I went on to marry and have two children, one of whom had severe epilepsy for many years that resulted in us needing to be very vigilant day and night. When the children were still very small my breathing deteriorated and my condition became very unstable requiring many stays in hospital (including 'intensive care'). At this stage my husband decided to leave work in order to become the 'carer' for both our son and myself. I carried on 'going downhill' physically and for the first time became acutely aware of the lack of support for someone in my situation. I was repeatedly told I was very young and had an illness that was normally associated with people in their eighties who had smoked heavily. Later I was to discover I was not alone in floundering with no support – I was the wrong age, in the wrong area, and with the wrong condition!

I carried on living in and out of hospital, being asked the same questions and hitting the same brick walls. A support group for people with breathing difficulties was suggested but I went and found all the members were much older than myself and I felt like I didn't fit in. I never went again. I was now reliant on a wheelchair to get about as even minimal exertion left me extremely breathless. I could get around my home but I could not now go further unaccompanied as I would be exhausted in just a few steps. At this time we moved our bedroom downstairs separating us from our children. I tried not to let the children see me unwell so would keep away from them on particularly bad days. Trips to the hospital consultant would leave them unsettled as often I was kept in. We all ended up hating the hospital and trips there.

By my mid-thirties I was told my breathing condition was called COPD. I asked if there was any information or support available to help me prepare for what I had ahead of me. I had a friend with breast cancer who had a buddy (someone who also had breast cancer and who was there to support her and her family) and also a hospice nurse to offer advice and support. The answer to my question was 'no'. There was the support group I had previously tried but nothing else. I had met a respiratory nurse at the hospital but she could only see me at the hospital. I felt very alone and I was left wondering if people with other conditions had this same lack of support.

I did receive social services home care provided to assist me with hygiene and dressing some weekday mornings. I was struggling with the simplest things in life and needed support from others for these tasks. I have now been told my condition is life limiting. I tried to access my local hospice as I thought a short respite stay would give us all a break – I was told I wasn't suitable (they mainly deal with people who have cancer). I had come to feel totally lost and I wondered if there was anything I could do to turn my life around. I felt I had nothing for me, only things against me.

Reflecting on the involvement

Mandy has shared this here in order to convey a little of the sense of isolation and separateness she has experienced over time. We are describing involvement in research of people with life limiting conditions but the result of other types of marginalization in other settings will be similar. In our joint endeavour finding the right level of support was essential to enable the group to be fully involved in the research over time. This support needed to be tailored to individuals dependent on their situation.

It is interesting to reflect on why, with such issues to contend with, the people Phil approached agreed to become involved. There are probably several factors at play here. Firstly a great deal depended on the personal contact. In many ways we were not meeting as equals but openness about the possibilities for the group and an explicit up-front statement that the group itself would make decisions on its remit and responsibilities helped. Sharing the unknownness of what journey the research would take illustrated some honesty as did the acknowledgement that positive outcomes for those involved and others with life limiting conditions was not guaranteed. There was however a clear commitment to make the involvement experience as positive and influential as possible. Phil presented the research in a way that indicated it would be a journey shared together. He also shared his feelings of uncertainty and anxiety alongside his belief in the research and the SURAG. Developing trust, between researcher and service user, has been acknowledged elsewhere as an important aspect that has a positive impact on the effectiveness of this type of research (Blackburn *et al.*, 2010). This was certainly the case in the research we are describing here. Another factor concerns the aim of the research. With its focus on identifying the needs of people with life limiting conditions it is likely that the topic was in tune with those approached to join the SURAG. Mandy reflects that the opportunity to try and highlight the needs of people in a similar position to her was appealing. Having a research focus on an issue (or issues) that is a priority for service users is of clear importance in terms of people from marginalized groups deciding to become involved or not.

Issues and gains

Service user involvement in research brings about both positive and challenging outcomes – these are well documented. We argue that the involvement of marginalized groups in research has the potential to heighten these outcomes in either positive or challenging ways. Those who can be identified as 'marginalized' often have more to lose from becoming involved but also, we argue, more to gain. In a position paper focused on maximizing the involvement of marginalized groups in social care, four key areas in need of attention were identified: attitudinal, organizational, cultural, and practical issues (Robson *et al.*, 2008). For us in our research, attention was required to all of these issues in order to enhance the involvement experience.

In our context, as mentioned above, a starting point concerned illustrating to people that they could actually play an active part and influence research. Another important point is that the possibility to become involved, that you are approached and told that you could be of help, and therefore offered a choice, can be a massive boost to some people. For Mandy, a background of feeling useless and a burden was suddenly challenged. No group members had been previously involved in research of any kind and, as made clear by Mandy's experience of life with her condition, all were to differing degrees unsure of what they might contribute and what personal cost involvement might bring. This was as a direct result of experiences of isolation and marginalization over long periods of time for many. We argue that such uncertainty and apprehension is not restricted to the context we are describing here. We described earlier how potential group members were approached and that time was taken to share understandings of the research and people's lives. A central issue for many in our experience concerns listening and being heard. This sounds obvious but later experience of involvement for both Phil and Mandy has shown how frequently involvement can be damaging and tokenistic and, as we have claimed, this is more so for those groups of marginalized people than for others.

Even with thorough preparation, the first meeting of the SURAG in particular caused heightened anxiety for some members of the group. The attitude of researchers is crucial then as explaining the research, clarifying roles and expectations, and facilitating a 'safe space' is of central importance. Such explanations need to be verbal but also in writing and in other ways suitable for those contemplating involvement. The direct experience that people have of the condition or situation being researched is central to why someone is being involved. It is right then to expect this to be of central import and focus when involved. All need to be in agreement about how this experience is to be negotiated once the formal research work begins. For example, is there an expectation that service users should not recount any of their direct experiences? How much of their experience may they be willing to share? Are there particular times in the research where drawing on direct experiences may be more acceptable than others? On joining in with research it is only right that people know what to expect and know that thought has been put into getting involvement right.

The organization of the research and research meetings is important and much thought is required here. We acknowledge that meetings, even if designed to be informal and supportive as ours were, are not always the most suitable way to involve some people. For Mandy though there was a normalizing aspect of joining in with the SURAG in meetings. Seeing others who were experiencing similar problems and barriers was supportive. Given thought, such meetings can provide the time to think through and reflect on wider aspects of one's own situation. Aspects of process concern getting the pace of meetings right, enabling clear communication, time for personal as well as business discussion, and getting scene setting right. For us meeting in someone's home with 'home comforts' present, hospitality, and travelling arranged was essential.

Of course, even with good planning and clear and honest intentions, the nature of this type of research with marginalized people is likely to raise challenges. In our experience some of these challenges were emotional and physical. SURAG members lived with ongoing physical problems and over the course of the research these problems posed a problem regarding involvement. As an example Mandy, who requires oxygen via a cylinder 24 hours daily, experienced breathing difficulties whilst in meetings at times. Having a room to take a break in when required was essential. Others experienced pain or discomfort and needed to take medication or to stand and walk around a little to relieve it. The group was accepting of the need for this type of behaviour, probably due to 'everyone being in the same boat' as a SURAG member said. A formal 'study management group' meeting is more likely of course to raise difficulties in relation to this. Perhaps particularly because of the setting of our research there were emotional challenges encountered. We have already mentioned the anxiety experienced on joining the group. It took some time for relationships to flourish and for people to feel comfortable with each other. Once established though friendships were made although occasional issues arose with relationships that caused some distress. We think that we were lucky in that the group self-managed these problems, although key to this was having time in the group to discuss and address the problems. Ultimately time to see the situation from the other's perspective was enough to lead to resolution.

For many SURAG members, some of whom also worked on the analysis of data, our emerging research findings had a personal and emotional impact. For example the research raised several issues concerned with social services home care provision of which members of the group had first-hand experience (Cotterell et al., 2007b). Hearing of the difficulties research participants had in terms of accessing and negotiating helpful home care packages brought home SURAG members' own struggles. It also affirmed members' experience of insensitivity and disrespect when in receipt of home care and this brought such negative experiences to the fore afresh. Such issues constitute some of the potential risks for those who may be termed marginalized when being actively involved in research.

Our method of analysing data collectively (Cotterell, 2008b), whereby service users alongside researcher (Phil) undertook a structured thematic analysis, clearly influenced the findings. Interviews focused on what service users with a range of life limiting conditions identified as their key experiences and needs generally and, specifically, from health and social care services. Findings included themes of 'anger/frustration,' 'fear' and 'grief' as well as 'difference/individuality' and the overarching theme of 'independence/dependence'. Early provisional analysis led by the researcher began raising more 'professional' and sanitized themes. Only when we all focused our efforts together did we see the findings shift into the more powerful and perhaps meaningful ones stated above. This analytic process was more user led and had a significant impact on the outcomes of the research.

Conclusion

Our reflections here have tried to explore positive and challenging aspects to the involvement of people in research from marginalized groups, and to do so by drawing on our own experiences. We feel proud and fortunate to have worked together with other members of the group on a research study that led to many positive outcomes. We have described how engaged and personally empowered members of the SURAG were as a direct result of being involved with this research. This in turn enabled members to become involved in other initiatives and even to be at the centre of a feature in a social care journal (Sale, 2005).

We have tried though to also cast a critical light on such an endeavour that has included negative or unintended consequences. These will vary dependent on context and should not be minimized. Careful and thoughtful efforts are required in designing such research in order that possible negative issues are avoided. The involvement of service users from the earliest possible point in the research process is likely to greatly assist with making involvement in this setting as positive an experience as possible. Commissioning research that is user led or with strong and genuine involvement throughout, those using participatory methods for example, needs to be a prerequisite when funding studies focused on marginalized groups.

References

Anderson, W., Florin, D., Gillam, S. and Mountford, L. (2002) *Every Voice Counts: Primary Care Organisations and Public Involvement*. London: Kings Fund.

Barber, R., Boote, J.D. and Cooper, C. (2007) 'Involving consumers successfully in NHS research: a national survey.' *Health Expectations 10*, 4, 380–391.

Barnes, M. and Cotterell, P. (eds) (2011) *Critical Perspectives on User Involvement*. Bristol: Policy Press.

Becker, S., Sempik, J. and Bryman, A. (2010) 'Advocates, agnostics and adversaries: researchers' perceptions of service user involvement in social policy research.' *Social Policy and Society 9*, 3, 355–366.

Beresford, P. (2001) 'Service users, social policy and the future of welfare.' *Critical Social Policy 21*, 4, 494–512.

Beresford, P. (2007) 'User involvement, research and health inequalities: developing new directions.' *Health and Social Care in the Community 15*, 4, 306–312.

Blackburn, H., Hanley, B. and Staley, K. (2010) *Turning the Pyramid Upside Down: Examples of Public Involvement in Social Care Research*. Eastleigh: INVOLVE.

Branfield, F. and Beresford, P. with Andrews, E. J., Chambers, P., Staddon, P., Wise, G. and Williams-Findlay, B. (2006) *Making User Involvement Work: Supporting Service User Networking and Knowledge*. York: Joseph Rowntree Foundation.

Cotterell, P. (2006) *Living with Life Limiting Conditions: A Participatory Study of People's Experiences and Needs*. Unpublished PhD thesis. Brunel University, UK.

Cotterell, P. (2008a) 'Striving for independence: experiences and needs of service users with life limiting conditions.' *Journal of Advanced Nursing 62*, 6, 665–673.

Cotterell, P. (2008b) 'Exploring the value of service user involvement in data analysis: "Our interpretation is about what lies below the surface".' *Educational Action Research 16*, 1, 5–17.

Cotterell, P., Clarke, P., Cowdrey, D., Kapp, J., Paine, M. and Wynn, R. (2007a) 'Becoming involved in Research: A Service User Research Advisory Group.' In L. Jarrett (ed.) *Creative Engagement in Palliative Care: New Perspectives on User Involvement.* Abingdon: Radcliffe Publishing Ltd.

Cotterell, P., Cowdrey, D., Kapp, J. and Paine, M. (2007b) 'Home care for people with life limiting conditions.' *Community Care*, 18–24 January, 30–31.

Cotterell, P., Harlow, G., Morris, C., Beresford, P., Hanley, B., Sargeant, A., Sitzia, J. and Staley, K. (2011) 'Service user involvement in cancer care: the impact on service users.' *Health Expectations 14*, 2, 159–169. DOI: 10.1111/j.1369-7625.2010.00627.x

Department of Health (2005) *Research Governance Framework for Health and Social Care.* London: Department of Health (Second Edition).

Department of Health (2006) *Best Research for Best Health: A New National Health Research Strategy.* London: Department of Health.

Hanley, B. (1999) *Research and Development in the NHS: How Can You Make A Difference?* Leeds: NHS Executive.

Hanley, B. (2005) *Research as Empowerment? Report of a Series of Seminars Organised by the Toronto Group.* York: Joseph Rowntree Foundation.

Hanley, B., Bradburn, J., Gorin, S., Barnes, M., Evans, C., Goodare, H., Kelson, M., Kent, A., Oliver, S. and Wallcraft, J. (2000) *Involving Consumers in Research and Development in the NHS: Briefing Notes for Researchers.* Winchester: Consumers in NHS Research Support Unit.

O'Keefe, E. and Hogg, C. (1999) 'Public participation and marginalized groups: the community development model.' *Health Expectations 2*, 4, 245–254.

Oliver, S., Clarke-Jones, L., Rees, R., Milne, R., Buchanan, P., Gabbay, J., Gyte, G., Oakley, A. and Stein, K. (2004) 'Involving consumers in research and development agenda setting for the NHS: developing an evidence-based approach.' *Health Technology Assessment 8*, 15, 1–148.

Robson, P., Sampson, A., Dime, N., Hernandez, L. and Litherland, R. (2008) *Seldom Heard: Developing Inclusive Participation in Social Care.* London: Social Care Institute for Excellence.

Small, N. and Rhodes, P. (2000) *Too Ill to Talk: User Involvement and Palliative Care.* London: Routledge.

Staley, K. and Minogue, V. (2006) 'User involvement leads to more ethically sound research.' *Clinical Ethics 1*, 2, 1–6.

Staniszewska, S., Jones, N., Newburn, M. and Marshall, S. (2007) 'User involvement in the development of a research bid: barriers, enablers and impacts.' *Health Expectations 10*,2, 173–183.

Staniszewska, S., Mockford, C., Gibson, A., Herron-Marx, S. and Putz, R. (2011) 'Moving Forward: Understanding the Negative Experiences and Impacts of Patient and Public Involvement in Health Service Planning, Development and Evaluation.' In M. Barnes and P. Cotterell (eds) *Critical Perspectives on User Involvement.* Bristol: Policy Press.

Steel, R. (2005) 'Actively Involving Marginalized and Vulnerable People in Research.' In L. Lowes and I. Hulatt (eds) *Involving Service Users in Health and Social Care Research.* Abingdon: Routledge.

Thompson, J., Barber, R., Ward, P.R., Boote, J.D., Cooper, C.L., Armitage, C.J. and Jones, G. (2009) 'Health researchers' attitudes towards public involvement in health research.' *Health Expectations 12*, 2, 209–220.

Sale, A.U. (2005) 'Who are the real experts?' *Community Care*, October, 32–33.

CHAPTER 10

The Key Contributions of User-led Services
What Does the Evidence Tell Us?

Colin Barnes

Introduction

Since the politicisation of disability by disabled activists in countries across the world in the latter half of the last century the various disadvantages encountered by people with impairments and labelled 'disabled' can no longer be explained away with reference to their 'disabilities'. It is now widely recognised in policy circles that disabled people encounter a range of economic, political and cultural barriers that inhibit their ability to achieve a comparable lifestyle to non-disabled peers. Disabled people are often viewed as dependent, a burden to themselves, their families and the state, a view exacerbated by a range of dependency creating services staffed by non-disabled professionals (Davis, 1990; Oliver, 1990; Finkelstein, 1991, 1999; Morris, 1993). Consequently, a key aim of the disabled people's movement around the world has been to achieve 'independent living' (Charlton, 1998).

This chapter discusses the growth of organisations controlled and run by disabled people in the UK and their contribution to the design and delivery of services to enable service users to achieve this goal. It begins with an overview of the arrival of the disabled people's movement and the origins of user-led disability services in the 1970s and 1980s with particular emphasis on the UK experience. A major catalyst and unifying factor for this development was the social model of disability's focus on the social barriers that create disablement. There follows a discussion of the political and social context in which user-led services evolved in the 1980s, in particular the critique of the welfare state and the promotion of user involvement in public services. The next section discusses findings from a national study of user-led organisations conducted at the turn of the new millennium by the British Council of Organisations of Disabled People's (BCODP) National Centre for Independent Living (NCIL) (Barnes and Mercer, 2006). The concluding section looks at recent developments in the promotion of user-led services.

Disability politics and independent living

Although disability activism in the UK can be traced back to the nineteenth century, it came to prominence in the 1960s. It was fuelled by disabled people's exclusion from mainstream economic and social activity, poverty and a rejection of 'residential care' and control by what Finkelstein (1999) termed 'professionals allied to medicine' (PAMs). Until the late 1960s, support for 'severely' disabled people was generally unavailable outside institutions and there were no disability related welfare payments. Consequently 'severely' disabled people were either incarcerated in residential homes run by professionals or living in relative poverty and social isolation in the community (Barnes, 1991). Britain's first overtly political disability organisation, the Disabled Incomes Group (DIG), was founded in 1965 by two disabled women and quickly became a focus for disability activism across the UK.

Besides a focus on the need for welfare payments to cover the cost of living with impairment, attention quickly turned to the need to reform public services. From the outset, DIG had become a magnet for disability activists, throughout Britain, several of whom would later leave to form other more radical organisations such as the Union of the Physically Impaired against Segregation (UPIAS). The founders of UPIAS had become disillusioned with DIG's narrow incomes approach and its colonisation by non-disabled 'experts' (UPIAS, 1976). The first official acknowledgement of the need for welfare reform came with the introduction of the Chronically Sick and Disabled Person's Act in 1970 following a Private Members Bill by a Labour MP, Alf Morris. The Act is widely regarded as the first piece of legislation in the world to introduce policies to improve equal opportunities for disabled people in community-based services, education, housing and public buildings (Topliss and Gould, 1981).

As the number of organisations controlled and run by disabled people, the disabled people's movement, began to increase, the focus shifted from lobbying for public service reform to user-led initiatives fuelled by news of developments in the USA. The American Independent Living Movement (ILM) emerged partly from within the campus culture of American universities and partly from repeated efforts by American disability activists, swelled by the growing numbers of disabled Vietnam War veterans, to influence US disability legislation. During the 1960s, some American universities had introduced various self-help programmes to enable students with 'severe' physical impairments to attend mainstream courses. Such schemes were rarely available outside university campuses. This prompted some disabled students to develop their own services under the banner of Centres for Independent Living (CILs). America's first CIL opened in Berkeley, California in 1972. With legislative encouragement and federal funding, the number of CILs quickly expanded to over 200 over the following decade (Crewe and Zola, 1983).

The activities of the ILM had a significant impact on activists across the world. Part of the reason for this apparent success is the almost universal appeal of the phrase 'independent living' within western culture. It is apolitical in the sense that it appeals directly to advocates of the politics of the right and of the left. It is apolitical in that the environmental and cultural changes needed to facilitate meaningful 'independent living' for disabled people will benefit everyone regardless of impairment or status. Yet some disability activists in the UK supplanted the term 'independent' with 'integrated' or, later, 'inclusive' living in recognition that no one regardless of impairment is truly independent, all humans are interdependent and everyone needs human interaction and support of one form or another (Barnes, 1993). However, despite terminological differences the phrase 'independent living' represents both a philosophy and a practical solution to the problem of disablement. It is founded upon four basic assumptions:

- All human life, regardless of the nature, complexity and/or severity of impairment, is of equal worth.

- Anyone, whatever the nature, complexity and/or severity of their impairment, has the capacity to make choices and should be enabled to make those choices.

- People who are disabled by societal responses to any form of accredited impairment – physical, sensory or cognitive – have the right to exercise control over their lives.

- People with perceived impairments who are labelled 'disabled' have the right to participate fully in all areas, economic, political and cultural, of mainstream community living on a par with non-disabled peers (adapted from Bracking, 1993; Brisenden, 1986; Morris, 1993).

The practical solution to the problems encountered by disabled people revolves around services controlled and run by disabled people themselves: CILs or user-led services. An early example of a user-led initiative in the UK is the Spinal Injuries Association (SIA) established in 1973 which provided various services such as information and 'care attendant' schemes for people with spinal cord injuries (Barnes and Mercer, 2006). As the decade progressed disabled activists developed a range of innovative user-led initiatives including a national network of telephone Disability Information and Advice Lines (DIAL) (Davis, 1981) and integrated accessible housing schemes for disabled and non-disabled residents (Davis and Woodward, 1981). In 1979 residents at Le Court Cheshire Home, Hampshire, persuaded the local authority to direct the funding equivalent to the costs of their 'care' in the home, through to residents to fund accessible accommodation in the community and employ their own support staff: 'personal assistants' (PAs) (HCIL, 1981). Although technically illegal under the 1948 National Assistance Act these 'direct payment schemes' attracted interest amongst disabled people as they gave them greater choice and control over their support within the community. This was in marked contrast to community-based services and support provided by local authority Social Services Departments (SSDs) and charities staffed by non-disabled professionals (Barnes, 1993; Oliver and Zarb, 1992; Zarb and Nadash, 1994).

Consumerism and the growth of user-led services

The 1980s and 1990s provided a fertile political climate for the growth of user-led services due to the election of Margaret Thatcher's Conservative Government in 1979. Criticism of state involvement in public services was central to 'New Right' thinking. The growing size and cost of state-sponsored public services and welfare dependency was a major concern. Government rhetoric prioritised the introduction of market forces to improve efficiency and effectiveness of health and social 'care' services and the importance of consumer sovereignty.

This found expression in the 1986 Disabled Persons (Services, Representation and Consultation) Act: legislation which promised much but delivered little. As is common with much subsequent legislation it was never properly implemented either nationally or locally (Barnes, 1991). The year of 1988 saw the introduction of the Independent Living Fund (ILF) a national means-tested scheme to help disabled people with the cost of support and employing their own PAs. However, the number of applications far surpassed government expectations. In its first year, applications exceeded 900 a month; by 1992, this had risen to 2000. When the original ILF ceased operations in March 1993, it was providing direct payments to 22,000 disabled individuals (Zarb and Nadash, 1994). It was replaced by two new charities: The Independent Living (Extension) Fund, which continued to make payments to existing users, and the Independent Living (1993) Fund set up to supplement local authority sponsored services to coincide with the implementation of the 1990 Community Care reforms (Oliver and Barnes, 1998). The ILF ceased operations entirely in 2011.

The 1990 NHS and Community Care Act stated that 'consumers' must be fully informed and consulted about services backed up by a complaints procedure and redress. It also allowed local authority SSDs to buy in services from the private and voluntary sectors including user-led organisations. In 1995, the Disability Discrimination Act was passed and the Community Care (direct payments) Act came into force a year later. The former claimed to prohibit unfair discrimination against disabled people, the latter empowered local authorities to offer direct payments to service users rather than conventional provider-led provision. The New Labour government elected in 1997 reiterated the importance of these initiatives and located users 'at the heart of social care' in its modernisation agenda for public services. Suffice to say that hitherto these developments have had only a marginal impact on the empowerment of the majority of service users (Prideaux et al., 2009). It is notable too that in many ways these developments were influenced by the activities of the disabled people's movement (Campbell and Oliver, 1996).

Disability activism intensified during the early 1980s at national and international levels. The BCODP, renamed the United Kingdom's Disabled People's Council (UKDPC) in 2006, the UK's national umbrella for organisations controlled and run by disabled people, was formed in 1981 by seven organisations. A decade later BCODP membership had risen to 80 organisations. The international equivalent of BCODP, Disabled Peoples' International (DPI) formed in 1981. DPI's first world congress was held in Singapore in the following year and attracted 400 delegates representing national organisations run by disabled people from around the world including representatives of BCODP. DPI's stated policy revolves around the promotion of grass roots organisations and the development of public awareness of disability issues in the struggle for equality. Its slogan 'nothing about us without us' has been embraced by disabled people's organisations around the world (Charlton, 1998).

Both BCODP and DPI adopted a socio/political or 'social model' definition of disability based on the impairment/disability distinction advocated by UPIAS at its formation in 1974 (UPIAS, 1976). Mike Oliver, a disabled writer and lecturer in social work, coined the phrase 'the social model of disability'. His aim was to provide an accessible key to understanding the importance of the UPIAS' definition of disability and its implications for policy and practice for social work students. Hence the social model: 'involves nothing more or less fundamental than a switch away from focusing on the physical limitations of particular individuals to the way the physical and social environments impose limitations upon certain categories of people' (Oliver, 1981, p.28).

It is therefore an aid to understanding. Contrary to subsequent critiques (Shakespeare and Watson, 2001), it is not a denial of 'impairment effects' (Thomas, 1999), appropriate medical or re/habilitative interventions, nor a comprehensive social theory. It is simply a tool with which to shift attention away from functional limitations of individuals with impairments onto the problems caused by disabling environments, barriers and cultures. It is a tool with which to provide insights into the disabling tendencies of modern society in order to generate policies and practices to facilitate their eradication (Oliver, 2004). Indeed, the social model had become the 'big idea' (Hasler, 1993) and key factor in the mobilisation of disability activism during the 1980s and 1990s. Notable examples include: the struggle for anti-discrimination legislation to outlaw discrimination against disabled people (Barnes, 1991) and the campaign to legalise direct payments to enable disabled people to employ their own support workers (Barnes, 1993; Oliver and Zarb, 1992; Zarb and Nadash, 1994), and it was a key factor in the development of user-led CIL-type services in the UK (Barnes and Mercer, 2006).

The UK's first CILs, Hampshire Centre for Independent Living (HCIL) and the Derbyshire Centre for Integrated Living (DCIL), opened in 1985. DCIL opted for the term 'integrated' (later inclusive) rather than 'independent' living to reflect the view that no one is truly independent and the importance of working in 'partnership' with health and local authorities. Nevertheless, both organisations held that the long-term aim was not simply alternative service provision, but to transform the bases of social exclusion (Davis and Mullender, 1993).

Mainly because disabled activists in Hampshire had pioneered direct payments in the UK, HCIL initially concentrated on providing information, advice and peer support for people wishing to employ PAs (HCIL, 1990). By contrast, DCIL adopted a more holistic approach commensurate with social model thinking and *integrated* or *inclusive* living. In a paper inspired by a 'social barriers model of disability' Ken Davis described how DCIL had developed a comprehensive 'operational framework' for service support based on the collective experience of disabled people often referred to as 'the seven needs for independent living'. These include information, peer counselling and support, accessible housing, technical aids and equipment, personal assistance, accessible transport and access to the built environment (Davis, 1990, p.7). Once these needs had been secured, other secondary needs arose in order for disabled people to achieve full participation. Following this line of thought in 1989, HCIL added four additional needs: education and training, employment, income and benefits (HCIL, 1998). Subsequently there was a sizable growth in the number of user-led initiatives of one form or another. By the year 2000 there were 85 known CIL-type agencies offering or aspiring to offer these and other services for disabled people and their families (Barnes and Mercer, 2006).

From theory to practice

What then are the principal strengths and weaknesses of CIL-type services? Findings from the first and only national study of this form of provision provide some useful answers to these questions. This project was initiated by the BCODP Research Committee in 1998 and developed in conjunction with the National Centre for Independent Living (NCIL). NCIL was set up by BCODP in 1999 to promote a co-ordinated voice for the development of 'independent living' type services but political differences led to a BCODP/NCIL split in 2002.

The research

The research was co-ordinated by a research advisory committee comprising members of NCIL, researchers from the Centre for Disability Studies (CDS) at the University of Leeds, and a research advisor: Peter B. Beresford, Professor of Social Policy at Brunel University. From 1990 until 2002 CDS had housed the BCODP Disability Research Unit. Five of the seven committee members including Professor Beresford and the principal investigator, Colin Barnes, are disabled people. Funded by the BIG Lottery Fund, the project had three primary aims:

1. to provide a critical evaluation of the development, organisation and services provided by CILs and similar user-led initiatives in the UK

2. to identify the principal forces – economic, political and social – hindering their further development

3. to produce and disseminate, in a variety of accessible formats, findings and recommendations to disabled people, their organisations, and policy makers in both public and private sectors.

It ran for two years from January 2000 and comprised four key stages.

Stage One included a literature review to provide background information and identify organisations for inclusion in the study. This was followed by four seminars to explain the aims of the research and determine key issues for analysis to disabled people and their organisations, and a survey of all known user-led organisations providing 'independent living' services to disabled people. Seventy-five organisations were invited to the seminars and 48 sent representatives. Forty-nine of the 50 participants were disabled people representing a diversity of experiences of user-controlled initiatives. The seminars were held in London, Birmingham, Glasgow and Newcastle in March and April 2000. Seminar topics included the social model, control and accountability, finance, employment policies and services. Summaries of each seminar were produced and circulated to all participants for comment.

The survey was designed by the research team and advisory committee in April 2000. The key issues relating to the form and content of the survey were gathered from the literature review and seminars. The questionnaire included both closed and open-ended questions and addressed such topics as organisational structure, wider networks, resources, activities and services, campaigning and aspirations. Eighty-five surveys were distributed, to a sample of user-led organisations gleaned from BCODP/NCIL membership lists and other sources. A total of 69 were returned giving a response rate of 84 per cent. To ensure equal access, questionnaires were produced in a variety of formats – large print, Braille, disk and email. Their experience confirms the relatively late development of user-led organisations, particularly those identifying as CILs, at least compared with the USA. Thus, over 80 per cent were established after 1986, mostly in the 1990s. Data from the surveys provided the basis for the second and third stages of the research.

Stage Two involved in-depth studies of nine organisations. Notably, all the organisations surveyed agreed to participate in this element of the project. Selection for inclusion was made by the research team and advisory group and based on the following criteria: geographic location, year of origin, membership, user numbers, and services offered. To ensure the project provided a useful insight into the main issues associated with user-controlled services it was important that the research focused on large well-established organisations and those that have emerged in the last decade.

Data collection included content analysis of relevant documents and semi-structured interviews with people involved at different levels in the development, organisation and delivery of services. These comprised 32 individual and ten group interviews. In all, 30 women and 26 men took part in Stage Two. These included members of the controlling body, executive officers, core service managers and providers, clerical and reception staff, voluntary workers and representatives of key funding bodies such as local authority SSDs.

The 42 interviews lasted between 1 and 2.5 hours. Each conversation was recorded and transcribed in full. The transcriptions were then returned to the interviewees for verification and comment.

The third phase of the project involved further visits to the nine organisations from Stage Two in the early months of 2001 to interview service users. The aim was to elicit their experiences and views of user-led services, both past and present, when compared to conventional provision provided by local authorities and other agencies. Also, because hitherto CILs had provided an important forum for the generation of disabled activism and this was reaffirmed in the findings of Phases One and Two, items on campaigning were included in the interview schedules for service users. Participants were also given an opportunity to talk about how user-led services might be improved.

Participation was voluntary. Seventy six individuals and nine representatives of user organisations were interviewed. This comprised 40 women and 36 men who self-identified with a variety of impairments. Although the majority had 'physical' conditions, some identified with multiple impairments including 'learning difficulties' and 'mental health problems'. As indicated in Figure 10.1 the sample were all over 18 but the majority was in the middle age range.

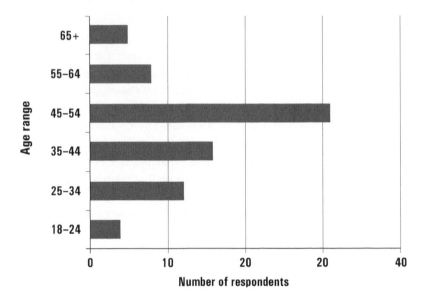

FIGURE 10.1 AGE DISTRIBUTION OF SERVICE USER SAMPLE
Source: Barnes, Mercer and Morgan, 2000, p.11

The final stage of the study centred on dissemination and validation of findings. This involved members of the research team presenting the preliminary findings to participants from each of the nine participating organisations in seminars and focus groups. Everyone involved was invited to these discussions and people had the opportunity to discuss, make suggestions and generally comment on the research and how it related to their particular situation.

Additionally, short summary reports were produced following each stage of the project and distributed by NCIL to all 69 organisations that had taken part in the research (Barnes, Mercer and Morgan, 2000; Morgan, Barnes and Mercer, 2001; Barnes, Morgan and Mercer, 2001). These were also produced in accessible formats and made available on disability websites such as the Disability Archive UK sponsored by the CDS at Leeds University (DAUK, undated). Stage Two concluded with a free national conference for 100 disabled people, participants and service providers at Old Trafford Cricket Ground in Manchester on 6 December 2001 (Barnes, Mercer and Morgan, 2002). A short follow-up study was conducted in 2004 to supplement findings for the book Independent *Futures: Creating User-led Disability Services in a Disabling Society* (Barnes and Mercer, 2006).

Findings

Findings indicate that there is a broad consensus that user-led organisations offer a distinctive and preferable approach to disability-related provision and support. This warrants the adoption of social model principles, democratic accountability and the promotion of 'independent living' through widening user choices and control for *all* disabled people regardless of the nature and severity of impairment. However, the translation of social model insights into provision and practice was often difficult and contentious due to the policy context in which they operated as it was often geared to an individual, medical approach to disability.

Seventy-five per cent of CIL-type organisations had formal links with other organisations and coalitions controlled by disabled people. Sixty-two per cent had ties with other voluntary agencies and around a third, 39 per cent, with organisations of people with specific impairments. Some, 21 per cent, were linked to organisations for people with specific impairments and 15 per cent had ties with 'carers' groups.

However, 39 per cent were formally attached to local authority SSDs and 21 per cent to health authorities. Indeed, it was reported by all interviewees that there was a symbiotic but often uneasy relationship between user-controlled organisations and traditional service providers such as SSDs and health authorities, for example, that often inhibited the development of services and support. Seventy-four per cent of organisations are formally attached to national organisations. Eighty-two per cent are attached to national organisations *of* disabled people with less than a quarter attached to national organisations *for* disabled people: 23 per cent. Ten per cent were associated with national organisations *of* and *for* disabled people with specific impairments.

The organisations surveyed worked with a variety of agencies at different levels. The majority, 93 per cent, with local groups, generally around the provision of services. A significant number operate on a national level, 65 per cent, working with organisations such as NCIL, BCODP, and DIAL: Disability Information Advice Line. Scottish and Welsh organisation operated more on a regional/national basis with agencies like Disability Wales or Disability Scotland. Sixteen per cent had operated in Europe and 10 per cent at the international level with organisations such as ENIL: European Network for Independent Living or DPI: Disabled Peoples' International.

All participating organisations stressed the importance of accountability to members and service users with almost 75 per cent requiring at least 50 per cent user representation on their management committees, all of which had a majority of disabled people. Over half restricted committee membership to people with impairments only. One third included representatives of their funders and 17 per cent included 'carers'. All the organisations sampled had a written constitution and/or a mission/policy statement setting out key aims and objectives. However, some concern was expressed about the limited involvement of service users and members in organisational policy and service development.

The services offered reflected local user priorities and resources. As indicated in Table 10.1 on the next page, information provision is the predominant activity, 82 per cent, followed by peer support, 67 per cent, Disability Equality Training, 58 per cent, and personal assistance support, 54 per cent. The other main areas covered are employment advice/training 38 per cent, housing advice, 32 per cent, and education advice/support, 30 per cent. Survey respondents broadly agree on their desire to expand on their current activities, with a significant minority hoping to take on the mantle of a fully-fledged CIL.

Although only half of the organisations sampled could provide accurate weekly figures of people using their services there was considerable variation. The smaller more recent organisations estimated that they supported around 25 people a week while the figure for the larger and older agencies was between 80 and 300 users. All participants felt that more could be done to recruit users. But several respondents were critical of 'mainstream' providers, both national and local, for routinely obstructing their attempts to expand and provide the full range of 'independent living' services. In particular, mainstream providers appeared 'unaware' or 'reluctant' to publicise user-led initiatives and refer potential users to their organisations. Notably, less than half the user participants in the NCIL/DCS research had been referred to user-controlled services by representatives of statutory agencies such as SSDs and health authorities.

TABLE 10.1 SERVICES CURRENTLY OFFERED BY USER-LED ORGANISATIONS

Service	Currently offered	Hope to offer
Information	82%	65%
Peer support by disabled people	67%	13%
Disability/distress awareness/ equality training	58%	9%
Personal assistance	54%	8%
Employment advice/training	38%	12%
Housing advice	36%	15%
Environmental access	32%	13%
Education advice/support	30%	12%
Transport	22%	6%
Counselling	16%	20%
Health/impairment related	15%	9%
Technical aids and assistance	13%	6%

Source: Barnes, Mercer and Morgan, 2000, p.22

However, the main limitation on the development of their aims and objectives for all the organisations studied was a severe lack of adequate or appropriate resources: funding, staffing and premises. As indicated, there was a general dependence on local authorities, 83 per cent, for core funding, grants and service level agreements. Typically, these were insufficient to sustain the desired level and range of services offered. Furthermore, most funding is short term, for three years or less, although over 85 per cent of organisations manage to avoid the obvious drawbacks in relying on only one funder.

TABLE 10.2 MAJOR SOURCES OF FUNDING OVER THE LAST THREE YEARS

	local authority	health authority	central government	lottery grants	European funding	charities	membership fees	service income
CIL – A	X							
CIL – B	X	X		X		X	X	X
CIL – C				X				
CIL – D	X		X				X	X
CIL – E	X			X	X		X	X
CIL – F	X		X		X			X
CIL – G	X		X	X		X	X	X
CIL – H	X			X				X
CIL – I	X	X	X	X		X	X	X

Source: Morgan, Barnes and Mercer, 2001, p.21

For example, Table 10.2 shows the various funding sources of the nine organisations that participated in Stage Two of the project.

Community Fund/BIG Lottery grants were also widely used, 55 per cent, followed by income from services and membership fees: 33 per cent. Opinions were divided over the merits of receiving money from other sources, particularly charities, or where it was linked to specific impairment groups. A major concern was that funding was increasingly 'conditional' on implementing, monitoring and evaluation and bureaucratic procedures that placed excessive demands on scarce resources without any obvious benefit to either the organisation or service users.

Inadequate staffing levels were a particularly crucial issue. Thirteen per cent of responding organisations were operating without any paid staff and 12 per cent had only one. Conversely, a small number of large well-established agencies had over 30 full or part-time employees. Most participant organisations opted to employ only disabled staff unless no suitable disabled applicants were available. Thirty six per cent employed unpaid voluntary workers whilst 20 per cent chose not to employ any; several respondents were uncomfortable about the potential exploitation of unpaid labour. Yet many volunteers appreciated the opportunity to acquire work training and experience. Moreover, all the organisations encouraged and provided formal training for all staff, including Disability Equality Training (DET) and independent living skills including direct payments training and support.

Securing accessible and affordable office accommodation was a major problem for all participant organisations. Less than half had exclusive use of their premises, with the majority sharing with other voluntary agencies. In some cases, this was in close proximity to other professionally led agencies and charities which had different values and priorities and/or were concerned with impairment specific groups only. The ensuing relationships were often uncomfortable resulting in unnecessary duplication and sometimes conflicting information and competition for users.

Even so, the emphasis on providing services was sometimes at odds with other CIL activities. Several organisations' representatives were acutely aware that their campaigning role might be viewed as compromised by their charitable status and might generate a negative reaction from potential funding agencies. Notwithstanding that several CILs and user-led service providers had informal links with but were formally separated from local coalitions of disabled people and other campaigning groups. Nonetheless, 70 per cent of organisations sampled campaigned on various disability issues. These included service cuts, access and charging for services, particularly at the local or regional levels, with some mobilised nationally and internationally around disability rights.

All respondents including providers and users were very critical of the way in which the independent living concept had been adopted and adapted by mainstream national and local service providers and organisations *for* disabled people. A major concern was the 'colonisation' of direct payment schemes for personal assistance by national and private agencies and the adoption of the phrase 'independent living' by traditional 'professionally' led service providers. One example cited was the renaming of Artificial Limb and Appliance Centres (ALACs) as Independent Living Centres, staffed by professional non-disabled independent living advisers and often attached to hospitals. These are charged with diluting the philosophy of independent living and the re-medicalisation of disability.

Interviews with 72 users reinforced the important differences between traditional professionally led and user-led services. The former were criticised for their complex and demeaning assessment procedures. Key concerns revolved around the 'professional knows best' approach, the priority placed on financial concerns over and above those of service users, lack of reliability and flexibility, and poor helper/helped relations. This was attributed to the little credence given to users' views and the high staff turnover within orthodox provider agencies. Making complaints was widely regarded as a waste of time. In comparison, user-led organisations were rated as far more responsive to users' needs and valued for their peer support, while the participation of disabled people at all levels is regarded as both essential and empowering.

Notwithstanding the broad consensus that CIL-type organisations are the preferred suppliers of independent living services, survey respondents also noted areas where improvement is required. These included the urgent need for secure and long-term funding with which to purchase larger, more accessible premises and recruit and train more staff. Other areas for improvement revolved around the need for greater publicity for user-led independent living services by statutory agencies, automatic referral by health professionals and more involvement in the assessment, design and evaluation of services generally.

Final word

Since the 1970s user-led organisations and CILs have been significant instigators of a range of services to enable people with impairments to achieve an independent lifestyle within the community. Yet despite suggestions that these services are the 'shape of things to come' (Morris, 1993), this research has indicated that their general impact and expansion has been relatively slow. This is due to various factors not least of which is that many local authorities have neither the resources nor inclination to secure their long-term development by providing adequate funding and support. This has had obvious implications for the type and range of services that CIL-type organisations are able to provide. Nevertheless, the emergence of CIL-type initiatives have confirmed the potential of disabled people's collective organisation and capacity to realise user-friendly and enabling services. The enduring impression is of progress in facilitating 'ordinary lives' and maintaining a concerted challenge to the dependency creating services of the past.

Moreover, the significance of the role of user-led organisations in the future development of user-friendly services was formally recognised in 2005 in the *Improving the Life Chances of Disabled People* report produced by the then New Labour Government's Prime Minister's Strategy Unit. Besides adopting a social model definition of disability this report promised the introduction of a range of practical measures designed to ensure that all disabled people achieve independent living by the year 2025. Significantly, this report specified that CIL-type organisations should be at the heart of these policies: 'By 2010 each locality (identified by the area covered by a council with social service responsibilities) should have a user-led organisation modelled on existing Centres for Independent Living' (PMSU, 2005, p.76).

However, due to several factors this directive has yet to be fulfilled (Barnes and Mercer, 2010; Beresford, 2011). These include local authority and professional service provider intransigence, underpinned by individualistic 'medical' understandings of disability, and the increasing emphasis on market forces within the context of social care provision by both the New Labour Government and its successor the Conservative Liberal Democrat Coalition (Roulstone and Prideaux, 2012).

However, the importance of the role of user-led organisations has been reiterated in recent government statements on the reform of public sector services. The express aim is to empower disabled people as consumers under the guise of 'personalisation' (Carr, 2010). In conjunction with this the Department of Health (in conjunction with the Office of Disability Issues) has produced design criteria for minimum standards for these organisations. Developing 'new' services that address 'user wants' such as 'support brokerage' it is claimed will enable them to secure contracts. But they will have to make 'persuasive arguments and business cases for continuation funding' (Carr, 2010) Moreover, as yet, it is not clear how the personalisation funding agenda will impact on services for disabled service users financed by local authorities and other statutory agencies. So user-led organisations may not be able to access funding from previous income sources (NCVO, 2011). Further, given the unprecedented cuts in social welfare provision introduced by the coalition government, due, it is claimed, to the recent and ongoing global economic crisis, its fulfillment in the foreseeable future seems less likely than ever (Oliver and Barnes, 2012). As a consequence, the likelihood of disabled people and indeed all service users achieving independent living by 2025 seems equally remote.

References

Barnes, C. (1991) *Disabled People in Britain and Discrimination: A Case for Anti-discrimination Legislation.* London: Hurst and Co, in association with the British Council of Organisations of Disabled People. *

Barnes, C. (ed.) (1993) *Making Our Own Choices: Independent Living, Personal Assistance and Disabled People.* Belper: British Council of Organisations of Disabled People. *

Barnes, C. and Mercer, G. (2006) *Independent Futures. Creating User-led Disability Services in a Disabling Society.* Bristol: The Policy Press.

Barnes, C. and Mercer, M. (2010) *Exploring Disability.* Cambridge: Polity Press (Second Edition).

Barnes, C., Mercer, G. and Morgan, H. (2000) *Creating Independent Futures: An Evaluation of Services Led by Disabled People. Stage One Report.* Leeds: The Disability Press. *

Barnes, C., Mercer, G. and Morgan, H. (2002) *Creating Independent Futures: An Evaluation of Services Led by Disabled People. Conference Report: Preliminary Findings and Policy Implications.* Leeds: The Disability Press. *

Barnes, C., Morgan, H. and Mercer, G. (2001) *Creating Independent Futures: An Evaluation of Services Led by Disabled People. Stage Three Report.* Leeds: The Disability Press. *

Beresford, P. (2011) *Supporting People: Toward a Person Centred Approach.* Bristol: The Policy Press.

Bracking, S. (1993) 'Independent/Integrated Living: a brief overview.' In C. Barnes (ed.) *Making Our Own Choices.* Derby: The British Council of Organisations of Disabled People. *

Brisenden, S. (1986) 'Independent living and the medical model of disability.' *Disability, Handicap and Society 1, 2,* 173–8.

Carr, S. (2010) *Personalisation: A Rough Guide.* London: Social Care Institute for Excellence. Available at www.scie.org.uk/publications/reports/report20.asp, accessed on 4 April 2012.

Campbell, J. and Oliver, M. (1996) *Disability Politics: Understanding Our Past, Changing Our Future.* London: Routledge.

Charlton, J.I. (1998) *Nothing About Us Without Us: Disability Oppression and Empowerment.* Berkeley, CA: University of California Press.

Crewe, N.M., Zola, I.K. and Associates (1983) *Independent Living for Physically Disabled People.* San Francisco, CA: Jossey-Bass.

Davis, K. (1981) '28–38 Grove Road: Accommodation and Care in a Community Setting.' In A. Brechin, P. Liddiard and J. Swain (eds) *Handicap in a Social World.* London: Hodder and Stoughton, in association with the Open University.

Davis, K. (1990) *A Social Barriers Model of Disability: Theory into Practice – The Emergence of the Seven Needs.* Paper prepared for the Derbyshire Coalition of Disabled People. *

Davis, K. and Mullender, A. (1993) *Ten Turbulent Years: A Review of the Work of the Derbyshire Coalition of Disabled People.* Nottingham: Centre for Social Action. *

Davis, K. and Woodward, J. (1981) 'DIAL UK: Development in the National Association of Disablement Information and Advice Services.' In A. Brechin, P. Liddiard and J. Swain (eds) *Handicap in a Social World.* London: Hodder and Stoughton, in association with the Open University.

DAUK (undated) *The Disability Archive UK.* Leeds Centre for Disability Studies, University of Leeds. Available at www.leeds.ac.uk/disability-studies/archiveuk/index.html, accessed on 4 April 2012.

Finkelstein, V. (1991) 'Disability: An Administrative Challenge (The Health and Welfare Heritage).' In M. Oliver (ed.) *Social Work: Disabled People and Disabling Environments.* London: Jessica Kingsley.

Finkelstein, V. (1999) 'A Profession Allied to the Community: The Disabled People's Trade Union.' In E. Stone (ed.) *Disability and Development: Learning from Action and Research in the Majority World.* Leeds: The Disability Press. *

Hasler, F. (1993) 'Developments in the Disabled People's Movement.' In J. Swain, V. Finkelstein, S. French and M. Oliver (eds) *Disabling Barriers – Enabling Environments.* London: Sage, in association with The Open University.

HCIL (1981) *Project 81, One Step UP: Consumer Directed Housing and Care for Disabled People.* Hampshire: Hampshire Coalition of Disabled People. *

HCIL (1990) *HCIL Papers: Independent Living.* Hampshire: Hampshire Coalition of Disabled People. *

HCIL (1998) *Facing Our Future: Experts Seminar on Independent Living and Direct Payments.* Hampshire: Hampshire Coalition of Disabled People. *

Morgan, H., Barnes, C. and Mercer, G. (2001) *Creating Independent Futures: An Evaluation of Services Led by Disabled People. Stage Three Report.* Leeds: The Disability Press. *

Morris, J. (1993) *Independent Lives, Community Care and Disabled People.* Basingstoke: Macmillan.

NCVO (2011) *Personalisation, User Led Organisations and the VCS.* London: National Council for Voluntary Organisations. Available at: www.3s4.org.uk/drivers/personalisation-user-led-organisations-and-the-vcs, accessed 4 April 2012.

Oliver, M. (1981) 'A New Model in the Social Work Role in Relation to Disability.' In J. Campling (ed.) *The Handicapped Person: A New Perspective for Social Workers.* London: RADAR.

Oliver, M. (1990) *The Politics of Disablement.* Basingstoke: Macmillan.

Oliver, M. (1996) *Understanding Disability: From Theory to Practice.* London: Macmillan.

Oliver, M. (2004) 'The Social Model in Action: If I Had a Hammer?' In C. Barnes and G. Mercer (2004) (eds) *Implementing the Social Model of Disability: Theory and Research.* Leeds: the Disability Press. *

Oliver, M. and Barnes, C. (1998) *Social Policy and Disabled People: From Exclusion to Inclusion.* London: Longman.

Oliver, M. and Barnes, C. (2012) *The New Politics of Disablement.* Tavistock: Palgrave.

Oliver, M. and Zarb, G. (1992) *Personal Assistance Schemes.* Greenwich: University of Greenwich. *

PMSU (2005) *Improving the Life Chances of Disabled People: Final Report.* London: Prime Minister's Strategy Unit, Cabinet Office. Available at: www.strategy.gov.uk/downloads/work_areas/disability/disability_report/index.htm, accessed on 4 April 2012.

Prideaux, S., Roulstone, A. Harris, J. and Barnes, C. (2009) 'Disabled people and self directed support schemes: re-conceptualising work and welfare in the 21st century.' *Disability and Society 24*, 5, 557–570.

Roulstone, A. and Prideaux, S. (2012) *Understanding Disability Policy.* Bristol: Palgrave.

Shakespeare, T. W. and Watson, N. (2001) 'The Social Model of Disability: An Outdated Ideology?' In S.N. Barnartt and B.M. Altman (eds) *Exploring Theories and Expanding Methodologies: Where Are We And Where Do We Need To Go? Research in Social Science and Disability, Vol. 2.* Amsterdam: JAI Elsevier.

Thomas, C. (1999) *Female Forms: Experiencing and Understanding Disability.* Buckingham: Open University Press.

Topliss, E. and Gould, B. (1981) *A Charter for the Disabled.* Oxford: Blackwell.

UPIAS (1976) *Fundamental Principles of Disability.* London: Union of the Physically Impaired Against Segregation. *

Zarb, G. and Nadash, P. (1994) *Cashing in on Independence: Comparing the Costs and Benefits of Cash and Services.* Derby: British Council of Organisations of Disabled People. *

* Available at the Disability Archive UK: www.leeds.ac.uk/disability-studies/archiveuk/index.html, accessed on 4 April 2012.

CHAPTER 11

No Blame, No Shame

Towards a Social Model of Alcohol Dependency – A Story from Emancipatory Research

Patsy Staddon

Introduction

If I were a member of Alcoholics Anonymous (AA) this chapter might begin with: 'Hello, my name is Patsy and I am an alcoholic.' My identity and my medical condition would be seen as inseparable, synonymous, a view still very common in academic journals, taught in medical schools and, unsurprisingly, held by many GPs: 'I *always* refer people to AA and I tell them they must go for the rest of their life' (GP respondent in one of my research projects, 'Treatment Approaches' (Staddon, 2006)). It is not surprising that, both for this reason and for others, it is also commonly the view of the general public (Ettorre, 2007; Fingarette, 1988).

In this chapter I will be challenging these views and providing evidence that on the contrary there are many who recover completely from 'alcoholism' (Hall *et al.*, 2001) and that the many ways in which people recover, like the many reasons which lead them into serious drinking, are most likely to be caused by social factors. I will be offering as evidence not only the views of senior academics (Raistrick, Heather and Godfrey, 2006; Sobell and Sobell, 1995) but also the practical outcomes of my service user-led research, which was grounded in my own personal experience of recovery. The project was perceived as emancipatory, in that its Advisory Group was made up entirely of service users, who designed the work, discussed its outcomes at all stages, were able to criticize and to comment on the final report, and were active in setting up and running the survivors' group which emerged at the end. I will be suggesting how such outcomes may be replicated.

In this way, a social model of alcoholism emerged, one which might relieve shame and hopelessness, and which addresses social issues such as poverty, inequality and abuse. I will be showing how such a model is grounded in a social model of disability.

Problems I encountered with the medical approach

As you will have gathered, I do not support a view of 'alcoholism' which sees it as a monolithic condition, typified by lifelong dependence, with varying remissions. For me, the need to drink disappeared in 1988, after more than 20 years of serious problematic drinking, a not uncommon but seldom acknowledged phenomenon (Klingemann, 2004). In my own case, I believe a major factor was the entry into my life of two other lesbian women who gave me confidence in my self-worth, housed me, comforted me, and took me out socializing with them, disregarding my continuing use of alcohol. Over a period of about a year I found that what mattered was having a glass in my hand, as opposed to having alcohol in the glass. Eventually I was also able to dispense with the glass!

However, I was persuaded, some time after my last drink, to attend a conventional treatment centre, because the GP to whom I told my story assured me I would drink again if I did not. Its 12-step philosophy was based on that of AA, and the centre was funded by the NHS.

I have no wish to denigrate any individuals working in such centres. Their belief in their methods is substantiated by much medical and health research, so they cannot be blamed for following them. Unfortunately, these are based on confusion as to the medical role (Tidmarsh, Carpenter and Slade, 2003). Inadequate understanding of the reasons why people drink too much alcohol is worsened by the belief that as medical experts they are also moral arbiters (International Centre for Drug Policy, 2007). Thus, for example, a woman who is drinking in a way which may not only be harmful to her body but which also causes disapproval and distress to her family, is likely to be regarded with distaste by a GP. The GP may believe this reaction to be based on alarm at the physiological consequences of considerable use of alcohol, but it is at least equally likely to be based on social expectations as to women's proper conduct (Vogt *et al.*, 2006). These will certainly be reinforced by public opinion and by most treatment centres. Some GPs will look seriously for the reasons behind the drinking, but a limited understanding of gendered issues around shame and guilt may prevent their realizing the unsuitability of most currently available treatment (Ettorre, 1997; Raine, 2001).

The alcohol treatment centre provides a fascinating example of how medicine may truly desire to heal the sick, but appears unable to refrain from flexing its moral muscles. Those whose philosophy is based on that of AA will be quick to cite aphorisms such as: 'Gratitude is an attitude', 'We suffer from alcohol-ISM, not alcohol-WASM', 'There is no gain without pain', 'Keep it simple, stupid (K.I.S.S.)'.[1] Attendees are seen as having a moral responsibility to stay 'sober'. They are encouraged to do this by meeting frequently with each other in groups, and reflecting on their own moral inadequacy and likelihood of failure. Centres such as these proliferate, basing their treatment on AA's well-known Twelve Steps, with AA attendance expected and its methods and outlook seen as one's only option. This model emphasizes personal responsibility for 'failure'. Shaming and moral opprobrium are common in such establishments (Women's Resource Centre, 2007) since staff may see it as part of their professional duty to ensure that patients know their behaviour has let them down in the eyes of family, society and friends. Later, newly 'sober' patients may be invited to speak to trainee GPs at local medical schools, emphasizing how their lives have been changed by such an approach. In my research I was unable to find any GPs who had heard from recovered 'alcoholics' with a different story to tell, so the whole wretched system continues, from one generation of GPs to another. Such a way of seeing such an illness has even been referred to as the 'medical model' (Moncrieff, 1997) of alcohol treatment. Alcoholism is seen as an incurable disease, yet one with a moral dimension (Warner, 2009). This ignores social learning theory (Heather and Robertson, 1997) and could additionally be infringing human rights: what Cresswell (2009) terms 'experiential rights', whereby people suffering from a condition may be seen to be suffering further by their experience of treatment.

I was fortunate in that I had such excellent support outside, and independent of, the treatment centre and its ethos. At the time, I did not question its approach, or that my ruin was my own fault. Slowly, however, doubt began to creep in. Over my two decades of drinking I had frequently attempted to stop, including several near-successful

---

1   AA aphorisms copied from placards on the wall at AA meetings.

suicide bids and lengthy stints of AA attendance, but it was too like Sunday school, like being treated as a naughty child. I have mentioned that when I had finally stopped drinking it had been in the environment of lesbian discussion groups, pubs and clubs, where I had found the accepting comradeship, and the political awareness, which my previous life had lacked. Alcohol had become less, and finally not at all, important, but it was always around in the places I frequented. I found that I could not share this aspect of my life at the treatment centre, where we were advised by staff to cross the road if we saw a pub. I was also unwilling to attend the (effectively) compulsory AA meetings, where I had to re-live the shame, humiliation and distress which had been part of my life for so many years, but which I was beginning to lose.

When I left the treatment centre, I was still calling myself 'an alcoholic' but I returned to university, this time to study sociology. I began slowly to understand both my drinking, and society's view of it, very differently. I learnt about the purposes and effects of labelling certain groups (Staddon, 2005a), and the contribution to social control made by, for example, viewing women's drinking differently from that of men (Staddon, 2005b). Eventually, despite ongoing mental health problems and other disabling conditions, I was able to obtain funding to do my PhD in the sociology of women's alcohol issues and their treatment. My aim was to find out the extent to which my experience was mirrored in that of other women, and whether other treatment providers also included a moral perspective within their treatment mission.

My service user-led research

The research I undertook was planned together with other women who had survived both alcohol issues and their treatment, and who sought change and improvement in the system (Stanley, 1990). We acknowledged that alcohol use could be emancipatory for disempowered groups, enabling them to escape 'the posture of social controls and self-imprisonment' (Gusfield, 1996, p.72) and hoped to move beyond the culture of 'problem' and 'solution' to one of personal growth and greater social understanding (Ettorre, 2007). We were very aware already that our ways of seeing were quite different from those of the so-called experts in the field, the treatment centres, the GPs, the mainstream alcohol research publications (Wells and Wright, 2003).

The first of two research projects, 'Making a Start', in which I interviewed women who had or had had alcohol issues, is the one to which I will be referring here. It was this first project which was to provide the foundation from which the service user controlled WIAS (Women's Independent Alcohol Support) was to develop. For the research project, I advertised across a large area, both urban and rural, using the press, radio and notices in shops, as well as on notice-boards in treatment centres, asking women who had or had had alcohol issues to get in touch with me. I said I was a woman who had had them herself and was now doing research. I used words like 'has recovered' to indicate that I was not coming from a traditional, medically based approach, whereby 'once an alcoholic, always an alcoholic'. I also hoped that by addressing women across the community, as opposed to the more frequently used approach of recruiting only those in touch with treatment centres, I would reach women who had decided against treatment or who had not yet tried it. In other words, I sought a wider range of service user experience than that which I believed had informed most 'addiction research'.

There was an excellent response, both from the women themselves and from family members, eager to speak of the difficulties encountered in these more traditional approaches and of how they were coping now. I interviewed 23 women in depth, and a recurrent theme was their wish to meet other women with similar issues, in a safe space, without feeling they had to accept any particular 'solution' to their 'alcoholism'.

With the help of the research Advisory Group, I set up focus groups to facilitate the discussion of what problems they had in their lives, why they felt alcohol helped them, and how they had experienced the responses of friends, family, GPs and treatment, including AA groups. I made the times and places easily accessible according to the needs of the different women. These focus groups were a great success. They were attended not only by some of my interviewees but also by some of the service users who made up the project's research Advisory Group. Once people began talking it was as if the floodgates had opened. Some spoke of the fear they felt in AA meetings when it was easy to say the 'wrong thing' and to be 'spoken to' about it after the meeting. All agreed that there was nowhere they could discuss their feelings, their problems and their experiences, without feeling judged. Most found it hard to socialize without a drink, and were full of a mixture of defiance, anger and shame (Ettorre, 2007).

If I had not been a service user, as well as a researcher, if the research Advisory Group had not been made up of service users – perhaps nothing more would have come from these meetings. But the pain and anger of these women resonated with us all. They wanted to go on meeting so we agreed to set up another session, at a time and in a place which we would all agree, even though there was no funding for such a thing at that stage. A Saturday afternoon was fixed upon, which seemed to be when the largest number could get away.

Women's Independent Alcohol Support

Within a short time, a regular group had been established. We had no funding for most of the four years in which this group met regularly. Money was scraped together from here and there to pay for room hire, and one year the Scarman Trust funded us, which was wonderful. We had speakers, went to concerts, and held discussion forums. We joined in events with other service users such as those in the national service user organization, Shaping Our Lives, who also funded our having an Open Day. The great thing was feeling that you were among a group of people who had come through the same fire as you had, but who were now going forwards, rather than continually revisiting the past. We did not intend to let the sufferings of ourselves and of others in our lives become a source of lifelong shame and blame. To the best of my knowledge, none of the women involved throughout, even on a casual basis, has returned to problem drinking. Some came only to a few meetings and then disappeared, but some of these contacted me later to say how much they had benefited from meeting us. Friendship and shared understanding, in a safe place, were what had helped them most, even if they had decided our group was not the right place for them at that time.

We remained a women-only group, because those involved preferred the intimacy of a single-sex group, and the greater opportunity to focus on the issues of importance to them. This preference is amply supported by other research (Barron, 2004; Eliason, 2006; Neville and Henrickson, 2005; Niv and Hser, 2007; Women's Health Council of Ireland, 2005; Women's Resource Centre, 2007). We also disliked having what we were doing seen as 'treatment'. We often felt that it was society that needed 'treating', rather than us. Between us, we had experienced racial hatred and homophobia, sexual and domestic abuse, often from childhood and on into adult relationships, chronic poverty and lack of opportunity, and cripplingly low self-esteem. We saw ourselves as fortunate but determined survivors of an unjust society.

For related reasons, some members also disliked the fourth word of the group's title, 'support'. They felt they were neither offering nor providing support, but reinforcing friendship and socializing. I would say we saw ourselves more as a springboard and a resource and a network than as a support group. This is a subject to which I return in the next section. However the idea of a group called 'wise women' was attractive, and at the time no one could think of a better word than 'support' which also began with 's'.

Gradually meetings became less frequent, as people's lives and timetables became fuller, but the core group has kept in touch, and still meets up occasionally. There are numerous reasons why relatively short periods of 'support' may better reflect and serve the different patterns of women's lives than the lifelong commitment expected of certain mutual aid groups (Currie, Kelly and Pomerantz, 2006; Lavack, 2007). Perhaps most commonly, the family's situation changes; children grow up; work outside the home becomes more important; violent partners leave or die. Additionally, attending groups like WIAS even for a few months may supply the confidence needed in forming new social networks, changing friendship patterns, and beginning new lives. A more positive identity may be developed, and isolation greatly reduced.

Developing a social model of alcohol 'misuse'

My development of a social model of alcohol 'misuse' was rooted in my understanding of the politics of disability whereby people with impairments are disabled by social structures (Beresford, 2002). In the case of 'alcoholism', these social structures, which may engender poverty, abuse, gendered and sexual inequalities, are usually disregarded, in favour of the belief that the person with the impairment, in this case the 'alcoholic', holds sole and personal responsibility for the 'illness' and must seek to amend the 'fault'. A controlling, moral framework is employed, supported by self-help philosophies, which often pay little attention to social components such as gender, shame and marginalization (Ettorre, 1997, 2007; Raine, 2001). This is particularly pertinent to women, whose crucial role, as takers of responsibility for everyone, is emphasized by magazines aimed at them (Roy, 2008). The public health approach is demonstrated in such documents as the Department of Health's *Safe, Sensible, Social* [drinking] (Department of Health, 2007) suggesting that the future for those *who do not look after their health properly* (my emphasis) is bleak.

I have described how lives, including my own, have been changed, over time, so that wounds may heal and more satisfying ways of resolving issues may be found. It would be misleading to call such a socially based process 'treatment', and the WIAS women would not have accepted a definition of their group's function as offering 'mutual aid', with its connotations of taking responsibility for each other's personal rescue. This would have challenged their view of their problems as being primarily external in origin and their solution as being best advanced by active involvement in social change. They saw WIAS more as somewhere to meet like-minded people who were dissatisfied with traditional ways of seeing 'alcoholism' as a lifelong, relapsing condition (Weisner et al., 2003). Its core component was the refusal to judge or be judged, and to challenge morally and medically informed critiques of their lives. Such a challenge has become critical to the wellbeing of particularly disadvantaged groups such as 'alcoholics'.

Discourses of alcohol and drug use offer insights into how social groups exert and retain power over each other. Such use serves different functions, and is seen as acceptable and unacceptable to different degrees, in different societies at different times (Bacon, 1958). Drunkenness may be seen as a privilege, a crime, a disgrace, or a religious rite, according to who is using it and in what way. Its use is always understood locally in very precise ways, deviance from which causes discomfort, and finally alienation from the majority. In this way, it illustrates many aspects of the society in which it occurs (Winlow, 2007). Even the effects of the alcohol on the body may be governed largely by expectation, and these expectations, being based on local mores, are culturally determined: 'the capacities officially attributed to a substance stem, in priority, from moral and political preoccupations' (McDonald, 1997, p.7). Not only the substance is required but also a recognition by the user of what symptoms to expect, in order to experience them. More recent research, using placebo trials, has confirmed that the effects of alcohol on a variety of social, affective, cognitive, and motor behaviours may be heavily influenced by expectation (Peele, 1989; Testa et al., 2006).

Context, then, is crucial. While the powerful public health model has become the dominant way of viewing alcohol issues (Hunt and Barker, 2001), a more multi-disciplinary approach including the sociology of alcohol use, medical anthropology, and public policy might lead to an increased awareness of their diversity and complexity (Marshall, Ames and Bennett, 2001). Gender differences around drinking alcohol are 'universally evident' (Plant, 1997, p.14). The problematizing of women's alcohol use in our society is particularly well illustrated by the way that young women's binge drinking is viewed and documented (Van Wersch and Walker, 2009). Young women are seen as needing to have particular care of their bodies, in preparation for childbirth and nurture, and as mature women are meant to be icons of reliability and security for everyone else (Kelly-Weeder, 2008). Their right to disport themselves in an 'unseemly' way is consequently questioned. Alcohol use is perceived as recreation, to the liberal use of which women may be seen, or may see themselves, to have less right than men (Strang, 2001). However women are 'overwhelmingly' (McDonald, 1997, p.20) more likely to be prescribed tranquillizers than men, and these do not carry a similar stigma, since such drugs as benzodiazepines and Prozac are seen as culturally acceptable for women on a prescribed basis. They are not recreational, and are not even seen as 'drugs', enabling them to continue to support the rest of society, often at the expense of the activities they would have preferred to pursue (McDonald, 1997). They have even been referred to as 'Mother's Little Helper' (song by the Rolling Stones). Problematization too appears to be socially influenced, rather than medically determined.

Alcohol has often provided an opportunity for women and men to behave in differently gendered ways, to experiment with different roles without fear of giving offence and to eschew behaviours which in their everyday lives are seen as their responsibility. Such behaviours are of particular importance to groups who otherwise feel themselves to be oppressed in their daily lives. Carnival, the place of transgression on the borders of society (Presdee, 2000) is often experienced as an opportunity to express dissent and grotesquerie within a designated social space. However the disapproval of the Protestant Evangelist churches endorses the Northern European focus on drunkenness as problem, missing the connection between its providing such opportunities, or indeed the necessity for similar opportunities to be provided (Harvey, 1997). It is this moral focus on drunkenness, as unproductive and wasteful, and even sinful, that has been adopted by organizations such as AA. It is seen as not only a problem but also a *personal* problem, which may affect society, rather than a number of *social* causes which may affect the person. At this point it becomes clear that the problematization is political, at least in its effect.

These aspects of using alcohol were all mentioned at different points in their interviews and focus groups by the women who took part in my research. The more generally held belief that as 'alcoholics' they were women who had failed, who were morally substandard, evoked rage as well as misery. Sometimes the alcohol had been necessary in coping with domestic abuse, poverty, low-paid and uninteresting work, and a lack of opportunity. Sometimes it had lent them the illusion that their lives could be different, more exciting, more glamorous (Bell and Hugh-Jones, 2008). It had often been a friend: their only friend. Most of all, it had offered them a new, and an otherwise inaccessible, perspective.

Engineering change: reflections

The medical model of seeing alcohol 'abuse' as a disease of the will is widespread (Perryman *et al.*, 2011), while the failure of such an approach to produce change in individuals so afflicted is significant (Willenbring, 2010). The cost to society, in terms of physical health and emotional well-being, of incompetent 'treatment' and colossally expensive interventions, is enormous (Kushlick, 2007). Is it possible that a group of women service users has come up with even a part of the answer?

The women in my research described issues which made them 'sick', that made them want to drink. There was depression: 'it's like a big black cloud that follows me about' (H); sexual abuse: 'my father came up behind me and put his hands inside my vest, where I was just starting to develop, and started to fondle my breasts and I felt absolutely terrified' (U); agonizing childhood loss: '[my mother] went on the game; the NSPCC...said she was neglecting us...took us away...I thought it was my fault' (J). Others found alcohol helped with loneliness: 'it fills up the time, I don't notice the time so much' (K); others that it provided excitement that their lives lacked: 'having a laugh...fun...I liked it' (F); 'it's not when I'm upset, it's when I've got something to celebrate' (V).

These are stories of emotional deprivation, whereby the initial warmth of both alcohol itself and the camaraderie it often engenders, filled yawning gaps in the wellbeing of the women concerned. To address the causes of the deprivation requires a close look at what is expected of women, and providing routes to their both overcoming disadvantage and achieving authenticity (Holt and Griffin, 2003; Lyons, 2006), to the benefit of others as well as themselves. Small informal groups which are organized by women themselves, but are funded by a 'community chest', are one way to help achieve this, but there are many others. The ideas are likely to come from the survivors themselves, and they are often likely to be applicable to other disadvantaged groups. This is a way forward which must be small in scale but which may be replicated freely wherever a few service users feel able to meet.

I have referred often in this chapter to 'shame'. It is hard to remember that one is not to blame for the way that life's events have proved too difficult to manage without alcohol, when most of the people one meets see one as having made a 'choice' to wreck one's important relationships and demolish one's career. Yet most people, backed into a corner, will admit that if they found life to be really hard, they might easily kill themselves or take to the bottle. A social model of alcohol use involves looking differently at the sources of distress, seeking them not in the individual psyche but in the very fabric of our society itself (Wilkinson and Pickett, 2009).

References

Bacon, S.D. (1958) 'Alcoholics do not drink.' *The Annals of the American Academy of Political and Social Science 315*, 1, 55–64.

Barron, J. (2004) *Struggle To Survive: Challenges for Delivering Services on Mental Health, Substance Misuse and Domestic Violence.* Bristol: Women's Aid.

Bell, C. and Hugh-Jones, J. (2008) 'Power, self-regulation and the moralization of behaviour.' *Journal of Business Ethics 83*, 3, 503–514.

Beresford, P. (2002) 'Thinking about "mental health": Towards a social model.' *Journal of Mental Health 11*, 6, 581–584.

Cresswell, M. (2009) 'Psychiatric survivors and experiential rights.' *Social Policy and Society 8*, 2, April, 231–243.

Currie, D.H., Kelly, D.M. and Pomerantz, S. (2006) '"The geeks shall inherit the earth": girls' agency, subjectivity and empowerment.' *Journal of Youth Studies 9*, 4, 419–436.

Department of Health (2007) *Safe. Sensible. Social. The Next Steps in the National Alcohol Strategy.* London: Department of Health. Available at www.dh.gov.uk/en/Consultations/Liveconsultations/DH_086412, accessed on 4 April 2012.

Eliason, M.J. (2006) 'Are therapeutic communities therapeutic for women?' *Substance Abuse Treatment, Prevention, and Policy 1*, 3. Available at www.substanceabusepolicy.com/content/1/1/3, accessed on 4 April 2012.

Ettorre, E. (1997) *Women and Alcohol: A Private Pleasure or a Public Problem?* London: The Women's Press Ltd.

Ettorre, E. (2007) *Revisioning Women and Drug Use: Gender, Power and the Body.* Basingstoke: Palgrave MacMillan.

Fingarette, H. (1988) *Heavy Drinking: The Myth of Alcoholism.* Berkeley: University of California Press.

Gusfield, J.R. (1996) *Contested Meanings: The Construction of Alcohol Problems.* Wisconsin: University of Wisconsin Press.

Hall, M., Bodenhamer, B., Bolstad, R. and Hamblett, M. (2001) *The Structure of Personality.* UK: Crown House Publishing.

Harvey, P. (1997) 'Gender, Community and Confrontation: Power Relations in Drunkenness in Ocongate (Southern Peru).' In M. McDonald (ed.) *Gender, Drink and Drugs: Cross-cultural Perspectives on Women, Vol.10.* London: Berg.

Heather, N. and Robertson, I. (1997) *Problem Drinking.* Oxford Medical Publications. Oxford: University Press (Third Edition).

Holt, M. and Griffin, C. (2003) 'Being gay, being straight, and being yourself: local and global reflections on identity, authenticity, and the lesbian and gay scene.' *European Journal of Cultural Studies 6*, 3, 404–425.

Hunt, G. and Barker, J.C. (2001) 'Socio-cultural anthropology and alcohol and drug research: towards a unified theory.' *Social Science and Medicine 53*, 2, 165–188.

International Centre for Drug Policy (2007) *Substance Misuse in the Undergraduate Medical Curriculum.* A United Kingdom Medical Schools' collaborative programme. The International Centre for Drug Policy (ICDP). Available at www.sgul.ac.uk/research/projects/icdp/our-work-programmes/pdfs/substance-misuse-book.pdf, accessed on 2 May 2012.

Kelly-Weeder, S. (2008) 'Binge drinking in college-aged women: framing a gender-specific prevention strategy.' *Journal of the American Academy of Nurse Practitioners 20*, 12, 577–584.

Klingemann, H.K.H. (2004) 'Natural recovery from alcohol problems.' in N. Heather and T. Stockwell (ed.) *Essential Handbook of Treatment and Prevention of Alcohol Problems.* Chichester: Wiley.

Kushlick, D. (2007) 'Addicts' adventures in wonderland.' *Addiction Research and Theory 15*, 2, 123–126.

Lavack, A. (2007) 'Using social marketing to de-stigmatize addictions: a review.' *Addiction Research and Theory 15*, 5, 479–492.

Lyons, A.C. (2006) 'Going out and "getting pissed": Young adults, drinking and gender identity.' Report based on a presentation given at the International Society for Political Psychology Annual Conference, Barcelona, Spain, July.

Marshall, M., Ames, G.M. and Bennett, L.A. (2001) 'Anthropological perspectives on alcohol and drugs at the turn of the new millennium.' *Social Science and Medicine 53*, 2, 153–164.

McDonald, M. (1997) (ed.) *Gender, Drink and Drugs: Cross-cultural Perspectives on women, Vol.10.* London: Berg.

Moncrieff, J. (1997) *Psychiatric Imperialism: The Medicalisation of Modern Living.* Reprinted from Soundings, issue 6, summer 1997. London: Lawrence and Wishart. Available at www.academyanalyticarts.org/moncrieff.htm, accessed on 2 May 2012.

Neville, S. and Henrickson, M. (2005) 'Perceptions of lesbian, gay and bisexual people of primary healthcare services.' *Journal of Advanced Nursing 55*, 4, 407–415.

Niv, N. and Hser, Y. (2007) 'Women-only and mixed-sex treatment programmes: service needs, utilizations and outcomes.' *Drug and Alcohol Dependence 87*, 2–3, 194–201.

Peele, S. (1989) *Diseasing of America.* San Francisco: Jossey-Bass Publishers.

Perryman, K., Rose, A.K., Winfield, H., Jenner, J., Oyefeso, A., Phillips, T.S., Deluca, P., Heriot-Maitland, C., Galea. S., Cheeta, S., Saunders, V. and Drummond, C. (2011) 'The perceived challenges facing alcohol treatment services in England: a qualitative study of service providers.' *Journal of Substance Use 16*, 1, 38–49.

Plant, M.L. (1997) *Women and Alcohol: Contemporary and Historical Perspectives.* London: Free Association Books.

Presdee, M. (2000) *Cultural Criminology and the Carnival of Crime.* London: Routledge.

Raine, P. (2001) *Women's Perspectives on Drugs and Alcohol: The Vicious Circle.* Aldershot: Ashgate.

Raistrick, D., Heather, N. and Godfrey, C. (2006) *Review of the Effectiveness of Treatment for Alcohol Problems.* London: National Treatment Agency for Substance Misuse.

Roy, S.C. (2008) '"Taking charge of your health": discourses of responsibility in English-Canadian women's magazines.' *Sociology of Health and Illness 30*, 3, 463–477.

Sobell, M.B. and Sobell, L.C. (1995) 'Controlled drinking after 25 years: how important was the great debate?' *Addiction 90*, 9, 1149–1153.

Staddon, P. (2005a) 'Labelling Out: The Personal Account of an Ex-Alcoholic Lesbian Feminist.' In E. Ettorre (ed.) *Making Lesbians Visible in the Substance Use Field.* New York: The Haworth Press.

Staddon, P. (2005b) 'Women's alcohol treatment as social control.' *Journal of New Directions in the Study of Alcohol 30*, 47–62.

Staddon, P. (2006) *Treatment Approaches.* Research Report for Avon and Wiltshire Mental Health Partnership Trust and for North Bristol PCT.

Stanley, L. (1990) (ed.) *Feminist Praxis: Research, Theory and Epistemology in Feminist Sociology.* London: Routledge.

Strang, V.R. (2001) 'Family caregiver respite and leisure: a feminist perspective.' *Scandinavian Journal of Caring Sciences 15,* 1, 74–81.

Testa, M., Fillmore, M.T., Norris, J., Abbey, A., Curtin, J.J., Leonard, K.E., Matiano, K.A., Thomas, M.C., Nomensen, K.J., George, W.H., VanZile-Tamsen, C., Livingston, J.A., Saenz, C., Buck, P.O., Zawacki, T., Parkhill, M.R., Jacques, A.J. and Haywood, Jr., L.W. (2006) 'Understanding alcohol expectancy effects: revisiting the placebo condition.' *Alcoholism: Clinical and Experimental Research 30,* 2, 339–348.

Tidmarsh, J., Carpenter, J. and Slade, J. (2003) 'Practitioners as gatekeepers and researchers: family support outcomes.' *International Journal of Sociology and Social Policy 23,* 1–2, 59–79.

Van Wersch, A. and Walker, W. (2009) 'Binge-drinking in Britain as a social and cultural phenomenon: the development of a grounded theoretical model.' *Journal of Health Psychology 14,* 1, 124–134.

Vogt, F., Hall, S. and Marteau, T. (2006) 'General practitioners' beliefs about effectiveness and intentions to recommend smoking cessation services: qualitative and quantitative studies.' *BMC Family Practice.* Available at www.biomedcentral.com/1471-2296/8/39, accessed on 4 April 2012.

Warner, J. (2009) 'Smoking, stigma and human rights in mental health: going up in smoke?' *Social Policy and Society 8,* 2, 257–274.

Weisner, C., Ray, G.T., Mertens J.R., Satre D.D. and Moore, C. (2003) 'Short-term alcohol and drug treatment outcomes predict long-term outcome.' *Drug and Alcohol Dependence 71,* 3, 281–94.

Wells, S. and Wright, S. (2003) 'Stategies for Living.' Presentation by Strategies for Living at Mental Health Foundation (MHF). Social Perspectives Network (SPN) paper from SPN Study Day: 'Where you stand affects your point of view. Emancipatory approaches to mental health research.' 12 June.

Wilkinson, R. and Pickett, K. (2009) *The Spirit Level: Why More Equal Societies Almost Always Do Better.* London: Allen Lane.

Willenbring, M.D. (2010) 'The past and future of research on treatment of alcohol dependence.' *Alcohol Research and Health, Celebrating 40 Years of Alcohol Research, 33* (1 and 2), 55–63.

Winlow, S. (2007) 'T.M. Wilson: *Drinking Cultures.* Review.' *Sociology 41,* 2, 373.

Women's Health Council of Ireland (2005) *Women's Mental Health: Promoting a Gendered Approach to Policy and Service Provision.* Conference Proceedings 2005. Dublin: Desire Publications Ltd.

Women's Resource Centre (2007) *Why Women-only? The Value and Benefits of By Women, For Women Services.* London: Women's Resource Centre. Available at www.wrc.org.uk/includes/documents/cm_docs/2008/w/whywomenonly.pdf, accessed on 2 May 2012.

CHAPTER 12

'There's No Point in Doing Research if No One Wants to Listen'

Identifying LGBT Needs and Effecting 'Positive Social Change' for LGBT People in Brighton and Hove

Kath Browne, Leela Bakshi and Jason Lim

Lesbian, gay, bisexual and trans (LGBT) individuals and communities have long been regarded as 'sexual and/or gender dissidents', resulting in their marginalization and exclusion. While legislative changes during the New Labour era in the UK, to a degree, benefited some LGBT people, LGBT people continue to face marginalization, considerations which are more than scholarly but also have implications for policy and planning. Using an LGBT community-led research project, Count Me In Too, this chapter outlines how partnership working that is instigated right from the design of the research can empower marginalised LGBT people, and yet still contribute to the agendas of those 'in power'. However, even this impact is not uniform across different sectors. Using data on housing and suicide, we show that sexual and gender difference matters in different ways to different people, and that the organizational context in which partnership working takes place is crucial in making research 'do something'. We argue that participatory action research, and partnership working, more broadly, can affect social change, but this is not uniform because of the broader contexts into which the research data comes and is used or not. We conclude by contending that work across community–university–public sector divides has the potential to be productive.

Introduction

> [We] want to consult and engage... We have an open door – we're waiting for a response. (Amanda Fadero, Brighton and Hove PCT's director of strategy, Count Me in Too Bi and Trans launch)

> I'd like to see [Count Me In Too] actually turn into some fruition as opposed to end up as a bunch of statistics in some Council in-tray (Rosa, Trans focus group)

LGBT people have been subject to forms of institutional, cultural, social and personal regulation and often discrimination since these sexual/gender identities came into being. Recently commentators have been split in celebrating or vilifying the 'normalization' of LGBT lives in the UK that has taken place through civil partnerships, workplace and service delivery equality legislation. For those who see these as developing and progressing LGBT rights, such legislation delivers freedom and normalization; queer commentators have questioned this as capitulation to state recognition and regulation (Duggan, 2002; Richardson, 2004; Warner, 1999; Weeks, 2007). We tread a line between these (caricatured) positions in order to explore how LGBT research, which worked with legislative equalities and government imperatives to consult, can address marginalized LGBT people. The contemporary usefulness of examining the lives and specific needs of LGBT people (social, economic, housing, health etc.) is at times challenged on the basis that certain LGBT people do not report difficulties, or understand them as related to their gender/sexual identities. In other words, gender and sexual identities no longer matter where we are 'equal now'. This situation is very different to a UK context where LGBT people were understood as 'deviant' and a 'corrupting influence'. Those who had been 'adversaries' (particularly local council, police and other services) embraced an equalities agenda that sought to incorporate LGBT people through partnership working (see Browne and Bakshi, forthcoming; Cooper and Monro, 2003).

Count Me In Too was a participatory action that sought to explore the realities for LGBT people of legislative changes (University of Brighton & Spectrum, 2011). It was a research project that examined multiple forms of marginalization and addressed the under-engagement of some individuals and groups within LGBT communities from 2005 to 2010 in the 'gay capital of the UK', Brighton (see Browne and Bakshi, forthcoming). Focusing on data collection with LGBT people, rather than comparing between heterosexual/LGB(T), we explored differences between LGBT people. LGBT is a category that is often treated as if it is unified and uniform, and those located in it can be seen to have coherent experiences. The participatory approach to research used in Count Me In Too, which sought to empower marginalized LGBT people, enabled us to explore how gender and sexual difference continues to matter, for different people, and in different ways. Producing data in this way enabled us to purport that whilst some have benefited from legislative change and do not require forms of support, others within the LGBT communities need access to particular services, as well as to be catered for by mainstream health and social care services in ways that take account of, and respect, gender and sexual difference. Thus, considering and recognizing differences among the LGBT collective is not simply scholarly, it has implications for service planning and delivery.

This research was a product of the New Labour era in the UK where services were led by evidence-based practice and sought to operate partnership working (see, for example, Asthana *et al.*, 2002; Browne and Bakshi, forthcoming; Cooper and Monro, 2003).[1] Empirical (both quantitative and qualitative) evidence regarding higher likelihoods of particular kinds of difficulties or marginalization (such as homelessness or suicidal distress) was important in the prevailing climate of evidence-based practice models. Data was believed to have the potential to secure commitments to changing current practices and funding new or improved services. Key to Count Me In Too was not only participatory research that empowered LGBT people, but also partnership working in ways that incorporated policy and service priorities and key people from the outset. This meant contesting traditional divides between community, university and the public sector. Yet, as this chapter will

---

1   This data pertains particularly to the New Labour era and does not address the changes that have been put in place since the establishment of the coalition government and the elections of the Green Party to lead local government in the city of Brighton and Hove. It is valuable in identifying key issues but temporal and spatial factors must be accounted for.

show, feeding into policies and practices, by creating data and processes that were influenced by, and tailored for, providers and policy makers had uneven outcomes.

We begin this chapter by outlining the key processes that created Count Me In Too. This includes discussing data design, collection, analysis and dissemination, and how these used participatory and partnership approaches. We then use the data on housing and suicide to show that sexual and gender difference continues to matter, but how they come to matter is not uniform across LGBT people. Some LGBT people seek and require mainstream and LGBT services.[2] In each section we discuss how the data was 'used' by mainstream and LGBT services, illustrating the diversity between the adoption of changes and LGBT specific initiatives in housing and the lack of engagement with this research in terms of suicide prevention. Thus, just because data was created through participatory and partnership processes, its use is not uniform and cannot be predicted or assumed.

Process, participatory and partnerships

Participatory research can enable inclusion in the research process, as well as challenging dominant modes of research practice (see, for example, Cahill et al., 2007; Pain and Francis, 2003; mrs kinpaisby, 2008). The Count Me In Too research team (consisting of partners from the University of Brighton, University of Sussex and Spectrum)[3] worked not only with disenfranchised communities, but also with local statutory bodies and service providers to consider how they could better cater for a grouping – LGBT people – that was increasingly on their equalities agendas in the early twenty-first century. Figure 12.1 on the next page shows the cogs that can be seen as key for this research, namely 'community', 'university' and statutory partners. Rather than working in opposition to each other, as had at times been the case in the past, the key stakeholders for this research worked together to generate useful data, crossing and blurring boundaries between activism, service provision,

---

2   Mainstream services were often found wanting, and indeed at times perpetuating abuse (see Browne and Bakshi, forthcoming). LGBT services were at times also found to be exclusionary, particularly for bisexual and trans people (see Browne and Bakshi, forthcoming).

3   Spectrum is Brighton and Hove's Lesbian, Gay, Bisexual and Transgender Community Forum established in 2002 to provide infrastructure and community development support to LGBT communities and promote partnership work and community engagement in the planning of services and policy.

researcher, community member, LGBT, cisgendered,[4] heterosexual etc. Working to empower marginalized people (in part through marginalized LGBT people 'sitting at the table' with those perceived to be 'powerful'), as well as engaging with statutory services and those 'in power' in terms of local politics, this research not only examined sexual and gendered lives, it also offers insights into effecting social change through research-based partnership working.

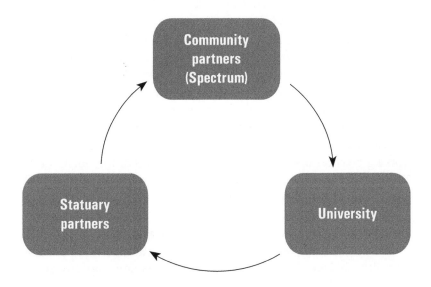

FIGURE 12.1 COUNT ME IN TOO PARTNERSHIPS

There is a danger in participatory work of overstating the power and place of research in addressing inequalities, even within the research process itself (Kapoor, 2005; Kesby, 2007; Pain, 2004; Taylor, 1999). Whilst there can be no doubt that Count Me In Too had an influence on services, policies and planning in Brighton, this is in part because of the context in which it was formed and subsequently fed into. Recognizing that this research operates within and informs broader structures enables an understanding both of how it is created through such a context, and

---

4   'Cisgendered' is used to discuss those whose gender assignment at birth continues to be the gender that they identify with and live within. 'Trans' is used to connote the broad umbrella of transgender, transsexual and other forms of trans identifications and categories, but these are complex and contested categories (see Browne and Bakshi, forthcoming).

how it can be used to effect positive social change. Count Me In Too was part of a broader context of people, groups and services working in a plethora of disparate ways to improve LGBT lives within Brighton. These people, organizations and services did not come together in a single unified body, but came together through practices such as LGBT working groups (for example, the LGBT housing working group) that consisted of organizations and services (across statutory and voluntary sectors and that included LGBT individuals with an interest in that area) who work or are interested in specific areas. These came together with the aim of progressing positive social change for LGBT people in that particular area. The Count Me In Too research was in part created by the working groups (they submitted questions for the questionnaire), who in turn wanted the findings to inform and support their work. Thus, participatory research informed the creation of the data and was then used by those who had an input in creating it. However, the impact that data can have is also dependent on how these networks, associations and working practices operate. This points to the limits of the Count Me In Too research as a research project that informs actions, planning and polices, rather than delivering them.

The chapter will now move to examine the design of the methods, the data collection and how the data was analyzed and reported, which all worked within a partnership/participatory framework. This allowed input by those who sought to 'progress positive social change for LGBT people' and sought specific forms of data to achieve this aim. The control of the research lay with LGBT people through a range of mechanisms during the course of the project, initially through the steering group. Moving through the data design and collection, analysis and dissemination, this section will now explore some of these partnerships and the processes of creating community–university research. The process is summarized in Table 12.1 on the next page.

TABLE 12.1 DETAILS OF COUNT ME IN TOO RESEARCH
PHASES, GROUPS, TASKS AND PARTNERS

Research phase	Leading group	Tasks of the group	Further inclusion of partners
Research design and data collection	Steering group: LGBT people, many of whom identified as multiply marginalized.	Research design: Create focus group questions. Offer insights into identifying/accessing multiply marginalized individuals. Final say regarding questions to be included in the questionnaire Help in the recruitment of participants.	All partners/ stakeholders submit questions for consideration to the steering group. All partners help in recruitment (recruitment is also undertaken through LGBT and mainstream press).
Initial analysis	Action group: LGBT people with the capacity to participate in extended data analysis meetings.	Undertake initial data analysis and identify key findings for initial report. Write community report (accessible summary of detailed initial findings).	All stakeholders invited to findings launch event.
Further analyses	Analysis groups: Closed and confidential groups – All relevant stakeholders – including police, council, health services, and non-aligned LGBT people. Funders and community involved as equal partners.	Analyse findings to produce reports and recommendations that are relevant (including policy and service provision, fitting into government and local agendas) for progressing positive social change for LGBT people. Decide on form of launch event and key stakeholders to be invited.	Reports on – domestic violence and abuse; housing; mental health; general health; bisexual people and trans people, drugs – all key local services have been involved in analysis groups.

cont.

TABLE 12.1 DETAILS OF COUNT ME IN TOO RESEARCH
PHASES, GROUPS, TASKS AND PARTNERS *CONT.*

Research phase	Leading group	Tasks of the group	Further inclusion of partners
Dissemination: Findings events	Open invite to all	Launch the findings. Panel of speakers is invited to discuss ways forward and take further points from the floor including: LGBT people and/or representatives from groups and services; key councillors; heads of service, strategic and policy development managers.	Findings are confidential until launch so no partner is favoured (no privileged access for funders) and media is embargoed until a joint press release is given that includes a discussion of partnership working moving forward.

Operationalizing participatory research in ways that are akin to the ethos of mutual respect and partnerships, Count Me In Too research processes from the outset sought to engage a range of people who identified with more marginal sectors of the LGBT communities. The steering group was thus made up of people who in some way felt part of and simultaneously marginalized from LGBT communities and collectives. This included, for example, people who identified as bisexual who recognized the place of bisexual identities in the LGBT collective alongside processes of exclusion in LGBT contexts (see Browne and Lim, 2008). Different partners were included in various aspects of the research, and the deployment of power, whilst never controllable, was managed by the research team in various ways.

Focus groups were created through partnerships to explore LGBT voices and needs that are often not included in large-scale questionnaires. The steering group listed identities that were disenfranchised from the mainstream LGBT communities in Brighton (see Browne, Bakshi and Law, 2009). For some, this was the first time they had shared experiences with people 'like them'. In order to make certain that everyone who wanted to participate in a focus group could do so, two 'general' focus groups were held. This was designed to ensure individuals' multiple areas of marginalization were acknowledged. Participants were invited to attend any focus group with which they identified, regardless of their attendance at other groups. There were 19 focus groups and one interview in all, with 68 participants. Using the list of 30 identified groups, it was possible to see where there was further work to be done to reach these groups, as well as the marginalizations and individuals that Count Me In Too did not 'reach'. This also informed the sections of the questionnaire that addressed marginalized groups.

The design of the questionnaire was based on a participatory process that crossed community–university–public sector boundaries. Individuals, community groups and statutory services were invited to submit questions that they could usefully employ in their work with LGBT people. Over 400 questions were submitted. Statutory services are often designed around quantification of experiences, framed as a set of issues to be tackled through 'packages of care' or 'service models'. The importance of statistical data was apparent in the questions submitted, and qualitative questions were put in alongside these to gather further information on experiences and opinions. This demonstrates the importance of statistics for setting and meeting targets for service providers in a climate of accountability through measurement. The lead researcher (Kath Browne) and the coordinator at the community partner group (Arthur Law) identified gaps in the questionnaire, particularly around multiple marginalizations as identified by the steering group and used stakeholders to address these. The steering group reviewed all the questions submitted, and reduced the number of questions, and changed the wording where appropriate. This meant that national-level questions, such as that applying to physical activity, also included categories such as 'trans-friendly spaces'. The final questionnaire had 238 questions and had a series of routings which allowed different experiences and identities to be explored in more depth. It was then piloted with all who submitted the questions. In this way, the research empowered LGBT people in the steering group, placing them above funders in deciding the direction of the research and what was to be included in the questionnaire.

The initial findings were released in Spring 2007 (Browne, 2007); these were analyzed with local LGBT people as part of an action group that developed university–community partnerships. We then operated a 'squeezing the sponge' model, in order to extract the maximum amount of data, using analysis groups that worked together in a partnership model across university–community–statutory sectors. During each analysis, the group advised on the information that would be most relevant to the analysis and that which would progress positive social change for LGBT people. The analysis groups met to discuss the data and which questions to ask of the data, and they advised on the reports and the recommendations in each of the reports. A series of additional analysis reports were published between 2007 and 2009; the additional analysis reports included: domestic violence and abuse, safety, housing, mental health, health, trans people, bisexual people and drugs and alcohol (see www.countmeintoo.co.uk for copies of all the reports, summaries of the research findings and details of the process). In this way the data from design to writing up was created through a participatory/partnership model.

The project sought to present its findings in a variety of ways, including launch events that brought together service providers, practitioners and members of LGBT communities; in-depth reports for analysis by service providers, policy makers and LGBT activists; quick read summaries of the findings for interested LGBT individuals; and an exhibition of the findings open to all (see www.countmeintoo.co.uk). Launch events were key, and illustrate the partnership working integral to this participatory project. Launch events were hosted by Spectrum, with relevant partner groups and organizations' top-level managers invited to ensure that the research engaged the services it sought to influence. They were designed to be beginnings rather than endings. In particular, presentation of the research made up less than half of the event. The recommendations were outlined by members of the analysis group (they 'owned' these recommendations as they were reflections of their expertise when combined with the messages from the data). Finally there was an extended question and answer session. During this time relevant and invited heads and representatives of services, commissioners, community and voluntary service representatives and members of the LGBT community took questions from the floor and gave their initial reaction to the data (they were not privy to the data ahead of the launch; however as a compromise to this rather unique position, the recommendations were given in advance where requested). This process sought to show support for progressing social change by working together rather than against those providing services, as well as holding the public sector and others to account for putting the findings into action.

This chapter now critically reflects on two of these findings reports with regard to housing and suicide and the subsequent action that resulted from these findings. We do this to emphasize the diversity of how 'positive social change' for LGBT people was actioned, and the need for participatory researchers to realistically take account of what 'policy changes' can be achieved. We hope for practitioners that this results in critical reflection on how data can be used and what forms of data 'count'.

Housing

What we found

For many LGBT people moving to Brighton and Hove was informed by LGBT identities and lives (Browne and Bakshi, forthcoming; Browne and Davis, 2008). Yet for some the 'gay capital of the UK' failed to live up to its promise and unplanned moves were particularly problematic. Over one-fifth (22%) of the entire sample had been homeless at some point in their lives, 12 per cent whilst in Brighton (see Table 12.2). There is extensive pressure on housing in Brighton (May, 2003) and it is one of the most expensive areas to purchase housing in the UK outside of London. Migration on the basis of sexual/gender identity, then, is always tempered with other social differences, such as gender identities, income, and experiences of domestic violence.

TABLE 12.2 HAVE YOU EVER BEEN HOMELESS?

	Frequency	Percentage	Valid percentage
Yes, while in Brighton and Hove	92	11.2	11.5
Yes, while elsewhere	80	9.8	10.0
No	629	76.8	78.5
Total	801	97.8	100.0
Missing returns	18	2.2	
Total	819	100.0	

Issues of gender identity were key in understanding the diversity between LGBT people and housing experiences. For example, 56 per cent of trans people had problems with accommodation, compared to 24 per cent of non trans people ($p<.0001$). Trans people were almost twice as likely to struggle getting accommodation, compared to other LGB people. One trans respondent relied on their cisgendered partner to find them privately rented accommodation because: 'I couldn't view the accommodation. I got my partner to do that because landlords discriminate against trans people' (Questionnaire).

Family rejection is a common experience amongst the LGBT grouping and includes disengagements with parents, children, partners and others who could act in supporting roles. Thus, 'home' may not be a safe place where coping and survival strategies that deal with gender and sexual discrimination are shared between family members:

> When I got together with my first partner her parents wanted me to stay away from her house and street, and my parents were hostile to her. We often didn't know where we were going to stay next week and sometimes that night. We stayed in very temporary accommodation and slept on floor/sofa/ 'house sat' for friends. It was years before I thought of this as being homeless, because we had a roof over our head. Due to stressful fall-outs with family, my partner started getting panic attacks and I know my mental health was not good. This made it harder to enter house-shares. One person who sublet to us told us to leave when a friend visited her and I think pointed it out we were a couple. (Housing and relationship questionnaire)

This quotation indicates family rejection and the potential for abuse. Thirty-three per cent of respondents who have experienced domestic violence and abuse[5] (this percentage is true of both those abused by family members and those abused by partners or ex-partners) had been homeless at some point in their lives. Survivors of domestic violence and abuse were more than twice as likely to experience homelessness compared to those who have never experienced domestic violence and abuse (16%). The reliance on friends came through strongly in the data. The need to find accommodation with friends to ensure one was not homeless highlights the practical support LGBT social networks can provide. In the qualitative data there was evidence of people staying in unhappy (and potentially) violent situations because the cost of moving was too expensive.

Perhaps unsurprisingly then, income was also a factor in experience of homelessness. Overall, one third of those earning under £10,000 had been homeless compared to 12 per cent of those earning above £40,000. It can be argued that experiences of homelessness are related to income and consequently LGBT people on lower incomes are more

---

5   Thirty per cent of the sample had experienced abuse, harassment or violence from a family member or someone close to them, defined here as domestic violence and abuse.

likely to have experienced homelessness. This can be seen as a form of multiple marginalization, making LGBT people on lower incomes more vulnerable to the risks associated with homelessness, as well as to the various perceptions of their sexual and income identities. There are also significant differences in the likelihood of experiencing homelessness based on sexual and gender identities (those who were bisexual, queer and of other sexualities, were more likely to experience homelessness), disability, HIV, isolation, and mental health (see Browne and Davis, 2008 for a full breakdown). There were also issues identified in how LGBT people coped with homelessness. Eight per cent of LGBT people (n. 59) have had sex or made themselves available to have sex in order to have somewhere to stay (see Browne and Davis, 2008; Cull, Platzer and Balloch, 2006).

Using the data

This data had significant implications for housing support and services across the city as well as beyond this geographic area. With the imperative to consult with local communities and find 'local problems', this research (along with Cull et al., 2006) was important in forcing the recognition of the issues that LGBT people may face, particularly when they are vulnerable and in need of housing support (see also Browne and Bakshi, forthcoming). The LGBT housing working group, consisting of a range of services including local youth housing services, Brighton and Hove housing team, and homelessness charities, held the process of conducting the housing analysis. The then housing officer Petra Davis co-authored the housing report, investing in it personally and professionally. She, along with all who were involved in the research, recognized the importance of both qualitative and quantitative data, such that service providers 'need statistical evidence'. Key service providers in this area, including housing services, the police, as well as local government elected councillors, attended the findings launch. Informal feedback after the event suggested some disconcertion around the findings, as it was presumed that housing services did not have 'a problem in this city' and catered well for LGBT people.

After the launch of the housing report, this data fed into the LGBT housing strategy for the city (see Brighton and Hove City Council, 2009). This was also written by Petra Davis and worked alongside other 'healthy housing' local government strategies such as those that address older people. The process of creating the housing strategy involved significant consultation with local groups and individuals, to ensure that the recommendations were accurate and appropriate. This process at times highlighted differences between what was desired by LGBT people and national government guidelines. (For example, the policy of 'local connection' means that if there are no local connections, work, family etc., then local councils return individuals to their 'home' town (see May, 2003)). However, for LGBT people who may be escaping abusive homes, such a policy may result in placing the person in danger (see Browne and Bakshi, forthcoming). Following the research, the housing officers who work in Brighton and Hove City Council received specific training with regards to particular LGBT issues, including bisexual and trans training. An LGBT housing options officer was also appointed as a result of this research.

The constructive impact of the Count Me In Too housing report can be read as resting in part upon engaging responsive local statutory services, made up of those who are interested and informed in issues of equalities. Housing services were willing to work with and for LGBT people, and housing officers were saddened, shocked and motivated by the findings. Such emotional engagements from service providers were not unusual in the research, particularly in a city where things were supposed to be 'good' for LGBT people. Whilst there are limitations, normalizations and other critiques can be levelled at any attempt to address marginalization. However, critiques that question the use of LGBT, or neoliberal structures that inform the provision of these services, should not overshadow or negate the potentials for an inclusive, collective politics that works alongside and with providers. Key activists within housing services sought to work for LGBT people within particular governmental controls, and issues such as a depleted housing stock, and house/rental prices in Brighton. The use of participatory partnership research thus in some ways 'worked' to effect positive social change with receptive and engaged providers. The data was both used and useful, being created with those who had a stake in actioning it.

Suicide

What we found

Twenty-three per cent of the overall sample had had serious thoughts of suicide in the past year.[6] Fifty-five people had thought about and

---

6   It should be noted that only those who identified with one or more of the mental health difficulties, from the list of significant emotional distress, depression, anxiety, anger management, fears/phobias, problem eating/eating distress, panic attacks, self-harm, addictions/dependencies, suicidal thoughts, were asked about having serious thoughts of suicide.

attempted suicide (7%), with 23 attempting suicide in the previous year, 2005–2006 (3%). Those who said they had some form of mental health difficulty and said they had serious thoughts of suicide varied by identity. Within this category bisexual, queer and sexualities other than lesbian, gay, bisexual and queer, were more likely to have had serious thoughts of suicide than lesbians and gay men. Trans people (56%) were almost twice as likely to have considered suicide in the last five years than non trans/cisgendered (28%) respondents who had had mental health difficulties in the past five years. Those who identified as having a physical disability or long-term health impairment (54%) were over twice as likely as those without a disability (25%) to have had serious thoughts of suicide. Young people (46%) were also more likely to have had serious thoughts of suicide than any other age category, although the figure is also higher for older people (35%). Those on a low income (49%) are twice as likely as those on a higher income (17%) to have had serious thoughts of suicide. Respondents who said that they felt isolated or felt isolated sometimes (47%) were also more than twice as likely to say that they had serious thoughts of suicide as those who did not feel isolated (20%).

TABLE 12.3 SUICIDAL THOUGHTS AND ATTEMPTED
SUICIDES IN THE PAST FIVE YEARS (2001–2006)

	Frequency	Percentage	Valid percentage
Have not experienced any mental health difficulties	139	17.0	18.1
Thought about and attempted suicide	55	6.7	7.2
Serious thoughts of suicide, but did not attempt	135	16.5	17.6
Mental health difficulties, but no serious thoughts of suicide	439	53.6	57.1
Total	768	93.8	100.0
Missing returns	51	6.2	
Total	819	100.0	

Brighton however did provide LGBT services that were understood as unique to the city. These can be life saving. MindOut, for example offered, among other things, advocacy, information and support for LGBT people with mental health concerns, and ran an LGBT suicide prevention project (www.mindout.org.uk). This and other services had positive impacts on LGBT people's lives:

> *Tom:* Well, there are one or two things that I can think of that I think are fantastic about Brighton and Hove, like the fact that there is the Mind LGBT project because there isn't, I believe, anywhere else in the country that has such a project so that's an excellent resource, and on the day of Brighton Pride, I think the access tent is also fantastic and has certainly enabled me to go to something that in the past I have found very difficult to go to and often not gone to despite it being an outdoor space because I am not entirely comfortable in outdoor spaces, I am just better in indoor spaces than outdoor spaces, and the Spectrum has been I think very effective with the access tent. It's fantastic.

> *Terry:* Without MindOut we'd be completely isolated. The MindOut has been a saviour to me and I'm tired of getting rejected, rejected, rejected, rejected and it is the one place that I haven't been rejected. I keep waiting for it [laughter]. I wait for it but it hasn't happened. (Disability focus group)

MindOut was repeatedly recognized as a valuable and important service, one that LGBT people who used it valued and found life saving. MindOut representatives sat on the analysis groups and in public meetings, and discussed how this valuable and important service struggled for funding. Given the existence of this service and the powerful evidence of quantified suicidal distress (alongside other powerful locally based qualitative research – see Johnson *et al.*, 2007), it could be presumed that the Count Me In Too data would be well used.

Using the data

The suicide data was reported alongside the mental health data, arising from and forming a part of the work undertaken by the local LGBT Suicide Prevention working group. The suicide data was not only one of the key findings in the mental health analysis, but also in other findings reports including housing, domestic violence and abuse, general health, safety, bisexual people, trans people. In this way, whilst the statistics were compelling, it was clear that one service could not by itself 'deal with' the issues of, and surrounding, LGBT suicidal distress, unlike housing. At the questions and answers session at the launch of the Mental Health findings, a diverse range of stakeholders were invited to the platform. This included commissioners for the local Primary Care Trust (who commission services for the NHS) and the Sussex Partnership Trust (who undertake the main mental health service provision/commissioning in the area), and these 'big players' sat alongside representatives from MindOut, the Gender Trust (a national trans support and advocacy organization) and Allsorts (the local LGBT youth service). The work of MindOut was celebrated on the night, alongside other local LGBT services such as Switchboard/Counselling Project, who were also present at the launch. Whilst LGBT people with mental health needs had clear lines of support, the need for services dealing with suicidal distress – as with mental health more generally – exceeds provision.

In contrast to housing, where specific needs and specific shortcomings in service provision could be identified and addressed through housing services, the diversity of risk of suicidal distress among LGBT people and the complexity of the causes means that addressing LGBT needs with regard to suicidal distress is not straightforward. Perhaps as a consequence initial discussions around the city's suicide prevention strategy made little mention of LGBT people or LGBT issues in their discussion of vulnerable groups, neglecting Count Me In Too and other local research (Johnson et al., 2007). This was met with disappointment from Spectrum, the community partner organization, and other LGBT activists. Nationally based research, that was located in peer-reviewed journals, was used to indicate that there may be an issue with LGB people (such as King et al., 2003), but locally specific data was still 'required'. One of the possible reasons for their inclusion of King et al.'s work and the exclusion of locally based research, was potentially the absence of peer-reviewed (medicalized) journal articles in the local work (Count Me In Too published most of the policy orientated reports to 'effect social change' before turning to outlets recognized in academic frameworks, such as this one). The data itself was also questioned. Moreover, this research did not use 'randomised control samples' favoured in medical research, and amongst those in the health arena who used 'evidence based practice'.

Research that engages with communities in its design, focuses on LGBT people and refuses to 'compare' between homogenous LGBT groups versus homogenous heterosexuals, does not stand up to the 'rigour' of specific forms of medical knowledge. Of course this argument fails to recognize the differences between 'drug trials' and examinations of social issues, and to us it illustrated the importance of academic outputs, as well as the regulation and control of knowledge. This illustrated how the recognition of what constitutes valid knowledge takes place within particular structures, processes and regulatory frameworks, which means that service providers and community groups do not necessarily share criteria for recognizing knowledge. However, in publishing peer-reviewed academic findings, and findings for the consumption of voluntary and community sector organizations and individual members of LGBT communities, Count Me In Too sought to produce knowledge that meets diverse criteria for recognition.[7] Moreover, the partnership model that Count Me In Too worked within also allowed us to pursue outputs from this research that blur the dividing lines between the needs of academic researchers and the needs of community partners. With both academic and community partners involved in publishing outputs, assumptions about who is able to produce academic knowledge and about what kinds of knowledge are useful for communities have been problematized. This example also indicates that the place and importance of statistics and quantitative data is not straightforward, but rather, through the context in which such knowledge is located, it becomes 'valid' and 'reliable' (or not) in different ways to various constituencies.

Although the process adopted by the Count Me In Too research team to produce the suicide data did not differ to that used for housing or mental health, and commissioners were committed to supporting LGBT people in suicidal distress, there were very different reactions and outcomes. Whilst Count Me In Too and Johnson's (2007) work was eventually included in the Suicide Prevention Strategy (2008–2012) after a significant amount of work by local LGBT groups, in 2010, the broader mental health charity Mind threatened a restructure which would mainstream the MindOut services so valued by participants in Count Me In Too, leading to the establishment of MindOut as a stand alone organization. Count Me In Too was amongst the research used both to justify the need for a specific service and to provide a rationale for the establishment of this charity. However, there remains a difference from housing in the sense that there is no one service that can (should?) cater for the diversity of suicidal distress amongst LGBT people. Even though the city's suicide prevention strategy recognizes the specificity of LGBT

7   Indeed a significant part of the reason for writing this paper is the creation of 'peer-reviewed' knowledge, as data that is validated through a (subjective) reviewing system.

needs, this constitutes only the first step in addressing these needs and the social conditions that often contribute to them. Thus, recognizing LGBT people using the Count Me In Too research is unlikely to be sufficient in itself, given the various and complex associations and the broader social issues that can manifest in suicidal thoughts for some. Elsewhere we have contested the criminal paradigm as the sole way of understanding LGBT safety (see Browne, Bakshi and Lim, 2011; Moran *et al.*, 2004), so too we need to rethink purely medicalized interventions (and services) in creating LGBT health and wellbeing. Further work is needed to explore this proposition, but we hope that this discussion opens this door. Here it is important to note that deploying the same participatory research tools does not necessarily yield identical outcomes, engagements and partnerships.

Critical conclusions: listening to 'them' so that they listen to 'us'

This chapter shows that gender and sexual difference continue to play an important part in defining the lives of LGBT people, particularly those who are multiply marginalized. LGBT communities are affected by suicide but levels of risk vary according to identity, experiences of marginalizations and other mental health issues. Similarly although the figures of homelessness are high and do need attention, this cannot be associated with all LGBT people. Indications of identities within the LGBT collective that are more likely to be subject to these can inform responses to these issues, both in terms of focusing service responses and informing understandings of issues for individuals accessing services. This diversity needs to be accounted for in policy and service provision, as well as through community and voluntary services, and informal support networks. In order to do this, we need to continue to embed participatory research into broader (institutional) processes (listening to 'them' so they listen to 'us'), working in partnership in ways that inform and use research findings. These need to be aware of power relations both external and within research processes. In the LGBT context, recognition of the differences between LGBT communities is important in managing these processes as well as subsequent outcomes. Reconsidering how LGBT research is undertaken and the possibilities of effecting social change, this chapter has not only presented these findings but also reflected on how these were created through partnership working that involved compromises as well as benefits, and how the findings were taken up by those whom the reports were targeting. After all, as more than one LGBT service provider has said, 'there is no point in doing research if no one wants to listen'.

The research grew, and empowered participation and leadership, from within Brighton's LGBT communities. This project, shaped by activists as well as academics, included services at a moment, and in a place, where they were listening hard for an LGBT voice, and sought to communicate diversity of experience within the collective in the language of 'evidence based practice' and partnership working (see Browne and Bakshi, forthcoming). It was key to this process that all partners had a stake in the findings. Using participatory research to bring communities, universities and statutory and voluntary services working alongside each other, puts 'hard' research, practitioner knowledge and experience, and service users' views and understandings into conversation. For us this created both community confidence in the research and generated the evidence needed to provide for marginalized individuals and groups through statutory services, grant provision and so on, as well as producing knowledge informed by a range of viewpoints. This offers a different model to policy makers and researchers (academic or otherwise) generating knowledge regarding marginalized communities without their input, or where research is undertaken without service providers and other input, such that the data generated cannot question or complement current understandings and practice, existing instead (and sometimes necessarily) outside of their 'remits', or fails to address their key targets/policies. The outputs of Count Me In Too were used to inform policy, as well as in demands for and the negotiation of improvements in support, understanding and services by LGBT activists from statutory bodies and other social and welfare service providers.

References

Asthana, S., Richardson, S. *et al.* (2002) 'Partnership working in public policy provision: a framework for evaluation.' *Social Policy and Administration 36,* 7, 780–795.

Brighton and Hove City Council (2009) *Housing Strategy 2009–2014: Healthy Homes, Healthy Lives, Healthy City.* Available at www.brighton-hove.gov.uk/index.cfm?request=c1188834, accessed on 4 April 2012.

Browne, K. (2007) *Count Me In Too: Academic Findings Report.* Brighton: Spectrum.

Browne, K. and Bakshi, L. (forthcoming) *Where we Became Ordinary? Lesbian, Gay, Bisexual and Trans Lives and Activism in the Early 21st Century.* London: Routledge.

Browne, K., Bakshi, L. and Lim, J. (2011) '"It's something you just have to ignore": understanding and addressing contemporary lesbian, gay, bisexual and trans safety beyond hate crime paradigms.' *Journal of Social Policy 40,* 4, 739–756.

Browne, K. and Davis, P. (2008) *Housing: Count Me In Too Additional Analysis Report.* Brighton: Spectrum and the University of Brighton.

Browne, K.B., Bakshi, L. and Law, A. (2009) 'Positionalities: It's Not About Them, It's About Us.' In S. Smith, R. Pain, S. Marston, Jones III, J.P. (eds) *The Handbook of Social Geography.* London: Sage.

Browne, K. and Lim, J. (2008) *Bisexual report: Count Me In Too additional analysis report.* Brighton: Spectrum and the University of Brighton.

Cahill, C., Sultana, F. *et al.* (2007) 'Participatory ethics: politics, practices, institutions.' *ACME: An International E-Journal for Critical Geographies 6*, 3, 304–318.

Cooper, D. and Monro, S. (2003) 'Governing from the margins: queering the state of local government?' *Contemporary Politics 9*, 3, 229–255.

Cull, M., Platzer, H. and Balloch, S. (2006) *Out On My Own: Understanding the Experiences and Needs of Homeless Lesbian, Gay, Bisexual and Transgender Youth.* Brighton: University of Brighton.

Duggan, L. (2002) 'The New Homonormativity: The Sexual Politics of Neoliberalism.' In R. Castronovo and D.D. Nelson *Materializing Democracy: Toward a Revitalized Cultural Politics.* Durham: Duke University Press.

Johnson, K., Faulkner, P. *et al.* (2007) *Understanding Suicidal Distress and Promoting Survival in the LGBT Communities.* Brighton: Brighton and Sussex Community Knowledge Exchange Project.

Kesby M. (2007) 'Spatialising participatory approaches: the contribution of geography to a mature debate.' *Environmental and Planning A 39*, 12, 2813–2831.

King, M., Eamonn, M., Warner, J., Ramsay, A., Johnson, K., Cort, C., Wright, L., Blizard, R. and Davidson, O. (2003) 'Mental health and quality of life of gay men and lesbians in England and Wales: controlled, cross-sectional study.' *British Journal of Psychiatry 183*, 6, 552–558.

May, J.O.N. (2003) 'Local connection criteria and single homeless people's geographical mobility: evidence from Brighton and Hove.' *Housing Studies 18*, 1, 29–46.

Moran, L.J., Skeggs, B. *et al.* (2004) *Sexuality and the Politics of Violence and Safety.* London: Routledge.

mrs kinpaisby (2008) 'Taking stock of participatory geographies: envisioning the communiversity.' *Transactions of the British Geographers 33*, 3, 292–299.

Pain, R. and Francis, P. (2003) 'Reflections on participatory research.' *Area 35*, 1, 46–54.

Pain, R. (2004) 'Social geography: Participatory research' *Progress in Human Geography 28*, 5, 652–663.

Richardson, D. (2004) 'Locating sexualities: from here to normality.' *Sexualities 7*, 4, 391–411.

Taylor, G. (1999) 'Empowerment, Identity and Participatory Research: Using social action research to challenge isolation for deaf and hard of hearing people from minority ethnic communities.' *Disability and Society 14*, 3, 369–384.

University of Brighton & Spectrum (2011) *Count Me In Too: Researching lesbian, gay, bisexual & trans lives in Brighton & Hove.* Available at www.countmeintoo.co.uk, accessed on 25 July 2011.

Warner, M. (1999) *The Trouble with Normal: Sex, Politics, and the Ethics of Queer Life.* New York: The Free Press.

Weeks, J. (2007) *The World We Have Won: The Remaking of Erotic and Intimate Life.* Abingdon: Routledge.

CHAPTER 13

Involving Children and Young People in Research
Principles into Practice

Louca-Mai Brady, Catherine Shaw, Rachel Blades and Ciara Davey

Introduction

In this chapter the authors discuss the involvement of children and young people in social care within the wider context of children's participation and rights, and models of child participation. They then outline how a focus on children's rights has, to some extent, been reflected in increasing interest in children and young people's involvement in research, both as participants (or research 'subjects') and through their active involvement in the research process, presenting a model for involvement developed by the National Children's Bureau (NCB) Research Centre. The practical implications of this model for social care research are then explored through case studies of three NCB Research Centre projects: involving young people in public health research; evaluating the Youth4U – Young Inspectors programme with a team of young evaluators; and involving young people in a study exploring why children who have been in care are disproportionately likely to be remanded or sentenced to custody. In the final section the authors consider the lessons from these projects for the involvement of children and young people in research and the implications for social care policy and practice.

Involving children and young people

As well as being located within the wider traditions of user involvement in social care and participative research, the involvement of children and young people in social care needs to be placed within the context of children's participation and rights. The term 'participation' in relation to children and young people is a multi-layered concept, involving many different processes (Kirby *et al.*, 2003; Sinclair, 2004) and covering a broad continuum of involvement in decisions from consultation to collaboration and young people-led projects. While 'participation' is commonly used to describe the process of listening to and engaging with children, the term is often contested (Lansdown, 2006) and there is no one agreed definition. Boyden and Ennew (1997) state that participation can simply mean taking part, being present and being involved or consulted. More commonly it is defined as the process by which individual children and young people, or groups of individuals, influence decisions which bring about change in themselves, their peers, the services they use and their communities (see Participation Works, 2010; Treseder, 1997).

The case for children and young people's participation in legal, political and social contexts has also been well documented (Sinclair and Franklin, 2000). However Kirby *et al.* (2003) found there was still work to be done in ensuring that participation is meaningful to young people, effective in bringing about change and sustained. A review of the child participation landscape in England from 2004 to 2010 (Davey, 2010) found that although children and young people's participation is becoming more common in relation to service delivery, it is still a long way away from being embedded in the commissioning, monitoring and evaluation of services. The review also noted that significant disparities still remained with regards to the characteristics of children likely to participate in decision-making, the types of decisions they were involved in making and the impact of their views in bringing about real change (Davey, 2010). In addition to the fact that funding for participation is vulnerable to cuts (Davey *et al.*, 2011), not all children and young people have equal opportunities for participation: young children (Waller and Bitou, 2011), disabled children and young people (Franklin, 2011) and those who are marginalised or perceived to be vulnerable[1] (Bolzan and

---

1   The 2003 Home Office Crime and Justice survey defines vulnerable young people as those who have ever been in care; those who have ever been homeless; truants; those excluded from school; and serious or frequent offenders (Becker and Roe, 2005).

Gale, 2011; Moore, Saunders and McArthur, 2011) are likely to have fewer participation opportunities than their peers.

Children's rights

McNeish and Newman (2002) suggest that the acceptance of children's and young people's participation and drive for increased participation has been influenced by a convergence of ideas:

- the growing influence of the consumer
- pressure from young people's groups
- the children's rights agenda and in particular the United Nations Convention on the Rights of the Child (UNCRC)
- the 1989 Children Act and subsequent Inquiry Reports
- the growth of citizenship as a policy issue.

Any consideration of children and young people's involvement needs to be located within this wider context, and in particular within the context of children's rights and the UNCRC (United Nations, 1989), which was ratified by the UK government in 1991. Article 12 of the UNCRC states that all children have a right to have a say in decisions that affect their lives and for their views to be given due weight in accordance with their age and maturity. The right to have a say is a key consideration in a rights-based approach to children and young people's involvement, however other rights contained in the UNCRC are also relevant to children and young people's involvement in social care research, policy and practice: the right to non-discrimination (Article 2); the right to have their best interests as a primary consideration (Article 3); the right to life, survival and development (Article 6); the right to the best possible health and health services (Article 24); and the right to information which is presented in a manner children can understand and use to inform their choices and decisions (Article 13). Within this framework, the right to have a voice is not an isolated right in itself, but can be seen as a means to achieving other key human rights. The UNCRC positions the child as the subject or holder of rights who is an individual and a member of a family and a community, with rights and responsibilities appropriate to his or her age and stage of development.

Models of participation

Models of children and young people's participation, in common with other models of user involvement, generally take a rights-based approach and make distinctions between levels of participation according to the degree of power that is shared or transferred. Hanley *et al.* (2004), for example, identifies the different levels of user involvement in research as consultation, collaboration and user control. Arnstein's (1971) ladder of citizen participation was adapted by Hart (1997) to include children and consists of eight rungs: manipulation, therapy, informing, consultation, placation, partnership, delegated power and citizen control. These eight rungs range from non-participation, through tokenism to the last three rungs, which are identified as citizen power or shared decision-making. Shier (2001) proposed a 'pathway to participation' and encouraged practitioners to explore the participation process, determine their current position and identify the next steps to be taken to increase the level of child participation. He identified five levels of participation:

1. Children are listened to.
2. Children are supported in expressing their views.
3. Children's views are taken into account.
4. Children are involved in decision-making processes.
5. Children share power and responsibility for decision-making.

Kirby *et al.* (2003) offer a similar model to Shier although in a non-hierarchical form (see Figure 13.1).Their model takes as its starting point Article 12 of the UNCRC and therefore only includes participation (i.e. not the lower three rungs of Hart's ladder or the first two elements of Shier's model).

The model is non-hierarchical as Kirby *et al.* (2003) argue that the type of participation activity should be determined according to the circumstances and the participating children and young people, therefore no level of participation in the above model is seen as 'better' than another. Likewise, Alderson (2001) argues that good practice should mean that practitioners ascertain from each individual the level of involvement that they desire, and continue to check this as wishes may change. These ideas are discussed further below in relation to children and young people's involvement in research.

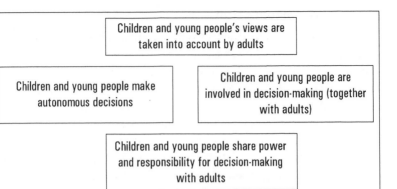

FIGURE 13.1 KIRBY *ET AL.*'S MODEL OF LEVELS OF PARTICIPATION
SOURCE: KIRBY *ET AL.*, 2003, P.22

Involvement in research

This focus on children's rights has, to some extent, been reflected in increasing interest in children and young people's involvement in research (e.g. Kirby, 2004; NCB, 2002; Powell and Smith, 2009; Shaw, Brady and Davey, 2011), both as participants and through their active involvement in the planning and process of research.

Involving those who are the focus of research has been found to have a positive impact on what is researched, how research is conducted and the impact of research findings (e.g. Staley, 2009). In recent years there have been theoretical and methodological shifts amongst many researchers from seeing children and young people solely as objects of enquiry, towards a view that children and young people are social actors with a unique perspective and insight into their own reality (e.g. Bolzan and Gale, 2011; James and Prout, 1990, 1997; Mason and Danby, 2011). As a result of this shift in thinking, and changing views of the nature of children and childhood, there is an increasing focus on the nature of children and young people's participation in research (Dockett and Perry, 2011). Increasing numbers of researchers are now seeking out new and creative ways of actively involving young people in the planning and process of research (Alderson and Morrow 2011; Franks, 2011; Kellett, 2005, 2011; Kirby 2004; Tisdall, Davis and Gallagher 2009).

For social care policymakers and practitioners research which actively involves young people, if used to inform decision-making or policy formation, could lead to policies and services that reflect children and young people's priorities and concerns, although evidence for this is currently limited. In organisations where participation is not already developed, involving children and young people in research could help to promote a more participative culture (Shaw *et al.*, 2011). It could also offer practitioners new ways of engaging with children and young people, highlighting existing or newly acquired skills and competencies and leading to greater mutual understanding and respect.

A model for involving children and young people in research

To be fully participative, children and young people should ideally be involved throughout the research process, but this is not always possible – because of the nature of the research, young people's availability or interest or because young people cannot be involved in designing and writing proposals for participatory research because funding is rarely available to make this possible (Franks, 2011; Shaw *et al.*, 2011). Franks (2011) suggests a model of: '"pockets of participation" where participants take ownership of sections of the research process once it has commenced' (p.23). Franks suggests that such ownership of parts of the research might be ring-fenced and made explicit in the proposal, which would mean that there is sufficient flexibility built into a project to allow for elements of collaboration or aspects which are young people-controlled. However in this model young people are unlikely to be involved in setting the broad parameters of the overall project or defining research questions, unless they do so as part of a project within a project. An example of this approach is discussed in Case Study 1 below in relation to funding ring-fenced for a group of young people to undertake their own research as part of the larger project.

The diagram in Figure 13.2 illustrates the NCB Research Centre model, which makes a clear distinction between children and young people as research participants (the single circle on the left) and their involvement in the planning and process of the research itself (the overlapping circles on the right). The three interlinked circles illustrate the varying degrees of control that children and young people may have in the planning and process of research. The circles are represented as overlapping (and porous), reflecting the fact that – within a single project – the nature of involvement may vary for different children and young people, or at different stages of the research process.

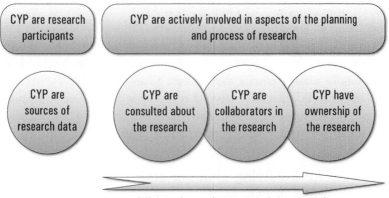

CYP have increasing control of the research process

FIGURE 13.2 MODEL OF CHILDREN AND YOUNG PEOPLE (CYP)'S INVOLVEMENT IN RESEARCH

Reproduced with kind permission from Shaw, C., Brady, L.M., and Davey, C. (2011) *Guidelines for Research with Children and Young People*. London: National Children's Bureau

As with Kirby *et al.* (2003)'s model discussed above the authors do not take the view that one or other form of involvement is inherently 'better' than another; rather, the approach taken will be determined according to the nature and resources of the particular research project or activity and the preferences of the children and young people concerned. This model is explored further in the three case studies below.

Principles into practice – involving young people in research

Case Study 1: The PEAR project

The Young People's Public Health Reference Group (YPPHRG) was a pilot project to explore how young people could contribute to public health research in the UK, linked to the Public Health Research Consortium (PHRC),[2] facilitated by NCB Research Centre and funded by the Department of Health and INVOLVE[3] (Brady, Law and Gibb, 2008). The success of this pilot enabled us to secure additional funding from the Wellcome Trust to continue and extend the work. The project which followed (renamed 'PEAR (Public health, Education, Awareness,

---

2   See PHRC (2010).

3   See INVOLVE (2011).

Research): our voices, our health' by the young people involved) supported 20 young people to contribute to the UK public health agenda from 2008 to 2010.

Two groups of young people aged 12–17 met in London and Leeds, with 16 meetings over the two years of the project (including two meetings and two residentials attended by both groups). Group members received training in public health and research skills, and worked with public health researchers on a variety of projects, including systematic reviews and project proposals. Group members also helped to develop a website[4] for the project, organised a conference attended by 150 adults and young people, and commissioned their own research project on the impact of cyber-bullying on young people's mental health (further information and reports are available on the PEAR project website).

Group members were also involved in various dissemination activities and events aimed at promoting young people's awareness of, and involvement in, public health related research including speaking at conferences, co-authoring articles (Brady and Ghosh, 2009; Brady *et al.*, in press) and producing their own guidance for researchers on how to involve young people in research (PEAR, 2010).

> Because the PEAR group has been involved in quite a few different research projects, lots of adults have asked us for our views on how to involve young people in research. Existing guidance for researchers is often written by adults, so we thought it was important to develop guidelines on how to support young people to get involved in the planning and process of research – giving our perspective on how we would like to be involved. (PEAR, 2010, p.1)

So, in relation to the model in Figure 13.2 on the previous page, in this example the young people were involved at several levels: they were consulted about research (when adult researchers came to seek their input on adult-led projects), worked collaboratively (e.g. when developing the website, co-authoring publications, and organising the conference) and had ownership of a 'project within a project' (when they decided to use the element of the project set aside for young people-led activity to commission the research on cyber-bullying, which they were involved in from drafting the project specification to disseminating the findings).

---

4   See NCB (2011).

An evaluation of the PEAR project by NCB Research Centre staff not involved in the project delivery (Davey, 2011) found that the project was perceived to be very successful by many of the adult researchers who had worked with the group, as well as by the young people involved, and that the group had received a lot of external interest from people wanting to know if it could be replicated elsewhere. The project was considered by one researcher who had worked with the group to be 'an exciting and innovative way of involving young people in an area, and aspects, of research where there was little history of coordinated user involvement'. But the project also uncovered some important lessons for future learning regarding the involvement of young people in public health and social care research, which are discussed further in the concluding section.

Case Study 2: Youth4U – Young Inspectors

Youth4U – Young Inspectors was a two-year programme (2009–2011) funded by the Department for Education to support 33 local authorities in England in recruiting teams of marginalised young people to inspect and report on services in their areas. In each area, the local authority (or a voluntary sector agency) provided a part-time local support worker to recruit, train and manage up to 30 young inspectors. The role of the young inspectors was to inspect local services and provide feedback on how those services could be made more amenable to the needs of young people. The young inspectors could choose to inspect health and social care services; information, advice and guidance services (IAG); extended services in schools; youth clubs and other leisure facilities; as well as more general provision used by young people such as police and transport. By March 2011, 1246 young inspectors had been recruited into the programme across England. Project evaluation found that young inspectors were motivated to join the programme for a variety of reasons, including the opportunity to gain experience, learn skills, and meet new people; they were also interested in playing a part in improving services and helping their community more generally. Young inspectors who carried out follow-up visits six months after their initial inspections found that in nine out of ten cases services had improved.

YOUNG PEOPLE'S INVOLVEMENT IN THE EVALUATION
OF YOUTH4U – YOUNG INSPECTORS

The NCB Research Centre was commissioned to evaluate the two-year Youth4U – Young Inspectors programme and to help them do this, 14 young people aged 14–19, from across England and a variety of socio-economic and racial backgrounds were recruited to work alongside the NCB evaluation team to:

- help design surveys and focus group questions to find out why young inspectors joined the programme and what they thought of it

- lead focus group interviews and other activities with young inspectors to gauge how well the programme was working

- help analyse, write-up and present the evaluation findings.

In relation to the model in Figure 13.2 (on p.232), the young people in this case study were collaborators in the evaluation, as decision-making during the research planning was shared or negotiated with adults. In the collaboration model, young people are potentially involved at any or all stages of the research which may involve (as in this case), young people helping design research tools, collect data, and report or disseminate information to their peers – but adult researchers still hold ultimate responsibility for the research.

Why recruit young people to be evaluators?

Relatively few evaluation projects involve young people as co-evaluators alongside adults, yet with the proper research training and support, there can be immense benefits for both the research and the young people themselves. In the first instance, young people have a unique perspective and can therefore generate fresh and interesting questions to pose in surveys or interviews. With the proper training they can also ask questions in a way that enables their peers to relate to them, and with the right support, they can identify new angles for thematic analysis and ways of presenting information that captures key findings in a way that keeps the research grounded in a young person's perspective. Benefits for the young evaluators also include learning about the research process, how to design data collection tools and conduct interviews, as well as how to analyse data and present information in a way that suits the needs of the audience. Through this project, the young evaluators also gained an insight into the range of services available in different areas and the rights of young people as clients of those services, to have a say in how they are run.

Given the complexity of the Youth4U – Young Inspectors evaluation (of which the data collected by the young evaluators constituted only one part of a much larger body of evidence), employing the collaborative model ensured that the research capitalised on the contribution young people could make to research, in a way which enhanced rather than compromised quality standards. The adult evaluators retained responsibility for the overall project, research ethics and quality, but the ongoing dialogue with and contributions from the Young Inspectors enabled the collection of richer and more valid data as the research was grounded in the lived experience of young people, and the training and support provided to the Young Inspectors ensured that the focus groups were conducted to appropriate quality and ethical standards.

Case Study 3: care – a stepping stone to custody?

In September 2010, the Prison Reform Trust commissioned the NCB Research Centre to conduct research exploring why children who have been in care are disproportionately likely to be remanded or sentenced to custody by exploring the views of young people with relevant experiences. The qualitative study explored the extent and ways in which young people felt that being in care contributed to the likelihood of offending and imprisonment, and what prevented or protected young people in care from offending or being imprisoned.

The research involved in-depth interviews with young people aged 13–17 who were:

- in care/care leavers who had no cautions/convictions
- in care/care leavers who had previously received cautions and/or convictions but who had never been in custody
- in custody or had been in custody (including remand), and had also been in care.

The sample included a mix of young people in terms of: gender; ethnic and cultural background; age; age of entry into care and length of time in care; care settings and experiences of custody.

To help the research team ensure that they approached the research in an informed and appropriate way, VOICE[5] was asked to set up an

---

5   See VOICE (2011).

advisory group. This group involved ten young people, aged between 17 and 24, who were in care or who were care leavers. Advisory group members met the research team three times during key points in the research study to give them advice about:

- the questions researchers should ask young people and how best to ask them

- what the findings mean and how the report should be written

- what recommendations the research should make to the Prison Reform Trust.

At the time of writing, the advisory group had informed the research design, carried out a snapshot analysis exercise, and suggested ideas for the full and summary reports. Each two-hour meeting involved an introduction to the session, the topic for discussion and an outline of the tasks. Young people were given key questions to consider for each task and encouraged to work as a whole and in smaller groups to complete the tasks, with the support of researchers from the NCB Research Centre and a participation worker from VOICE.

At the first meeting, young people discussed a draft topic guide produced by the research team. Their input led to changes in the way the researchers introduced the interview to young people and also influenced the structure and content of the topic guide, for example recommending that interviewees should be allowed to choose in what order issues were discussed. During the second meeting, the group helped the research team with the interpretation of findings, highlighting what stood out for them from a sample of interview data. Their perspectives helped to inform the interpretation, and their views were reflected in the report. In the third and final meeting the group discussed the research findings and helped to draw out learning points and recommendations for the final report.

By informing the research team's approach to the research in these ways, the advisory group has helped to make the study more relevant to social care policy and practice with regard to looked-after children. So, in relation to the model in Figure 13.2 (on p.232), in this case study the young people were consulted about the research. In this model young people are actively and directly consulted at key decision points in the research, in this case on an ongoing basis as members of an advisory group. The group also had an understanding of the wider policy context, as they were consulted by VOICE on a range of issues.

However their involvement in this project was not evaluated so data on group members' motivations for getting involved or feelings on their involvement in the project are not available. The need for evaluation of young people's involvement in research is discussed below but, given the lack of evidence in this area, further consideration should be given to how to evaluate involvement when time and resources are limited (for examples see Mainey, 2008).

Discussion

The case studies discussed in the preceding section took as their starting point the principle that children and young people have a right to be involved in matters that affect them, including active involvement in the research process. As argued by Kirby *et al.* (2003) and Alderson (2001) the level and type of participation should be determined by the circumstances of the project (e.g. funding constraints and limitations, proposed methodology and practical constraints such as resources and timing) and the wishes of participating children and young people. The three case studies illustrate how this can be applied to young people's involvement in research: using the model developed by the NCB Research Centre (Shaw, Brady and Davey, 2011) the approach taken in each project was determined by the nature and resources of the project or activity and the preferences of the children and young people concerned. The PEAR project (Case Study 1) illustrates how different types of involvement may be possible within a single project. But it is essential to be clear with young people involved from the outset about the scope and any limitations to their involvement.

From a children's rights perspective children and young people should ideally be involved in as many stages of a research project as possible, but as with levels of involvement this will be influenced by the views and preferences of children and young people themselves, the nature of the research and the resources available. For example in the PEAR project (Case Study 1) the young people chose to commission a research project rather than carry out all aspects of the research themselves as many of them needed to focus on exams and did not have the time available. In 'Care – a stepping stone to custody' (Case Study 3) young people's involvement was limited to a number of advisory group meetings rather than active involvement throughout the research process, with the aim of maximising their impact within the constraints of a limited budget.

In considering who is involved, Case Studies 1 and 2 were not focused on specific populations of children and young people and therefore conducted open recruitment. Although they recruited fairly diverse groups of young people, those involved tended to have prior experience of participation and/or involvement in research. By contrast Case Study 3 needed to recruit young people who were in care or who were care leavers in order to ensure that their input would be relevant to the research population; having an interest in research was secondary. In addition to personal and demographic characteristics researchers recruiting children and young people for involvement in research need to consider whether there are specific skills or interests that children and young people may have which are relevant to the research topic or methodology; and implications of the size and composition of the group (e.g. a very wide age range or very diverse needs can present challenges in designing activities that are accessible and stimulating for all members). A key aspect of Case Studies 1 and 2 was that a range of experience within the groups meant that young people with previous experience of participation or research could also provide peer support to other group members as well as consolidating and developing their own skills.

Other key lessons from the case studies, which echo the recommendations made by the PEAR group (Case Study 1) in their guidance for researchers (PEAR, 2010), were:

- Anticipate the likely availability of children and young people when planning their involvement (and ascertain their availability individually, once they are involved).

- Spend time making the research accessible and interesting to children and young people, using creative methodologies and group work to encourage all members to participate.

- Ensure that children and young people have sufficient ongoing training and support which is relevant to the activities they will be involved in.

- Provide feedback to children and young people on the impact their input has had as soon as possible after they have been involved, and in a way that is accessible to all members. Be honest about the impact the research is likely to have in bringing about change, and the time this may take.

- At the outset of the project, agree which channels of communication will work best for those involved and explore whether other modes of communication, such as social networking, can be set up so that children and young people can receive up-to-date project news and stay engaged with work in between meetings.

- Build in evaluation of involvement, both of children and young people's involvement in research and through their involvement in the monitoring and evaluation of services (see Case Study 2). There is currently a very limited evidence base on the impact of public involvement in research (Staley, 2009) and even less for children and young people's involvement.

Recognising that children and young people are experts in their own lives is vital to ensuring that their voices, including those from marginalised backgrounds or perceived to be 'harder to reach' or vulnerable, influence social care and other research, policy and practice. Involving commissioners, policymakers and practitioners, as well as young people in thinking creatively about how young people can be involved in social care research, will help to ensure that policies and services reflect children and young people's priorities and concerns. Involving children and young people in the commissioning, monitoring and evaluation of services as well as their delivery will help to ensure services that are relevant to children and young people and in which they are engaged as stakeholders. In an environment where resources are increasingly scarce the involvement of young people in research offers opportunities to develop evidence-based services which reflect the needs and experiences of current and potential young service users.

References

Alderson, P. (2001) 'Research by children.' *International Journal of Social Research Methodology 4*, 2, 139–153.

Alderson, P. and Morrow, V. (2011) *The Ethics of Research with Children and Young People: A Practical Handbook*. London: Sage.

Arnstein, S. (1971) 'A ladder of citizen participation.' *Journal of the Royal Planning Institute 35*, 4, 216–24.

Becker, J. and Roe, S. (2005) *Drug Use Among Vulnerable Groups of Young People: Findings From the 2003 Crime and Justice Survey*. Home Office Findings 254. London: Home Office.

Bolzan, N.P. and Gale, F. (2011) 'Expect the unexpected.' *Child Indicators Research 4*, 2, 269–281.

Boyden, J. and Ennew, J. (1997) *Children in Focus: A Manual for Participatory Research with Children*. Stockholm: Radda Barnen.

Brady, L. and Ghosh, G. (2009) 'Involving Young People in Public Health Research.' *INVOLVE Newsletter: Summer 2009*. Available at www.invo.org.uk/Newsletters.asp, accessed on 4 April 2012.

Brady, L.M., Davis, E., Ghosh, A, Surti B. and Wilson, L. (in press) 'Involving Young People in Research: Making an Impact in Public Health.' In M. Barnes and P. Cotterell (eds) *Critical Perspectives on User Involvement*. Bristol: Policy Press.

Brady, L.M., Law, C. and Gibb, J. (2008) *Young People's Public Health Reference Group: Pilot Project - Final Report*. London: NCB. Available at www.york.ac.uk/phrc/YPPHRG_FR_1.08.pdf, accessed on 4 April 2012.

Davey, C. (2010) *Children's Participation in Decision-making: A Summary Report on Progress made up to 2010*. London: NCB.

Davey, C. (2011) *Evaluation of the PEAR Project*. London: NCB.

Davey, C., Gill, C., Gibb, J., Lea, J. and Shaw, C. (2011) *An Evaluation of the Youth4U Programme*. London: NCB.

Dockett, S. and Perry, B. (2011) 'Researching with young children: seeking assent.' *Child Indicators Research 4*, 2, 231–247.

Franklin, A (2011 – in press) *Developing the Participation of Children and Young People: Literature Review*. London: NCB. Available at www.ncb.org.uk/cdc/wider_projects/participation_research. aspx, accessed on 4 April 2012.

Franks, M. (2011) 'Pockets of participation: revisiting child-centred participation research.' *Children and Society 25*, 1,15–25.

Hanley, B., Bradburn, J., Barnes, M., Evans, C., Goodare, H., Kelson, M., Kent, A., Oliver, S., Thomas, S. and Wallcraft, J. (2004) *Involving the Public in NHS, Public Health and Social Care Research: Briefing Notes for Researchers*. Eastleigh: INVOLVE.

Hart, R. (1997) *Children's Participation: The Theory and Practice of Involving Young Citizens in Community Development and Environmental Care*. New York: Unicef.

INVOLVE (2011) *INVOLVE* [online]. Available at www.invo.org.uk, accessed on 11 May 2011.

James, A. and Prout, A. (1990) *Constructing and Reconstructing Childhood*. Basingstoke: Falmer Press.

James, A. and Prout, A. (1997) *Constructing and Reconstructing Childhood: Contemporary Issues in the Sociological Study of Childhood*. London: Falmer Press.

Kellett, M. (2005) *How to Develop Children as Researchers*. London: Paul Chapman.

Kellet, M. (2011) 'Empowering children and young people as researchers: overcoming barriers and building capacity.' *Child Indicators Research 4*, 2, 205–219.

Kirby, P., Lanyon, C., Cronin, K. and Sinclair, R. (2003) *Building a Culture of Participation: Involving Children and Young People in Policy, Service Planning, Delivery And Evaluation*. London: DfES.

Kirby, P. (2004) *A Guide to Actively Involving Young People in Research, for Researchers, Research Commissioners and Managers*. Eastleigh: INVOLVE.

Lansdown, G. (2006) 'International Developments in Children's Participation: Lessons and Challenges.' In K. Tisdall, J. Davis, M. Hill, A. Prout (eds) *Children, Young People And Social Inclusion: Participation For What?* Bristol: Policy Press.

Mainey, A. (2008) *Evaluating Participation Work: the Toolkit and the Guide*. London: Participation Works. Available at www.participationworks.org.uk/resources/evaluating-participation-work-the-toolkit-and-the-guide, accessed on 4 April 2012.

Mason, J. and Danby, S. (2011) 'Children as experts in their lives: child inclusive research.' *Child Indicators Research 4*, 2, 85–189.

McNeish, D. and Newman, T. (2002) 'Involving Children and Young People in Decision Making: What Works for Children?' In D. McNeish, T. Newman and H. Roberts (eds) *Effective Services for Children and Families*. Buckingham: Open University Press.

Moore, T., Saunders, V. and McArthur, M. (2011) 'Championing choice: lessons learned from children and young people about research and their involvement.' *Child Indicators Research 4*, 2, 249–267.

NCB (2002) *Including Children in Social Research.* Highlight no.193. London: NCB.

NCB (2011) *PEAR Young People's Public Health Research Group.* Available at www.ncb.org.uk/PEAR, accessed on 11 May 2011.

Participation Works (2010) *Listen and Change: A Guide To Children And Young People's Participation Rights.* London: Participation Works (Second Edition).

PEAR (2010) *Young People in Research: How To Involve Us. Guidance for Researchers from the PEAR Young People's Public Health Group.* London: NCB. Available at www.ncb.org.uk/PEAR, accessed on 4 April 2012.

PHRC (2010) *Young People's Group* [online]. Available at phrc.lshtm.ac.uk/project_2005_2011_ ypphrg.html, accessed on 11 May 2011.

Powell, M.A. and Smith, A.B. (2009) 'Children's participation rights in research.' *Childhood 16,* 1, 124–142.

Shaw, C., Brady, L.M. and Davey, C. (2011) *Guidelines for Research with Children and Young People.* London: National Children's Bureau.

Shier, H. (2001) 'Pathways to participation: openings, opportunities and obligations: a new model for enhancing children's participation in decision-making, in line with Article 12.1 of the United Nations Convention on the rights of the child.' *Children and Society 15,* 2, 107–117.

Sinclair, R. (2004) 'Participation in practice: making it meaningful, effective and sustainable.' *Children and Society 18,* 2, 106–118.

Sinclair, R. and Franklin, A. (2000) *A Quality Protects Research Briefing: Young People's Participation.* London: Department of Health, Research in Practice and Making Research Count.

Staley, K. (2009) *Exploring Impact: Public Involvement in NHS, Public Health and Social Care Research.* Eastleigh: INVOLVE.

Tisdall, K., Davis, J. and Gallagher, M. (2009) *Researching with Children and Young People.* Sage: London.

Treseder, P. (1997) *Empowering Children and Young People Training Manual: Promoting Involvement in Decision Making.* London: Save the Children.

United Nations (1989) *Convention on the Rights of the Child.* Geneva: The Office of the United Nations High Commissioner for Human Rights.

VOICE (2011) *Voice.* Available at www.voiceyp.org, accessed on 11 May 2011.

Waller, T. and Bitou, A. (2011) 'Research with children: three challenges for participatory research in early childhood.' *European Early Childhood Education Research Journal 19,* 1, 5–20.

CHAPTER 14

'Involving People with Learning Difficulties and Self-advocacy'

Maggie Brennan, Vic Forrest and Jennifer Taylor

'Who we are and why this chapter is written as it is' (Vic)

'Three of us have written this chapter. We are called Jennifer Taylor, Maggie Brennan and Vic Forrest' (Vic). 'The three of us are all researchers' (Jennifer) 'and service users' (Vic). 'One is a supporter and two of us have got learning difficulties' (Jennifer). 'Vic is supporting Jennifer and Maggie to write this chapter and also writing himself about the support of people with learning difficulties' (Vic).

'We are making this chapter easy to read so professionals and some people with learning disabilities can understand it' (Maggie). 'We have our names next to what we said so people can see who wrote each part of the chapter' (Jennifer). 'So society can understand that people with learning disabilities can write a chapter' (Maggie). 'Also, so that the supporter on this project can be clear about what is his work and what is not; so he does not write his views into the work of the people with learning difficulties' (Vic).

'This is how Jennifer wanted to describe herself' (Vic): 'I am a parent with two boys who don't live with me. I am a researcher and I've done a book called *We Are Not Stupid* with people with learning difficulties (Taylor *et al.*, 2007). I have learning difficulties myself... I am a black woman and I go to a lot of meetings around the country and do a lot of speaking up for people with learning difficulties.'

'Maggie wanted to say the following about herself' (Vic): 'I have a learning disability. I have a job. I work as a self-advocacy worker. I go to loads of meetings. I go to Shaping Our Lives National User Group meetings and also I am on Lambeth's Partnership Board.'

'This is what Vic wanted to say about himself. I have worked with people with learning difficulties in supportive roles for around 30 years, and as a self-advocacy supporter for more than half of that time. I've been supporting people with learning difficulties on research and writing projects for the last ten years. I do my own research and writing as well, mostly about supporting people with learning difficulties.'

'About our writing' (Vic)

'Although we have been involved in and started research projects that include the experiences and views of other people with learning difficulties and their supporters, to some extent all three of us are writing from our own first-hand experience' (Vic). 'We have had a lot of experience... [in] the things we are writing about' (Maggie). 'This sort of writing can be seen as valuable information or evidence for understanding different social situations in life (Beresford, 2003; Etherington, 2004a, 2004b). When we talked about what evidence meant we thought it could be explained as information that can be used towards proving something.

We will also be mentioning some research we and other people have done. By mentioning research, some of which has people's first-hand experience in it and some of which doesn't, we will be adding some more evidence to what we are writing. It would be good if more people wrote about their experience and did research on this subject to get more evidence about' (Vic) 'supporting people with learning disabilities, [and people with learning difficulties] getting involved with people' (Maggie).

'People First Lambeth and self-advocacy' (Vic)

'We all work in People First Lambeth' (Vic). 'People First Lambeth is an organisation for people with learning difficulties. Also some of the supporters have got learning difficulties' (Maggie). 'It is a self-advocacy organisation' (Vic). 'People with learning difficulties run People First Lambeth... All the Management Committee members have learning difficulties' (Jennifer).

'This is a list that the Training Group at People First Lambeth made about what self-advocacy is' (Maggie):

- Self-advocacy is speaking up for yourself about how you want to live and what you want out of your life.

- Self-advocacy is people speaking up for themselves. They have got the right to speak up for themselves and for people to understand them.

- Self-advocacy is being in control of yourself and your rights and what you want to do, not what other people tell you to do.

- Self-advocacy is taking control of your own life, not letting people take over your life and make you do things you don't want to do in your life.

- Self-advocacy is living independently if you want to.

- Independence is quite a big thing. Independence means where you can live in your own flat without your parents being there. Being independent means doing what you want. If you want to fly a kite you can go and fly a kite. If you want to go to America you can (if you have the money). It is having a life, just being yourself. It is being respected. Sometimes you need support to be independent, to do what you want. Being independent doesn't just mean doing everything yourself without support.

- Self-advocacy is speaking up for other people with learning difficulties as well. Sometimes people can't speak. They do sign language. It is especially important to speak up for other people with learning difficulties in meetings.

- Self-advocacy is about being powerful and feeling strong.

- Self-advocacy is hard sometimes.

'Self-advocacy is important because it is for people like us to speak up for ourselves and to have a life of our own' (Jennifer). 'It is important to speak up for yourself and you need power and the rights to have control of your life, and people can't take over your life... People with learning difficulties can't be involved in anything if they have no power and no control [over]...their lives' (Maggie). 'People with learning difficulties should be in control of self-advocacy groups... People with learning difficulties should also be in control of self-advocacy organisations' (Jennifer).

'What involving people with learning difficulties means' (Vic)

'This book chapter is about involving people with learning difficulties in' (Vic): 'what is important to us' (Jennifer). 'Involving means getting people involved in the community' (Maggie). 'Some people need help with shopping and to get around in the community, like getting their bus pass, or helping them get their money, or helping them get support, or helping them get information that they want to find out – just getting out and about in the community, being part of the society as well' (Jennifer).

'People with learning difficulties can get involved in other things that are important to them like' (Vic): 'researching' (Maggie). 'Involving [also] means getting people with learning difficulties to get together with other people, but sometimes on our own, to do the work. Involving means joining in with other people to do the work and not being left out' (Jennifer).

'Some of the projects Jennifer and Maggie are involved in' (Vic)

Jennifer said: 'I get involved with SCIE [the Social Care Institute for Excellence's] Partners' Council and Shaping Our Lives National User Group, talking about how we want things to change... I am there to spread the word to people and get it across to them...our voices, and to make them listen to us as people with learning difficulties, what we want... I work with people to plan and make things better for people with learning difficulties across the country.

I also write things down for people with learning difficulties if they can't read or write at People First Lambeth. We do training at People First Lambeth to train staff up to get them to understand us better as people...and [we also train] people with learning difficulties as well' (Jennifer). 'We train them to speak up for themselves, [and explain to them that] people shouldn't tell them what to do' (Maggie).

Maggie said: 'I go to a lot of meetings and I've done a talk in Oxford about the book [*We Are Not Stupid* (2007) that Maggie and Jennifer have co-written with other people with learning difficulties]. [I have worked on] making things easy reading... A lot of people can't read so [I have been involved in choosing] more pictures so they can understand... I speak up for them [people with learning difficulties] if they have got a problem, because people do come in [to People First Lambeth] upset. If

I can't help them I get someone to help me. I speak to them... We did a conference in York [part of a research project] where we spoke to the service users with learning difficulties. They have lived in residential homes nearly all their lives, like institutions... I was telling them, don't you go shopping on your own? Is staff there with you all the time? Don't you get a choice to do what you want to do? You should have choices, don't you have choices in life? And don't you have power? We should have power and we should have choices in life, you know to have a boyfriend or a girlfriend, a relationship. They shouldn't have people walking into their rooms' (Maggie).

Vic asked 'Are you working to make things better just for people with learning difficulties?' Jennifer said 'and to get the society to listen to us and stop calling us nasty names and look up to us as people with learning difficulties, because they are the ones that are pulling us down and making us look small, and we're not, and things need to change for the better in future... People should not push us away, because it seems they're pushing us away in the society, not making us be in the society and be part of it and they don't see eye to eye with people with learning difficulties right now... They [people in society] should work with us, like a partnership and just make a difference you know. Even if we go in the restaurant or café, cinemas or to a night club or something, and just be part of the society [they should] not just push us underneath the carpet like some people do all the time.'

Vic asked 'So are you working to make things better just for people with learning difficulties or other people too?' Jennifer said: 'Other people too yeah'... Maggie said: 'We are helping people who have got mental health problem[s] to blind [people], [people] in wheelchairs [and people with a] hearing [and/or] speech impediment.' Jennifer said: 'Sometimes...it is good to work...with people with mental health problems and people who are disabled and people who are blind as well... I like to help with other service users as well.'

WHAT WE ARE SAYING (JENNIFER AND MAGGIE)

'Jennifer and Maggie do a lot of work on research, and other work as well, getting people to speak up for themselves and...be involved in activities and...the society' (Jennifer)... [They also work at] 'supporting people just to be themselves, and have power' (Maggie) 'in their lives' (Jennifer). 'They don't just work with people with learning difficulties... They work with social care staff...and professionals like the Fire Brigade and social services...and disabled people as well' (Jennifer).

'The point of being involved and why it is important' (Vic)

'Jennifer said the point of being involved is' (Vic) 'to stop the society being nasty to people with learning difficulties...and people with mental health issues and people who are disabled. That is what we are trying to do in all of our meetings, stop society bullying us and giving us dirty looks because they don't understand where we are coming from... We are trying to get across to them [society] that we can do research, [or be part of a] Partnership Board. [We can do] anything with a bit of help.'

'Vic asked Jennifer and Maggie why it is important for people with learning difficulties to be involved in things that are important to them. Jennifer said the following' (Vic): 'to be somebody as a person with learning difficulties and to show the whole world what we can do without people bringing us down all [the] time, making us look stupid when we are not. We want to be the person we want to be in our lives' (Jennifer).

Maggie said this: 'People with learning difficulties are no different to anyone else. They can do jobs... We've got the power. We've got the choice. People can't take over us. People with learning difficulties are not stupid and we should be involved in research, getting more high power jobs. We can do it. We should go and visit more people in power.'

'Vic asked why people with learning difficulties should be involved in society and the running of the services that are there for them. This is what Maggie said' (Vic): 'We've got the right haven't we. I've got a job... We [also] know what it is like to get services. Some services are good, some are bad... (Taylor et al. 2007). I've had bad social services in the past...putting me in homes I don't like. We know what it is like to have bad power... Well, people take over and they don't give us a chance. In the past people have not given me a chance. I've been hit across the head [by a social care worker]'.

'We want to change the society for the better, for the future, to stop people without learning difficulties pulling us down' (Jennifer). 'Some people try and take over our lives' (Maggie). 'The point of being involved is...us having our own decisions [and] making them (the people without learning difficulties) look up to us rather than down at us, and being proud of what we are doing, achieving something in our lives... We want a life like everybody else – like being ourselves, like having confidence and doing things for ourselves, not for people out in the world, ourselves... The society doesn't see people with learning difficulties as full citizens but we want the society to see us as full citizens, because we are people with learning difficulties...living a life like everybody else' (Jennifer).

'Some people with learning difficulties do get treated really badly' (Jennifer). 'People get bossed around' (Maggie) 'and get told what to do all the time' (Jennifer). 'They don't get a choice to go out in the evening or have a say [about] what they want to do' (Taylor *et al.*, 2007; House of Lords House of Commons Joint Committee on Human Rights, 2008; Beresford *et al.*, 2005) (Maggie). 'It is wrong because they don't own people with learning difficulties' (Jennifer)... 'We have got power... We have got rights' (Maggie).

'It is important to talk about culture (Department of Health, 2001), and as a black woman with learning difficulties I think, for me, it's for people to stop being racist to black people...and people of every culture... I like to have black people around in People First [Lambeth] because they have got a right to be here as well as white people...I like to see people mixing in and getting on...being friendly' (Jennifer).

WHAT WE ARE SAYING (JENNIFER AND MAGGIE)

'We want to be part of this society to get people to start thinking about what they are doing to us... We want to show people how it feels to have learning difficulties' (Jennifer). 'We want to show them that we have got the power and the rights, that we can do it..., groups and meetings, our way and no one can take over' (Maggie). 'We want everybody to get on with everybody with a different culture and people who are gay and people with learning difficulties, everybody, and then the world would be a better place to live in' (Jennifer).

'Not getting involved in meetings' (Jennifer)

'Not all the meetings that we've been to are good meetings, because they don't get people with learning difficulties involved…sometimes. If the meeting is important to…just them they…want us there for the fun of it, just sitting there listening to what they've got to say, not asking us questions, not [giving us a chance to say] what we want to say to them' (Jennifer). Jennifer said 'once I went to a meeting. It was a social services meeting and they were talking among themselves and they didn't ask me if I wanted to say anything in the meeting. They just wanted me to be there just to listen to them really… It was like a big round table with all the social workers there and there was just me there with a learning difficulty and they didn't ask me if I wanted to join in. So I just walked out really.'

Maggie said 'I have had bad experiences in inspection [when Maggie took part in a particular inspection of services]. They just left me out… They didn't introduce me to people. We went to some day centres and they used too many long words and they didn't understand me. They didn't look at me. They just left me out. I went to loads of meetings [to do with that inspection] and you just sit there and they avoid you. It was a bad experience. Some of the meetings I didn't understand them. They were so long.'

'Involving people with learning difficulties in meetings' (Vic)

'We like working with other people with learning difficulties…because we know what it is like to have learning difficulties, and we know what it is like to live with learning difficulties as well' (Jennifer). 'I like working with other people with learning difficulties because when we are all together no one can take over and interfere… We work out what things to say and what power is' (Maggie). 'We want to know where we are coming from as people with learning difficulties. [When we get together with other people with learning difficulties] we learn who we are inside…as a person with learning difficulties, and to be proud of who we are as well…and not to be ashamed about it' (Jennifer).

'We like to do things with people who haven't got learning difficulties as well… [and] we need things to make it easy for us' (Maggie). 'We like to talk about the [agenda] with a supporter before the meeting, to talk about what we have got to do in it' (Maggie), 'to get what the meeting is all about and to know what they are talking about in the meeting'

(Jennifer). 'Ground rules help us because we want to make sure that no one is nasty towards us in the meeting. So it is important to put that down in every meeting that we go to... It is important to put your hand up...(everyone at the meeting)...because people don't get a chance to say what they want to say...if everyone doesn't put their hand up' (Jennifer) 'they just jump in [to the conversation] and they don't give us a chance to talk' (Maggie).

Jennifer said: 'I have noticed with some people with learning difficulties they don't like big groups or being in a big room with a lot of people... If they are having a workshop they like to have a small group... Sometimes I like big groups because I want to get it out in the open, and other times I like small groups as well because it is easier for me to put my views across.'

'We want people to be friendly and nice to us and come up to us... and be in a conversation with us' (Jennifer). Jennifer said: 'It is very hard to go up to a person I don't know. You don't know what to say to them.' Maggie said: 'Sometimes I find it hard to talk to strangers myself.' 'We want people to talk in English... Plain English not jargon words, for us to understand them' (Jennifer).

'People shouldn't talk fast because a lot of people don't understand... what they are saying' (Maggie). 'People need to write things down for us – what they [the people at the meeting] said in the meeting... We want the minutes after the meeting, to be posted to us...so we can go over them to know what they were talking about in the meeting... We like to get the papers easy to read and understand [them] before we do the meeting' (Jennifer). 'We like to get pictures because some people can't read well... The pictures help us with [understanding] the writing. We should train more people to learn how to work with us' (Maggie). 'We train professionals to do a better job...working with people with learning difficulties' (Jennifer).

'We need supporters to help us do what we want to do' (Jennifer)

'People with learning difficulties need support to help them do things in their lives – what they want to do' (Jennifer). 'Good power is a good worker, a good support person. They don't tell you what to do. They don't take over. That's good power... They help you to do what you want in life' (Maggie).

'My supporters at People First [Lambeth] help me to write things and they type them out for me and help me with organising things like making telephone calls that I can't understand sometimes...and to read and understand letters sometimes. They are good at supporting me because they are good support workers, because they make sure they don't take over. They support me if there are any problems to do with my work. They help me run the groups [at People First Lambeth]' (Maggie).

'A supporter is to help you... They have to be helpful and know what they are doing. They have got to be kind and caring. That is part of their job. They have got to listen, [give you] eye contact [and] treat you like an adult' (Maggie). 'The supporter should be friendly towards people with learning difficulties because it is important to us... It could be hard to get on with a supporter who was not friendly... We like to have a laugh and a joke... It makes us feel comfortable'.

They have to be confident [in] what they do in their job and not take over what the client wants to do in their life. They need to be supporting people to do what they want to do... Supporters need to listen to the client and understand them. ... If I had a bad supporter I would feel very upset and be very uncomfortable, if she kept on my back all the time... A bad supporter is someone who takes over a person's life... We need supporters to do a good job... They are there to support you to do what you want to do.

A supporter shouldn't be nagging at a person with learning difficulties. It has happened to me a little bit but not all the time at [a named residential home]. They were kind of telling me to go and tidy up my bedroom and go and have a bath and come to the group meetings and telling me to go and do my shopping and all that and I knew what I had to do, because I knew what I was doing... It made me feel really uncomfortable it did. This is what some people with learning difficulties find... They (the staff) are on their backs all the time (Taylor et al., 2007)...and if it's not that, they come into your bedroom to see what you are doing' (Jennifer).

'Vic asked what we mean by the word "supporter" in this chapter... Maggie said' (Vic): 'We mean all the people who give support. Not just in self-advocacy organisations but outside organisations as well... Like I get support doing budgeting, [and with] going out from [a named organisation that supports people to live in their own homes].'

> ### WHAT WE ARE SAYING (JENNIFER AND MAGGIE)
>
> 'We need supporters to help us do things we can't do' (Maggie). 'Not all support workers are nice. There are some nice ones' (Maggie). 'People who support people with learning difficulties outside, not just here [in People First Lambeth], should give us the right support...it's just the same [it's all support]. No one can take over your lives and tell you what to do' (Maggie). 'Good supporters are kind and very friendly. They treat you like an adult and they don't take over at all' (Jennifer).

'The role of the supporter' (Vic)

'In his research about self-advocacy, Dan Goodley (2000) has written that supporters can have a lot of power. He has argued that there may be a need for supporters to understand and challenge the ways that people with learning difficulties are silenced and have power taken away from them. He has written that there may be a need for supporters to work in ways that support the *self-empowerment* of people with learning difficulties. This is the way that supporters in People First Lambeth try to work – supporting people with learning difficulties to do what they want to do, in their own ways (Forrest and Taylor, 2010).'

'The social model, training, education and self-advocacy' (Vic)

'Understanding and taking on board the social model of disability and what it could mean in the lives of people with learning difficulties (Aspis, 2002; Boxall, 2002; Goodley, 2001) can be useful for supporters and people with learning difficulties alike. Doing this can give both sets of people a political focus for their work that takes into account the ways that people with learning difficulties have power taken away from them within society' (Vic).

'The social model of disability says that people with learning difficulties don't have to change, because it is not us that needs to change it's the society itself because they're the ones that are putting us down... They also leave us out of things like getting a job or being part of the society itself' (Jennifer). 'They use too much jargon words... they leave us out and don't give us a chance to get involved [in the] society' (Maggie).

'What this could mean for people who support people with learning difficulties is that our aim is not to change people so that they can fit in. If we take the social model of disability to heart it seems that we should be there to support people as they are, to have their rights met and deal with the issues that they face as people with learning difficulties in society. This is different to what can happen' (Vic).

Maggie said: 'Some people think we should be going to college and go round and round in circles and be trained… I think it is terrible. I think it is silly…I know a lot of people go to college for ages and ages. They don't learn a lot, they go to college, doing the same thing all the time, doing the same course.'

'The sort of education and training mentioned above is not the same as supporting people with learning difficulties to get what they want out of life and deal with their problems in ways that they choose to – working with their own agendas and being in control of their own groups' (Vic).

'Up to some point courses are good [but] some of them can be bad courses as well. [The problem is] they have got the same students there year after year after year. People go to college and job training and all that but [they are] not getting nothing [anything] out of it and they think it is boring as well… They have the courses but when it comes to getting a job there is nothing out there for them to do' (Jennifer).

'Self-advocacy and people with learning difficulties being in control' (Vic)

'Maggie and Jennifer have made clear that they want to be supported to do what is important to them. Also they don't want the supporter to take over and tell them what to do. This is not a new idea. Other people involved in self-advocacy have also written that the people with learning difficulties should be in control of what is talked about in the self-advocacy group (Williams and Shoultz, 1982) and the support that is offered to them (Dowson and Whittaker, 1993). These points were made in the earlier days of self-advocacy. However, apart from work we have done we could not find any recent work that made either of these points clear' (Forrest, 2009; Forrest and Taylor, 2010; Taylor *et al.,* 2007) (Vic). 'It should be people with learning difficulties being in control in self-advocacy groups…and organisations' (Jennifer).

'Supporters can take control away from people with learning difficulties in ways that can seem quite small. For example, control can be taken away if a supporter says something like the following to the group, in a way that suggests they are in charge: "Come on everybody. The break is over. It's time to start work now"' (Vic). 'Some supporters can do this and that is wrong' (Maggie). 'Supporters should never tell a person with learning difficulties what to do. They shouldn't take over. They shouldn't be in control of us. It should be us who decides when we have a break and when we stop and get on with the work' (Jennifer).

Vic said: 'I think the supporter could say that they were aware of an issue, like time running out on a piece of work that the people with learning difficulties were being paid to do by a certain time, for example (that is if none of the people with learning difficulties seemed to have noticed) but that is very different to taking over the group as if the supporter is the boss of everyone. It is a different attitude altogether. I like to hold in mind that the people with learning difficulties are my boss.' 'Well, we are the boss in the group. We go and get the coffee and the biscuits and we get on with the work after that' (Jennifer).

'So before going any further it is important to say now that the support issues that are written about here are to do with trying to support people with learning difficulties in a way that is not taking control away from them at all. That is not to say that supporters should not have some personal boundaries (Forrest and Taylor, 2010). For example, I have personal boundaries around touch and space. I don't like people to hug me from behind unexpectedly or suddenly and I don't feel comfortable if people stand or sit extremely close to me. If anyone did this (and people with and without learning difficulties have, occasionally), in most circumstances I would tell people that I was not comfortable' (Vic). 'If someone grabbed me by my arm or something I'd say "Let go please, can you let go"' (Jennifer).

'Maggie and Jennifer have said that people with learning difficulties being in control of what happens in their lives and their support is not something that can or should only happen in self-advocacy organisations. The Department of Health are also saying this should happen throughout social care. They call it personalisation, self-directed support and person-centred planning (Department of Health, 2010a; Web and Members of Skills for People, 2002). However, they have not written about how the people who work face to face with people with learning difficulties might behave when supporting them to be in control of their own lives' (Forrest, 2009) (Vic).

Vic asked 'Are there any times when a supporter should take over?' Maggie said: 'Not usually but if someone is crying for help and tries to jump out of the window...the supporter should help them. It has never happened though has it? I'm just saying they could be in danger.' Vic asked 'What if a supporter was crying out for help and trying to jump out of the window or a manager from one of the organisations that we work with?' Maggie said: 'We would have to help them or get someone else to help them.' 'The point is that in any situation if people were trying to seriously harm themselves or others there might be a need for someone else to take control, but except for that sort of situation there is no need for supporters to' (Vic) 'take over' (Maggie). 'That is not to say that the supporter will have no influence [make no difference to what people with learning difficulties choose]' (Vic).

'Making information understandable: what the supporter says makes a difference' (Vic)

Maggie and Jennifer pointed out that they need their supporters to make information understandable. 'Other authors have written about making information understandable [or accessible] to people with learning difficulties. For example a Google search on the internet will reveal a lot of information on this subject – too much to list here. Also the Department of Health (2010b) have recently put out detailed guidelines about making written information understandable for people with learning difficulties. The subject of making information understandable has been written about much more than the issue of supporting people with learning difficulties without controlling them, which is an under-researched subject (Forrest, 2009).

However, part of the supporter role is making complicated information accessible to the people with learning difficulties they are supporting. This means that at times people with learning difficulties only get what the supporter understands and picks out to tell them. Also when a supporter is told about a situation where a person with learning difficulties is being treated badly it is important at times to let the person with learning difficulties know that they think it is wrong and should not be happening in their lives.

Because the supporter will have some influence [make some difference] it seems particularly important that they care about what happens to people with learning difficulties in society and see themselves as an ally [a person who is on the same side] to the people they support, siding with them in the struggles they face in the community (Forrest and Taylor, 2010). The supporters should be on our side to fight the problems we face in the society' (Jennifer).

'Not taking over' (Vic)

'People with learning difficulties can lead lives that are controlled by other people (House of Lords House of Commons Joint Committee on Human Rights, 2008). The people who wrote *We Are Not Stupid* said that some support workers offer choices but they took over at the point where they disagreed with them' (Taylor *et al.*, 2007) (Vic). 'Vic doesn't take over' (Maggie) 'and he is not bossy towards us either, or tell us off in any way' (Jennifer). 'Vic said he works hard to not take over in his work with people with learning difficulties. He found in his own research into his support role (Forrest, 2009) that it is not easy to support people with learning difficulties without falling into controlling them. However he also found that there are some steps that can be taken that might help the supporter to avoid taking over people with learning difficulties, and that there are also some actions supporters can take that might help people with learning difficulties to feel more confident about being in control of their own work and self-advocacy group.

It might be helpful if the supporter watches how they react towards people with learning difficulties and has strong rules for themselves about how they behave. For example the supporter could make sure they don't ever behave as if they are annoyed or irritated by the people with learning difficulties' (Vic). Maggie said: 'In the past support workers have come into my flat in a bad mood and they [have] take[n] it out on me and they shouldn't.' 'Not ever behaving annoyed or irritated could help people with learning difficulties to be more confident to speak up about what they really want and to disagree comfortably with the supporter.

It could be helpful if the supporter understands themselves well so they are able to notice when they are experiencing feelings that could lead to them wanting to take control of the group. For example, these sorts of feelings could come up when the group is taking longer to complete a project than the supporter expected or when what the group is doing or saying touches on something that could upset the supporter in some way, like talking about a subject that she or he finds painful for personal reasons' (Forrest, 2009) (Vic).

'Working against being in a powerful position' (Vic)

'As the supporter can be in a very powerful position in the group they may need to prove to the people with learning difficulties that they will not take over. When Vic supports groups to do their own work he says to them that they have the final say over what happens and he sticks to this and makes it clear to the group members that they really do have the power to do what they want. For example one time when Vic was supporting a group throughout a long research project of theirs and doing research into his own support role the group decided they were going to stop meeting for a time and decide later if they would get back together. Vic did not want this to happen but did nothing to try and stop the group doing it (Forrest, 2009). Jennifer said this is what happened at that time' (Vic): 'We were getting fed up with the [name of a particular service they had been meeting with to try and make improvements] and they weren't doing what they said they were going to do...so we decided not to meet for a while... For me I was fed up because [of] the way they were coming out with it...and not paying attention to what we wanted to do in our lives, 'cause they were talking about money issues and all that, where they were going to get the money and all this.'

The supporter can do other things to move away from being seen as a person who has more power than the people with learning difficulties. One thing they can do is accept responsibility for misunderstandings. For example they can take responsibility for not communicating clearly enough when people with learning difficulties don't understand what they are saying (Forrest, 2009). They can also let the group see any mistakes that they make so that the people with learning difficulties can see that everyone can make mistakes and that it doesn't really matter as they can be changed and worked on. Here is what one People First Lambeth supporter had to say about this issue:

> I find that showing that supporters make mistakes and being open about what you do not know is also helpful as it goes some way to equalling (in some small way) the power imbalance that can exist between paid "support" workers and people with learning difficulties who are used to "receiving" help... The supporter not taking themselves too seriously is also helpful to develop trust as this again can promote an atmosphere [of] mutual support where all skills are recognised but all errors are not taken too seriously so that "mistakes" are nothing to worry about. (Forrest and Taylor, 2010, p.34)

'Some more issues that could lead to the supporter taking over' (Vic)

'Supporters need to understand the subjects they are supporting people to do, like research or training. At the same time it is not helpful if they have particular ideas about what research or training is and what it should look like that lead to them stopping people with learning difficulties researching and training in their own ways.

Different managers, social care workers and funders can talk to the supporter like the supporter is in control of the group. They can put some pressure on the supporter to try and get the group to do what they want. This can mean supporters have to be very strong at times to be able to stand up to these people and say that the people with learning difficulties are in control of the group and it is not the supporter's job to try and make them do anything (Forrest, 2009).

Also the supporter could need to be aware of conflicts of interest that could get in the way of them supporting people with learning difficulties to do what they want to do. It could help if the supporter as far as possible tries to make sure that their own needs are not tied in with those of the people they are supporting (Forrest, 2009). For example on this project (the writing of this book chapter) it has helped that we have all had our names next to what we have written. This has meant that Vic has been able to separate better the act of supporting people with learning difficulties to say what they want from the act of writing what he wants' (Vic).

'Building up a support relationship takes time' (Vic)

'It needs time to get to know a new supporter and get on with that supporter as well... You have got to know somebody first before you trust them... You have got to know what their personality is because they could easily talk to someone else about what you said. They could easily spread it to someone else outside instead of keeping it confidential or private' (Maggie). 'Vic said it takes time to get to know how to best support particular people with learning difficulties' (Lawton, 2007; Forrest, 2009) (Vic).

'Some people without learning difficulties 'teach' self-advocacy' (Vic) 'and stay in control' (Jennifer)

'Some people seem to think that people without learning difficulties can teach self-advocacy to people with learning difficulties' (Vic) 'and stay in control' (Jennifer). 'Some self-advocacy supporters we have seen teach self-advocacy skills and they are in control of the agenda and what people talk about each week. They say things like "This week we are looking at what self-advocacy means and next week we are going to look at something else. It is your turn to speak. It is not your turn to speak." Vic asked Jennifer and Maggie if they remembered seeing this in a particular group we have visited and what they thought about it. This is what Jennifer said' (Vic): 'I think that was out of order what she [the self-advocacy group supporter] said and the way she behaved towards them like they were kids, very strict on them... They weren't allowed to go anywhere till she said so... Someone wanted to go to the loo, and she said that you can't go to the loo yet because you haven't finished watching the video. Self-advocacy supporters shouldn't behave like that... She [the self-advocacy group supporter] shouldn't be in control of them. They should be in control of her... If he wants to go to the toilet he goes to the toilet' (Jennifer).

'People with learning difficulties need time to sort their own problems out' (Jennifer)

'Sometimes people with learning difficulties have problems in their lives and will choose to try and sort them out instead of moving forward with the project that they originally came together to work on (Forrest, 2009). Jennifer explained the problems some people faced when they worked together on one research project' (Vic): 'When we were doing our research people were having problems with their housing and someone was having problems at home, and somebody got attacked. Someone was having problems with the residential home where they weren't getting on with the staff... People came in and talked about what was going on, about the problem' (Jennifer).

'Vic asked Jennifer and Maggie if they thought it was up to the supporter to make the group stick to doing their work when people came in with problems in their lives. Maggie said' (Vic): 'I think if you have got a big problem it should be sorted out first. The supporter shouldn't make the people do the work if they've got problems.' 'Vic asked if the supporter should make them do the work at any time. Maggie said' (Vic): 'No not really, they shouldn't do, no.'

'Conclusion' (Vic): 'summing up what we said from the beginning to the end of this chapter' (Jennifer)

'We need to get people with learning difficulties...involved in the community and...meetings, groups that are going on – get them to speak up for themselves and take control of their own lives... We need to get the society to listen to us, stop bullying us on the streets and not look down on us and start looking up to us as people with learning difficulties... We need support but we want the right support not the bad support. The right supporters are friendly, joking around with us, they can help you go and do your shopping or help you with your bills or do research with you... It depends on what we want to do... They need to be kind and they need to care about you... They need to know what they are doing with us as well and not [be] taking advantage of us or nagging us or telling us what to do' (Jennifer).

'We just don't want the society to push us to one side. We are part of the society as well. We want the society to fit us in, into the community. People with learning difficulties need to be a part of everything that people without learning difficulties do like going to groups, going to meetings, being part of a partnership board or research [group]... We want to...make services and the society all together better for people with learning difficulties and for everybody. People who get pushed underneath the carpet like mental health service users, disabled people, people with learning difficulties, it could be people who are blind, we should make a difference and help each other out to stand up...and change the society. It is so slow, the society is pushing us away...but it is worth doing' (Jennifer).

'We go to meetings...and conferences...because it is important to go... They should listen to us because people walk over you sometimes. We have got the right to write things about ourselves...and speak up for ourselves and sometimes they don't let you... We need to be able to understand what people are saying. [We don't want people to use] too much jargon words. We want more pictures with the writing...because some people with learning disabilities don't understand [writing, or some writing]. We need supporters [in order] to go to different places where we don't know and to help us with different things. Support workers should be kind and respectful to us, not nasty, and listen to us, what we are saying, don't look on the ground, and have eye contact with us... People with learning disabilities should be involved in everything in life. We should have the same life as anyone else has... We should have our own lives. We should control our lives. People should listen to us... Other people shouldn't take over our lives' (Maggie).

'The Department of Health and the Committee for Human Rights have made clear that they think people with learning difficulties should be in control of their own lives. Supporters need to support without controlling and people with learning difficulties have told us that they often feel very controlled by the people who are supposed to be supporting them to do what they want to do.

While people have written about communication and how to make information accessible to people with learning difficulties a lot less has been written about how people can support people with learning difficulties without controlling them. Supporting people with learning difficulties to do what they want to do is not easy. Also it doesn't happen enough. It's a complicated job that requires a lot of thought from the supporter. It could be helpful if the supporter is clear about what they are doing in their relationship with people with learning difficulties, insofar as they understand that they are not there to tell people what to do or teach people in a way where they are in control of the agenda.

If supporters understand the difficulties people with learning difficulties face within society that could also be helpful. This doesn't just mean knowing about what people with learning difficulties need to understand information. It also means knowing and caring about how people with learning difficulties are treated within society and standing side by side with them in their struggles to be equal citizens' (Vic). 'Because people with learning difficulties are human beings on the planet as well, like anybody else but people without learning difficulties don't see us as we are, as human beings...sometimes' (Jennifer).

'Supporters who do not have learning difficulties are often in a powerful position when they are working. It could help if they do what they can to not be seen as being in charge in any way. This means working in a way where people with learning difficulties have the final say over everything that happens even if supporters disagree with them or feel uncomfortable about decisions that are made because of their own needs' (Vic). 'The people with learning difficulties should have the final say [about] what they want in their lives' (Jennifer).

'It could also be helpful if supporters present themselves in ways that make it easier for people with learning difficulties to disagree with them and say what they want. What might be useful here is if supporters are gentle, good humoured and friendly, and don't ever get annoyed with what people with learning difficulties say or decide' (Vic). 'We want people to be nice to us...all the time' (Jennifer). 'It might also be helpful if they take responsibility for any misunderstandings that happen in their working relationships between themselves and people with learning difficulties.

It is important that supporters try and make sure that their needs do not lead to them controlling people with learning difficulties. It could be useful if supporters keep their own needs, as far as possible, out of their working relationships with people with learning difficulties, to avoid them clashing with what the people with learning difficulties choose to do' (Vic). 'The supporters are working with our needs' (Jennifer). 'It may help if supporters develop skills around watching themselves and how they behave when they are with people with learning difficulties. If supporters are able to notice that they are getting close to wanting to take over at some point because of their own needs they may be able to stop themselves before they act on their feelings. It could also help if supporters know themselves well enough to understand what upsets them and might lead them to feeling as if they need to take over. As very little research has been done on this subject it would be useful if a lot more research was done in this area so we could understand more about the best ways to support people with learning difficulties to be in control of their own lives and the support they receive' (Vic).

References

Aspis, S. (2002) *Updating the Social Model, Activate.* British Council of Disabled People.

Beresford, P. (2003) *It's Our Lives: A Short Theory of Knowledge, Distance and Experience.* London: OSP for Citizen Press.

Beresford, P., Shamash, O., Forrest, V., Turner, M. and Branfield, F. (2005) *Developing Social Care: Service Users' Vision for Adult Support.* London: Social Care Institute for Excellence.

Boxall, K. (2002) 'Individual and Social Models of Disability and the Experiences of People with Learning Difficulties.' In D. Race (ed.) *Learning Disability: A Social Approach.* London: Routledge.

Department of Health (2001) *Learning Difficulties and Ethnicity.* London: Department of Health Publications.

Department of Health (2010a) *Personalisation Through Person-centred Planning.* London: Department of Health Publications.

Department of Health (2010b) *Making Written Information Easier to Understand For People With Learning Disablities: Guidance for People who Commission or Produce Easy Read Information. Revised Edition.* London: Department of Health Publications.

Dowson, S. and Whittaker, A. (1993) *On One Side: The Role of the Advisor in Supporting People with Learning Difficulties in Self-Advocacy Groups.* London: Values into Action.

Etherington, K. (2004a) *Becoming a Reflexive Researcher: Using Our Selves in Research.* London: Jessica Kingsley Publishers.

Etherington, K. (2004b) 'Heuristic research as a vehicle for personal and professional development.' *Counselling and Psychotherapy Research 4,* 2, 48–63.

Forrest, V. (2009) 'A qualitative enquiry into the process of supporting self-directed researchers with learning difficulties.' Unpublished PhD thesis.

Forrest, V. and Taylor, J. (2010) *Self-advocacy Matters: Self-advocacy and self-advocacy Support in People First Lambeth.* London: People First Lambeth.

Goodley, D. (2000) *Self-advocacy in the Lives of People with Learning Difficulties: The Politics of Resilience.* Buckingham: Open University Press.

Goodley, D. (2001) 'Learning difficulties: the social model of disability and impairment: challenging epistemologies.' *Disability and Society 16,* 2, 207–231.

House of Lords House of Commons Joint Committee on Human Rights (2008) *A Life Like Any Other? Human Rights of Adults with Learning Disabilities.* Seventh Report of Session 2007–2008 Volume 1. London: The Stationery Office.

Lawton, A. (2007) *Supporting Self-advocacy.* Position paper 6. London: Social Care Institute for Excellence.

Taylor, J., Johnson, R., Williams, V., Brennan, M. and Hiscott, I. (2007) *We Are Not Stupid.* London: Shaping Our Lives.

Web. T. and Members of Skills for People (2002) *Valuing People – A New Strategy for Learning Disability for the 21st Century: Planning With People: Towards Person Centred Approaches – Accessible Guide.* London: Department of Health Publications.

Williams, P. and Shoultz, B. (1982) *We Can Speak For Ourselves.* London: Souvenir Press (E&A) Ltd.

Conclusion
The Personal is still Political

Peter Beresford and Sarah Carr

'We should go and visit more people in power.'
(Maggie Brennan, Chapter 14)

This book presents some very diverse and dynamic examples of service user and community participation in research and development aimed at improving services and support in order to make a difference to people's lives. There are strong, successful examples of projects which demonstrate that it is possible to unleash the knowledge and expertise of people who services consistently label 'hard to reach' or 'seldom heard', such as African and Caribbean men who use mental health services; lesbian, gay, bisexual and transgendered people who are marginalised from many participation initiatives; older people with high support needs and people nearing the end of their life; people who have experienced drug or alcohol addiction; people living in poverty; people with learning disabilities who self-advocate and children and young people, including those with experience of the criminal justice system.

The people involved in the participation work presented in this book are not the so-called 'usual suspects' (a term which some service users involved with participation initiatives see as derogatory because it can be used to undermine their particular expertise and experience – professionals do not attract the same label). The discussions in the chapters challenge the workings of a wider system in social care and mental health which can create 'usual suspects' by being tokenistic or technical and therefore creating barriers to wider involvement meaning that certain people are under-represented or are not present at all (Shaping Our Lives, 2007), something explored in the first two chapters of the book. This conclusion looks at some of the key common themes and uniting principles across the chapters.

Political activism and social change

Despite the wide range of projects and people involved and the differences in age, race, culture, sexual orientation, gender and gender identity, disability, education and experience of poverty, service use, mental distress or substance use, it is clear that everyone is united in their commitment to make changes for the better. As has been observed elsewhere: 'The emphasis is...on democratisation, but now – out of the original impetus for differentiation – is emerging an interest in exploring ways of increasing strength and solidarity through the recognition of common causes' (Simmons, Powell and Greener, 2009, p.215). Contributors like Browne and colleagues, Staddon, Hoban, Barnes and Kristiansen make it clear that for their work this commitment to change is a political one as it addresses deeper issues of social inequality and power differentials as well as being about improving services and support.

Barnes outlines the political, rights-based nature of the disabled people's movement and Staddon describes political resistance to medicalised understandings of alcoholism, while Browne and Hoban are explicit in their use of the term 'activism' to describe the community participation projects they have been involved with. Kristiansen is clear that the quality assurance system developed with a user-led organisation in the Swedish drug rehabilitation field had to integrate elements which allowed understanding and assessment of social change. From these examples it is clear that service user and community participation maintains the political character of the collective action of the new social movements as described in Chapter 1. In Chapter 14 Jennifer Taylor makes the political and collective nature of participation very clear: 'We want to...make services and the society all together better for people with learning difficulties and for everybody...we should make a difference and help each other out to stand up...and change the society.'

New knowledge creation

The experiential knowledge of people who use services or experience social inequality is often contested in conventional academic circles and is regularly accorded less value by many professionals and academics (Beresford, 2003). Rose *et al.* have concluded that: 'the experiential knowledge of users may be valued for its authenticity but when set beside other form of knowledge which can claim the status of "evidence", that authenticity occupies second place' (Rose *et al.*, 2002, p.15). As Chapter 2 explored, the way people express themselves and the stories they tell can be sidelined in situations which demand the use of certain types of language and limit discussion to a few professionally defined topics, something which is well described by Jennifer Taylor and Maggie Brennan in Chapter 14 when they talk about being ignored in meetings. Again, this means that vital insights from the service user perspective risk being sidelined or devalued if the discussion is dominated by professional agendas and language. This situation can be particularly acute in university and academic cultures and several of the contributors to this book describe the challenges they both faced in and have posed to the traditional 'knowledge establishment'.

Newbigging and colleagues, along with Browne and colleagues, describe reframing and reforming traditional academic activity and presenting a genuine challenge to established ideas about knowledge production and values. Newbigging and her project team detail the challenges and possibilities of marginalised and stigmatised service users – African and Caribbean men who use mental health services – participating in one of the most technical forms of research: the systematic review, and later being questioned about the 'validity' of the resulting research by her academic peers at a mainstream, international academic conference. Browne and collaborators reflect on the need to disseminate research in a way that can 'effect social change' rather than using conventional academic outputs like peer review journals and observe some of the dynamics of 'the regulation and control of knowledge'. They also underline that for community-led research to make a difference, it should be co-owned by all parties, particularly those responsible for implementing any resultant changes: 'the data was both used and useful, being created with those who had a stake in actioning it'.

As with much of service user participation, these endeavours are not without their conflicts or tensions, particularly when engaging with people who have been marginalised or discriminated against, and the examples show that these tensions need to be recognised and addressed. Cotterell and Paine discuss the process of involving people with life limiting conditions in research, something which required openness, sensitivity and flexibility. Interestingly, several of the chapters are derived from PhD studies, with the doctoral scholars reflecting on their motivations and the effect of their user/survivor researcher identity in the case of Sweeney and Staddon, and on the dynamics of involvement in the case of Cotterell and Paine. Each chapter represents an important contribution to the growing body of collective service user and survivor knowledge, which in itself is becoming increasingly recognised as an essential part of the evidence base for social care and mental health (Beresford, 2003; Pawson *et al.*, 2003; Staley, 2009;).

Practical improvements and peer support

Common to all the chapters is the theme of practical improvement, be it through service users creating new ways of evaluating service quality, defining outcomes, developing entirely new ways of understanding and providing support or simply getting heard in support planning and assessment. In Chapter 1, service user participation is introduced as happening on both individual and collective levels. The chapters by Fleming and by Bowers and Wilkins show how significant it is to maintain a focus on self-determination and independent living as crucial outcomes for people using social care and support. Fleming underlines the importance of involvement meaning people having control over the day-to-day decisions about their lives. Bowers and Wilkins show that older people with high support needs can determine service standards and outcomes and equip local services and communities with ways to assess their progress and success in involving older people in decisions that affect them at all levels.

In his chapter, Barnes details the history and role of centres for independent living and user-led organisations (ULOs) which, among other things, offer unique types of peer support and advice to disabled people. Peer support is also a theme coming out of Staddon's and Browne *et al.*'s research work where it is apparent as a by-product of the process: 'for some, this was the first time they had shared experiences with people "like them"'. Staddon's research project even resulted in the unintended, spontaneous establishment of an informal women's alcohol support group. Finally, several chapters give accounts of service users developing formal quality assurance methods and being involved in evaluation of services. Most notable of these are contributions by Kristiansen who also shows how an academic can be commissioned by service user organisations to develop an appropriate quality assurance system for user-led drug rehabilitations services; Sweeney, who describes creating a user-defined outcome measure for continuity of care in mental health and by Brady and colleagues who discuss the involvement of young people in the inspection and evaluation of children's social care and criminal justice services.

Emotional and personal experience and motivation

Finally, the power of emotional and personal experiences and responses is apparent through nearly all the accounts in this book. This reflects the background discussion on some of the challenges service users may face for achieving change through participation, with one issue being the tendency of certain professionally led initiatives (or 'invited spaces') to sideline or disregard people's contributions because, as Rose *et al.* say, 'the direct experience of users and the way it is expressed may sometimes be dismissed as too distressing or disturbing' (Rose *et al.*, 2002, p.15). This situation can then result in the types of conflict also described in Chapter 2 and implied in many of the discussions presented here. However, there are also strong examples of how emotional and personal dimensions are an inherent and positive part of many participation processes, not least for motivation to get involved in the first place; as Hoban says of community work in Chapter 4 'people are motivated to act out of feelings of anger, frustration and concern for others'. This relates to the themes of political activism and wanting to make practical improvements.

People who use services will always bring a personal perspective, and participation often means reflecting on experiences or an identity which can sometimes make it an emotional affair, particularly if the power dynamics apparent in service use are replicated in the participation process or space. Sweeney gives a detailed exploration of the effects of having a 'double identity' of being both a researcher and a mental health service user/survivor working as a researcher, but with other service users/survivors to develop a continuity or care outcome measure. For people with life limiting conditions, as Cotterell and Paine discuss, it is very important to acknowledge how experiences of being marginalised and feelings of 'isolation and separateness' will affect how people may feel during the process. The project also highlighted that 'emerging research findings had a personal and emotional impact'. Similarly Newbigging and colleagues explore at length the dynamics of race and racism for research involving black men who have been through the mental health system, which for most has been an extremely negative experience, often characterised by racism. Browne and colleagues outline how one intention of their research project was to empower a marginalised community and Staddon's research surfaced a distinct need for women who had complex relationships with alcohol use to simply talk to each other without the moral ('shaming') and medical framework imposed by traditional alcohol treatment.

Conclusion

Over the past 20 years UK adult social care policy has slowly determined that service users should have greater influence over both frontline and strategic decisions about care and support (Barnes and Cotterell, 2012). Activity and expectation regarding the involvement of service users in social care research, either as research partners or leaders has increased greatly (Kemshall and Littlechild, 2000; Staley, 2009). The practical examples and thinking presented in this book are an important account of how such research and development is really happening in practice and demonstrate what is possible, even by and with people labelled 'hard to reach' or 'seldom heard'. In this way this book provides an account of the possibilities and realities which responds to some of the policy rhetoric about service user participation, the latest of which is associated with the personalisation agenda (HM Government, 2007).

Our contributors make it clear that people who use services can be productive and active citizens, despite the many limitations placed on them by traditional services and by wider society. It is such negative experience of services, which do not support people to live their lives, that motivates many to become involved in participation initiatives aimed at changing things for the better, or finding out what works well for people. Therefore personal experiences lead people to political action and this book demonstrates that this remains the core driving force for service users getting involved in social care research and development. This in turn can be seen as the basis for the truly person-centred and co-produced services for which there is now increasing public and political support.

References

Barnes, M. and Cotterell, P. (eds) *Critical Perspectives on User Involvement.* Bristol: Policy Press.

Beresford, P. (2003) *It's Our Lives: A Short Theory of Knowledge, Distance and Experience.* London: OSP for Citizen Press.

HM Government (2007) *Putting People First: A Shared Vision and Commitment to the Transformation of Adult Social Care.* London: HM Government.

Kemshall, H. and Littlechild, R. (eds) (2000) *User Involvement and Participation in Social Care: Research Informing Practice.* London: Jessica Kingsley Publishers.

Pawson, R., Boaz, A., Grayson, L., Long, A. and Barnes, C. (2003) *Social Care Institute for Excellence Knowledge Review 3: Types and Quality of Knowledge in Social Care.* London: SCIE.

Rose, D., Fleischmann, P., Tonkiss, F., Campbell, P. and Wykes, T. (2002) *User and Carer Involvement in Change Management in a Mental Health Context: Review of the Literature - Report to the National Co-ordinating Centre for NHS Service Delivery and Organisation R&D (NCCSDO).* London: NCCSDO.

Shaping Our Lives (2007) 'Beyond the Usual Suspects: Developing Diversity Get Together.' In *Shaping Our Lives National User Network Newsletter Issue 11,* Summer, 3–5.

Simmons, R., Powell, M. and Greener, I. (2009) *The Consumer in Public Services: Choice, Values and Difference.* Bristol: Policy Press.

Staley, K. (2009) *Exploring Impact: Public Involvement in the NHS, Public Health and Social Care Research.* Eastleigh: INVOLVE.

The Contributors

Leela Bakshi is an activist researcher in LGBT issues in Brighton. She volunteered with a couple of LGBT groups in Brighton between 2005 and 2010, including as a trustee with Spectrum, the local LGBT community forum at that time, and with the Count Me In Too project, initially as a participant and subsequently as part of the research team. This led to a role as an 'activist researcher', working with academic researchers on publications and participation at academic conferences, where academic fora offer opportunities for LGBT activism. Alongside volunteering, Leela works as a speech and language therapist with people who have learning disabilities.

Colin Barnes is Professor of Disability Studies, University of Leeds; founder of centre for Disability studies, the Disability Press, and the Disability Archive UK; co-author of *The New Politics of Disablement* (2012) and *Exploring Disability* - 2nd Edition (2010).

Peter Beresford OBE is Professor of Social Policy and Director of the Centre for Citizen Participation at Brunel University and Chair of Shaping Our Lives, the national service user and disabled people's organisation and network. He has a longstanding interest in issues of participation as writer, researcher, educator and service user activist. He is also co-author of *Supporting People: Towards person-centred support* (2011), Policy Press.

Rachel Blades is a Senior Research Officer at the NCB Research Centre. A geographer by background, Rachel has over ten years' experience of evaluating national and local targeted funding programmes and conducting research designed to identify and disseminate good practice, working for local authorities and a research consultancy before joining NCB. Her work has involved ensuring, wherever possible, that the views of children and young people are sought and reflected throughout the research process.

Helen Bowers is Head of Policy, Research and Evaluation at the National Development Team for Inclusion (NDTi). She has an interest in generating knowledge and learning that is co-designed and co-produced with all stakeholders and interest groups. NDTi is a social change organisation that works to achieve a society that is inclusive of all people, where factors like disability and age are not an obstacle to people achieving good life outcomes. For more information please visit www.ndti.org.uk. Helen has worked in and around public services for over 20 years and for most of this time has focused on delivering, designing and improving services for older people. She is passionate about public service reform that is shaped with and by local communities working in partnership with public agencies and other sectors to bring about real and lasting change.

Louca-Mai Brady is a freelance research consultant specialising in research with children and young people and public involvement in research and evaluation, and was previously a Senior Research Officer at the NCB Research Centre. She has 14 years' experience in commissioning, conducting and managing social research and her interests include research on and with children and young people; health, public health and social care; disability; education and participative research. Louca-Mai is a member of INVOLVE, the national advisory group, funded through the National Institute for Health Research (NIHR), which supports and promotes active public involvement in National Health Service (NHS), public health and social care research.

Maggie Brennan is a woman with learning difficulties and a travel buddy. She is a member of Shaping Our Lives' Management Committee and a People First Lambeth member. She used to be a Speak Up worker in People First Lambeth. In her work as a travel buddy she picks people with high support needs up from home and takes them to a day centre and back. Maggie has a lot of experience of helping other people with learning difficulties and listening to them. She also has experience of writing and has been involved in writing published work before.

Kath Browne is a Principal Lecturer at the University of Brighton. Her research interests encompass sexual identities, marginalisations and equalities, and gendered lives and sexed bodies. She has been working on the award-winning participatory research project Count Me In Too as the lead researcher since 2005. The book from this work, *Where we Became Ordinary? Lesbian, Gay, Bisexual and Trans Lives* is due in 2013, published by Routledge.

Sarah Carr PhD is a Senior Research Analyst at the Social Care Institute for Excellence (SCIE) and has led on the organisation's personalisation work and advising on the policy at a national level. Before this she led on work concerning service user and carer participation in social care services and research. Sarah is also an Honorary Fellow at the Faculty of Health, Staffordshire University, a Visiting Fellow of the Centre for Government and Charity Management, Faculty of Business, London South Bank University and a Fellow of the Royal Society of Arts. She is now a trustee of NDTi, the LGB&T Consortium of Voluntary and Community Organisations and of the National Survivor and User Network (NSUN). Sarah is a long-term user of mental health services and has written on her own experiences as well as general mental health practice and policy, LGB welfare and equality issues, service user empowerment and participation.

Phil Cotterell is a Clinical Nurse Specialist in palliative care at St Catherine's Hospice, Crawley, West Sussex. He is also a Visiting Senior Research Fellow in the Macmillan Survivorship Research Group, Faculty of Health Sciences at the University of Southampton. He has combined a nursing and research career. Phil has worked in palliative care delivering specialised end of life care for many years. His research interests and activities focus on cancer survivorship; service user involvement and social movements; and palliative and end of life care practice and provision. He has conducted research with many service user colleagues using a participatory approach.

Ciara Davey currently works as a senior researcher with *Which?* magazine. Before becoming a champion for consumer rights, she worked for 13 years in the field of children's rights specialising in the participation of children and young people in research and championing for the legalisation of Article 12 in domestic legislation. Prior to working at NCB she spent several years at the Children's Rights Alliance of England (CRAE) and has a PhD in education.

Jenni Fleming is a Reader in Participatory Research and Social Action and Director of Centre for Social Action at De Montford University.

Vic Forrest is a supporter for people with learning difficulties who are involved in self-advocacy. He is also a researcher, community activist and service user. He has worked as a supporter in People First Lambeth for over 20 years. He specialises in supporting people with learning difficulties to do their own research and training and did a PhD about the process of supporting self-directed researchers with learning difficulties. As well as being a supporter he continues to be involved in research and writing about the subject of support and empowerment. Vic is currently employed in several different roles on the

Joseph Rowntree Foundation's Change in Action Programme. In addition he is working on a project he initiated that is looking at how members of a large housing co-operative can develop support systems that could contribute towards them maintaining independence in their old age. This project is part of the Joseph Rowntree Foundation's A Better Life Programme.

Beverley French PhD is Reader in Evidence Based Healthcare, University of Central Lancashire. Beverley's research interests are in knowledge management, systematic review and evidence synthesis. She has participated in quantitative, qualitative and mixed method evidence syntheses for the Health Technology Assessment Programme, Social Care Institute for Excellence, National Institute for Health and Clinical Excellence and the Department of Health, in stroke care and public health.

Zemikael Habte-Mariam is a retired civil servant and works as an independent researcher on health and social care. Zemikael has been involved in supporting and empowering African Caribbean mental health service users to conduct research on mutual support leading to their recovery as well as being involved in a national research project for the Social Care Institute for Excellence on advocacy with African and Caribbean men. Zemikael has also worked with service users and survivors to produce a DVD that depicted their wellbeing and barriers to services, and with carers in setting up a self-advocacy service.

Martin Hoban is a part-time research worker for Shaping our Age. Martin has worked as a community worker in the South Wales Valleys, the North East of England and in Ireland. He has a background in the disability movement and has wide-ranging experience of involvement as a service user, community worker, educator and researcher.

Arne Kristiansen is Senior Lecturer at the School of Social Work at Lund University, Sweden. His research focuses on substance abuse, homelessness and service user participation. Before he gained a PhD in Social Work and began working as a researcher, he spent several years working as a social worker, especially with people who had substance abuse problems. He works closely with various service user organisations, which he involves both in the social work education and in research projects.

Mick McKeown is a Principal Lecturer, School of Health, University of Central Lancashire. Mick is variously mental health nurse, lecturer, researcher, union activist and supporter of service user involvement, notably in relation to UCLan's Comensus initiative. He has been involved in numerous research and teaching initiatives that have user involvement at their centre and helped to produce the collectively written text: *Service User Involvement in Education for Health and Social Care*, published by Wiley (2010).

Jason Lim is a Lecturer in Human Geography at Queen Mary, University of London. His research has considered intersections of sexualities, race, ethnicity and gender in everyday life. He has worked with Kath Browne, Leela Bakshi and others to research LGBT needs and experiences in Brighton and Hove, UK. He is co-editor of *Geographies of Sexualities: Theory, Practices and Politics* (2007), Ashgate.

Karen Newbigging is a Principal Lecturer, School of Health, University of Central Lancashire. Karen is a researcher in mental health policy, service user and survivor involvement, advocacy, equalities and related areas. Karen has developed research partnerships with service users, survivors and members of diverse communities over the last ten years. Her most recent project is a national evaluation of Independent Mental Health Advocacy, commissioned by the Department of Health, and the research has been undertaken in partnership with community groups and service users and survivors with a broad range of experience of mental health services.

Mandy Paine is a 50-year-old service user who has chronic obstructive pulmonary disease, a life limiting respiratory condition. Mandy spends her life turning negatives into positives. She has put her house in order by planning her own funeral, writing her own eulogy and her own music. She has a national and local media profile. Mandy takes information on death and dying into charity shops, schools and funeral directors, churches and nursing homes. She is an advocate for all aspects of death and dying. She offers her personal experience of thinking and talking about death and dying as an inspiration to others. 'It shows my illness hasn't rendered me useless and it gives me a sense of purpose and a mission by helping other people.' She is a member of the National Council for Palliative Care's People Bank, a Dying Matters champion, an All Party Parliamentary end of life care champion, an advisor to the Department of Health for patients on home oxygen therapy, a trustee for the Independent Living Association and recent co-chair of a local adult social services carer and user group.

Alastair Roy is a Senior Lecturer in the Psychosocial Research Unit based in the School of Social Work at the University of Central Lancashire. Alastair is particularly interested in issues of diversity and difference in health and social care policy and practice. He has undertaken a number of research projects using participatory methods. Recent publications include: 'Avoiding the involvement overdose: drugs, race, ethnicity and participatory research practice' in *Critical Social Policy* and 'Thinking and doing: "race" and ethnicity in drug research and policy development in England' in *Critical Policy Studies*.

Catherine Shaw is Assistant Director of Research at the National Children's Bureau and has 18 years' experience of conducting and managing social policy research and evaluation relating to socially excluded or marginalised children and young people. She has a particular interest in involving children and young people in the research process and leads NCB's work in this area.

Patsy Staddon PhD is a Member of INVOLVE, a Director of Shaping Our Lives, and a Visiting Fellow at the University of Plymouth. She is Convenor of the British Sociological Association's Study Group for the Sociology of Alcohol Use. 'She suffered from "alcoholism"' for over 20 years and has been recovered for nearly 24 years. She has mental health issues which include epilepsy and severe anxiety state. She became a sociologist in her forties, specialising in the development of social approaches to alcohol issues, particularly for women and LGBT people. She is active in service user controlled research and a consultant and reviewer of alcohol research proposals for the Department of Health.

Angela Sweeney PhD is a Research Associate at University College London. She is a survivor researcher at University College London. Her research focuses on survivors' perspectives on and experiences of mental health services. She is lead editor of the book *This is Survivor Research* (2009), published by PCCS Books, and has a PhD in Sociology as Applied to Medicine from the Service User Research Enterprise (SURE), Institute of Psychiatry (King's College London).

Jennifer Taylor is a People First Lambeth member and also a woman with learning difficulties. She is on the Management Board of Shaping Our Lives and is involved in doing a film for the Joseph Rowntree Foundation. Jennifer Taylor has done research and is an author. She has done a lot of talks and training about what it is like to live as a person with learning difficulties and be more powerful. She also used to be on the Partners' Council for the Social Care Institute for Excellence.

Anita Wilkins is the Evaluation Manager at the National Development Team for Inclusion (NDTi), overseeing the design and development of evaluation methodologies and materials, as well as project managing a number of medium and long-term evaluation and research programmes with particular experience in the field of ageing and older people's services. Over the last five years, she has set up and now co-ordinates a network of older people trained and supported to work with NDTi as local evaluators. Prior to joining NDTi, Anita worked in environmental research consultancy and community regeneration roles, with a passion for research/evaluation, inclusion and social justice being key threads throughout her work.

Subject Index

Author Index